T0213839

Lecture Notes in Computer Science 13576

Bhavna Antony · Huazhu Fu · Cecilia S. Lee ·
Tom MacGillivray · Yanwu Xu ·
Yalin Zheng (Eds.)

Ophthalmic Medical Image Analysis

9th International Workshop, OMIA 2022
Held in Conjunction with MICCAI 2022
Singapore, Singapore, September 22, 2022
Proceedings

🐴 Springer

Editors
Bhavna Antony (iD)
Alfred Health
Melbourne, VIC, Australia

Cecilia S. Lee (iD)
University of Washington
Seattle, WA, USA

Yanwu Xu (iD)
Baidu Inc.
Beijing, China

Huazhu Fu (iD)
Institute of High Performance Computing
Singapore, Singapore

Tom MacGillivray (iD)
University of Edinburgh
Edinburgh, UK

Yalin Zheng (iD)
University of Liverpool
Liverpool, UK

ISSN 0302-9743   ISSN 1611-3349 (electronic)
Lecture Notes in Computer Science
ISBN 978-3-031-16524-5   ISBN 978-3-031-16525-2 (eBook)
https://doi.org/10.1007/978-3-031-16525-2

This Springer imprint is published by the registered company Springer Nature Switzerland AG
The registered company address is: Gewerbestrasse 11, 6330 Cham, Switzerland

Preface

The 9th International Workshop on Ophthalmic Medical Image Analysis (OMIA 2022) was held on September 22, 2022, in conjunction with the 25th International Conference on Medical Image Computing and Computer-Assisted Intervention (MICCAI). This will be the first MICCAI conference hosted in Southeast Asia. Due to COVID-19, this year it took place as a hybrid (virtual + in-person) conference.

Age-related macular degeneration, diabetic retinopathy, and glaucoma are the main causes of blindness in both developed and developing countries. The cost of blindness to society and individuals is huge, and many cases can be avoided by early intervention. Early and reliable diagnosis strategies and effective treatments are therefore a world priority. At the same time, there is mounting research on the retinal vasculature and neuro-retinal architecture as a source of biomarkers for several high-prevalence conditions like dementia, cardiovascular disease, and, of course, complications of diabetes. Automatic and semi-automatic software tools for retinal image analysis are being used widely in retinal biomarkers research, and increasingly percolating into clinical practice. Significant challenges remain in terms of reliability and validation, number and type of conditions considered, multi-modal analysis (e.g., fundus, optical coherence tomography, scanning laser ophthalmoscopy), novel imaging technologies, and the effective transfer of advanced computer vision and machine learning technologies, to mention a few. The workshop addressed all these aspects and more, in the ideal interdisciplinary context of MICCAI.

This workshop aimed to bring together scientists, clinicians, and students from multiple disciplines in the growing ophthalmic image analysis community, such as electronic engineering, computer science, mathematics, and medicine, to discuss the latest advancements in the field. A total of 33 full-length papers were submitted to the workshop in response to the call for papers. All submissions were double-blind peer-reviewed by at least three members of the Program Committee. Paper selection was based on methodological innovation, technical merit, results, validation, and application potential. Finally, 20 papers were accepted at the workshop and chosen to be included in this Springer LNCS volume.

We are grateful to the Program Committee for reviewing the submitted papers and giving constructive comments and critiques, to the authors for submitting high-quality papers, to the presenters for excellent presentations, and to all the OMIA 2022 attendees from all around the world.

August 2022

Bhavna Antony
Huazhu Fu
Cecilia S. Lee
Tom MacGillivray
Yanwu Xu
Yalin Zheng

Organization

Workshop Organizers

Bhavna Antony   University of Edinburgh, UK
Cecilia S. Lee   University of Washionton, USA
Huazhu Fu   IHPC, A*STAR, Singapore
Tom MacGillivray   University of Edinburgh, UK
Yanwu Xu   Baidu Inc, China
Yalin Zheng   University of Liverpool, UK

Program Committee

Dewei Hu   Vanderbilt University, USA
Dongxu Gao   University of Liverpool, UK
Dwarikanath Mahapatra   Inception Institute of Artificial Intelligence, UAE
Emma J. R. Pead   University of Edinburgh, UK
Geng Chen   Northwestern Polytechnical University, China
Guanghui Yue   Shenzhen University, China
Hai Xie   Shenzhen University, China
Heng Li   Southern University of Science and Technology, China
Huazhu Fu   IHPC, A*STAR, Singapore
Huihong Zhang   Southern University of Science and Technology, China
Huiying Liu   I2R, A*STAR, Singapore
Jiong Zhang   University of Southern California, USA
Jui-Kai Wang   University of Iowa, USA
Kang Zhou   ShanghaiTech University, China
Melissa de la Pava   Universidad Nacional de Colombia, Colombia
Mingchen Zhuge   China University of Geosciences, China
Mohammad Shafkat Islam   University of Iowa, USA
Muthu Rahma Krishnan Mookiah   University of Dundee, UK
Oscar Perdomo   Universidad del Rosario, Colombia
Peng Liu   University of Electronic Science and Technology of China, China
Peng Yang   Shenzhen University, China
Pengshuai Yin   South China University of Technology, China
Ravi Kamble   AIRA MATRIX, India

Contents

AugPaste: One-Shot Anomaly Detection for Medical Images

Weikai Huang[1], Yijin Huang[1,2], and Xiaoying Tang[1(✉)]

[1] Department of Electronic and Electrical Engineering,
Southern University of Science and Technology, Shenzhen, China
tangxy@sustech.edu.cn
[2] School of Biomedical Engineering, University of British Columbia,
Vancouver, BC, Canada

Abstract. Due to the high cost of manually annotating medical images, especially for large-scale datasets, anomaly detection has been explored through training models with only normal data. Lacking prior knowledge of true anomalies is the main reason for the limited application of previous anomaly detection methods, especially in the medical image analysis realm. In this work, we propose a one-shot anomaly detection framework, namely AugPaste, that utilizes true anomalies from a single annotated sample and synthesizes artificial anomalous samples for anomaly detection. First, a lesion bank is constructed by applying augmentation to randomly selected lesion patches. Then, MixUp is adopted to paste patches from the lesion bank at random positions in normal images to synthesize anomalous samples for training. Finally, a classification network is trained using the synthetic abnormal samples and the true normal data. Extensive experiments are conducted on two publicly-available medical image datasets with different types of abnormalities. On both datasets, our proposed AugPaste largely outperforms several state-of-the-art unsupervised and semi-supervised anomaly detection methods, and is on a par with the fully-supervised counterpart. To note, AugPaste is even better than the fully-supervised method in detecting early-stage diabetic retinopathy.

Keywords: Anomaly detection · One-shot learning · Anomaly synthesis

1 Introduction

In recent years, deep learning has achieved great success in the field of medical image analysis [13]. However, the effectiveness of deep representation learning techniques, such as convolutional neural networks (CNNs), is severely limited by the availability of the training data. Most of the disease detection methods in the medical image field are fully supervised and heavily rely on large-scale annotated datasets [11]. In general, acquiring and manually labeling abnormal

B. Antony et al. (Eds.): OMIA 2022, LNCS 13576, pp. 1–11, 2022.
https://doi.org/10.1007/978-3-031-16525-2_1

data are more challenging and more expensive than normal data. Thus, a vast majority of anomaly detection methods in computer vision have been focusing on unsupervised learning through training detection models using only normal data, assuming no access to abnormal data at the training phase [1,2,21,24].

Typically, these methods use normal samples to train models to learn normality patterns and declare anomalies when the models have poor representation of specific test samples [16]. For instance, training an autoencoder that reconstructs normal samples by minimizing the reconstruction error can be used to detect anomalies when the reconstruction error is high in testing [25,27]. Generative models aim to learn a latent feature space that captures normal patterns well and then defines the residual between real and generated instances as the anomaly score to detect anomalies [17,22]. Recently, some approaches have been explored by synthesizing anomalous samples. For example, CutPaste performs data augmentation by cutting image patches and pasting them at random locations in normal images to serve as coarse approximations of real anomalies for anomaly detection [10]. DREAM synthetically generates anomalous samples to serve as the input to its reconstruction network and calculates anomaly scores based on the reconstruction results [25]. Since there is no prior knowledge of the true anomalies, these methods generally use very simple and rough methods to synthesize anomalous samples, although of high effectiveness. A major limitation is that the anomaly score defined as the pixel-wise reconstruction error or the generative residual relies heavily on the assumption on the anomaly distribution [20]. Therefore, these methods may not be sufficiently robust and generalizable in discriminating anomalies in real-life clinical practice.

In such context, we propose AugPaste, a one-shot anomaly detection (OSAD) method, which is the extreme case of few-shot anomaly detection [15,19,23]. Namely, we train an anomaly detection network with only one annotated anomalous sample. Requiring only a single labeled anomalous sample, AugPaste is highly flexible and accommodates well various settings even for rare diseases or other unusual instances. Our goal is to make use of the prior knowledge of true anomalies to synthesize artificial anomalous samples, at the cost of annotating anomalies in only a single anomalous sample.

In AugPaste, we first choose one annotated anomalous image and extract all lesion patches. Then, data augmentation is applied to the extracted lesion patches to construct a lesion bank. Afterwards, MixUp [26] is employed to paste lesion patches from the lesion bank to normal images to synthesize artificial anomalous images. Finally, we train an anomaly detection network by discriminating synthesized anomalous images from normal ones. The performance of our proposed AugPaste is evaluated on two publicly-available medical image datasets with different types of abnormalities, namely EyeQ [4] and MosMed [14].

The main contributions of this work are two-fold: (1) We propose a novel OSAD framework, namely AugPaste, to utilize the prior knowledge of true anomalies from a single sample to synthesize artificial anomalous samples. To the best of our knowledge, this is the first work that synthesizes artificial anomalous samples using real anomalies from a single sample, for a purpose of anomaly detection. (2) We comprehensively evaluate our framework on two large-scale publicly-available medical image datasets including fundus images and lung CT images. The superiority of AugPaste is established from the experimental results. The source code is available at https://github.com/Aidanvk/AugPaste.

2   Methods

2.1   Construction of Lesion Bank

As depicted in Fig. 1A, we first choose one annotated anomalous image and extract all lesions based on the pixel-wise lesion annotation. For the two anomaly detection tasks investigated in this work, the single annotated anomalous data are illustrated in Fig. 2. After lesion extraction, the Connected Component Labeling algorithm [6] is adopted to identify each isolated lesion region from which a corresponding lesion patch is extracted.

Following that, random resampling with repetition is carried out to select the lesion patches to be pasted. The number N of the to-be-pasted lesion patches is also randomly generated with $N \sim U(1, 1.5N_L)$, where N_L is the total number of the isolated lesion regions. The selected lesion patches are then sent to a subsequent transformation block for lesion patch augmentation to construct a lesion bank, for a purpose of synthesizing more diverse anomalies. Data augmentations

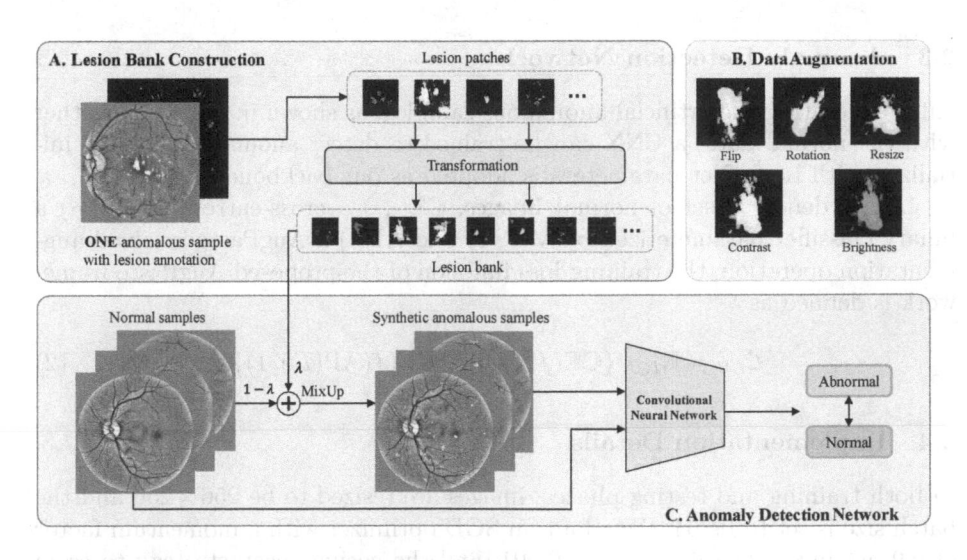

Fig. 1. The proposed AugPaste framework. In part A, lesion patches are extracted from an annotated anomalous sample. Then, the lesion patches are processed by a transformation block involving data augmentation operations in part B to construct a corresponding lesion bank. In part C, the transformed lesion patches in the lesion bank are randomly pasted to the normal samples via MixUp, yielding synthetic anomalous samples. Then a CNN is trained to detect the anomalies.

are conducted as shown in Fig. 1B, including flipping, rotation, resizing, contrast, and brightness changing, to generalize our anomalies from a single sample to various unseen anomalies during testing.

2.2 Synthesis of Anomalous Samples

We randomly sample a number of lesion patches from the lesion bank and paste them at random positions in the normal images to synthesize artificial anomalous images. Each normal image is used to generate one corresponding artificial anomalous image.

The MixUp technique is initially proposed as a simple data augmentation method in [26] to regularize model complexity and decrease over-fitting in deep neural networks by randomly combining training samples. Extensive experiments have shown that MixUp can lead to better generalization and improved model calibration. As such, to have the pasted lesion fuse more naturally with the normal image, random MixUp is employed when we paste a lesion patch L to a normal image I. The image after MixUp I_{MU} is defined as

$$I_{MU} = (1 - \lambda)(M \odot I) + \lambda(M \odot L) + \bar{M} \odot I, \tag{1}$$

where M is the binary mask of the lesion patch, $\bar{M}$ is the inverse of M, $\odot$ denotes the pixel-wise multiplication operation and $\lambda \sim U(0.5, 0.8)$.

2.3 Anomaly Detection Network

After generating the artificial anomalous samples, as shown in Fig. 1C, together with the normal data, a CNN can be trained to detect anomalies. VGG16 initialized with ImageNet parameters is adopted as our backbone model.

Let $\mathcal{N}$ denote a set of normal images, $\mathbb{CE}(\cdot, \cdot)$ a cross-entropy loss, $f(\cdot)$ a binary classifier parameterized by VGG16 and $\mathrm{AP}(\cdot)$ a AugPaste involved augmentation operation, the training loss function of the proposed AugPaste framework is defined as

$$\mathcal{L}_{AP} = \mathbb{E}_{I \in \mathcal{N}}\{\mathbb{CE}(f(I), 0) + \mathbb{CE}(f(\mathrm{AP}(I)), 1)\}. \tag{2}$$

2.4 Implementation Details

In both training and testing phases, images are resized to be 256×256 and the batch size is set to be 64. We adopt an SGD optimizer with a momentum factor of 0.9, an initial learning rate of 0.001, and the cosine decay strategy to train the network. All network trainings are performed for 50 epochs on EyeQ and 100 epochs on MosMed, with fixed random seeds. All compared models and the proposed AugPaste framework are implemented with Pytorch using NVIDIA TITAN RTX GPUs.

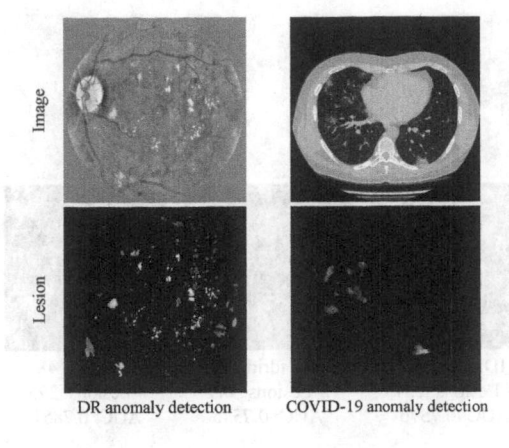

Fig. 2. The single annotated anomalous data for each of our two tasks.

3   Experiments and Results

3.1   Datasets

EyeQ. EyeQ [4] is a subset of the famous EyePACS [9] dataset focusing on diabetic retinopathy (DR), consisting of 28792 fundus images with quality grading annotations. The quality of each image is labeled as "good", "usable", or "reject". In our experiments, we remove images labeled as either "usable" or "reject", ending up with 7482/865/8471 fundus images for training/validation/testing. According to the severity of DR, images in EyeQ are classified into five grades: 0 (normal), 1 (mild), 2 (moderate), 3 (severe), and 4 (proliferative) [12]. The class distribution of the training data is shown in Fig. A1 of the appendix. Images of grades 1–4 are all considered as abnormal. All normal images in the training set are used to train AugPaste and all images in the testing set are used for evaluation. All fundus images are preprocessed [5] to reduce heterogeneity as much as possible, as shown in Fig. A1 of the appendix.

IDRiD. IDRiD [18] consists of 81 DR fundus images, with pixel-wise lesion annotations of microaneurysms (MA), hemorrhages (HE), soft exudates (SE) and hard exudates (EX) [8] (see Fig. A2 of the appendix). In our AugPaste, the lesions of a single fundus image from IDRiD are used as the true anomalies for DR anomaly detection. According to the clinical definition of DR grading, DR of grade 1 only contains MA, DR of grade 2 contains MA and HE, and DR of more severe grades contains more types of lesions. To enhance the performance of the detection CNN, we design a specific strategy for synthesizing the anomalous DR images: 80% of the normal fundus images are Mixed-Up with lesion patches containing MA only, 10% with lesion patches containing both MA and HE, 5% with lesion patches containing MA, HE and SE, and the remaining 5% with lesion patches containing all the four types of lesions (MA, HE, SE, and EX).

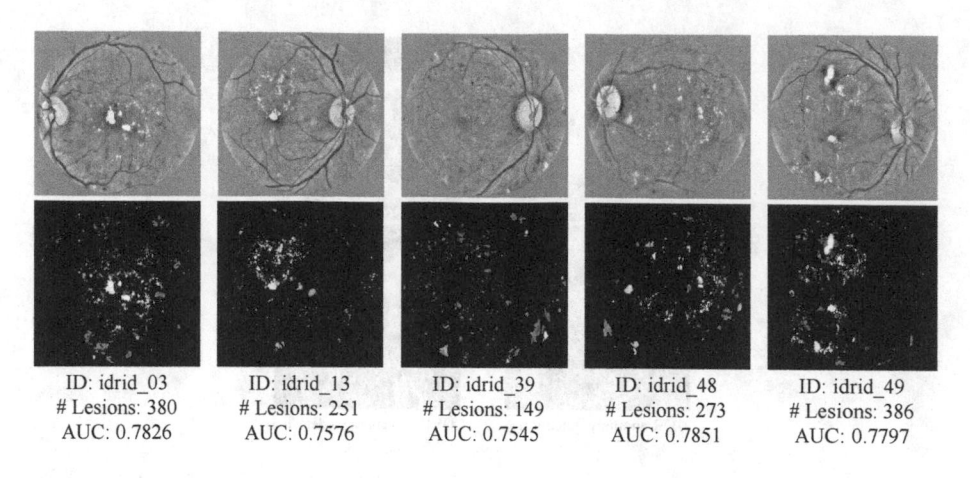

ID: idrid_03	ID: idrid_13	ID: idrid_39	ID: idrid_48	ID: idrid_49
# Lesions: 380	# Lesions: 251	# Lesions: 149	# Lesions: 273	# Lesions: 386
AUC: 0.7826	AUC: 0.7576	AUC: 0.7545	AUC: 0.7851	AUC: 0.7797

Fig. 3. The impact of using different annotated samples. ID denotes the image index in IDRiD, #Lesions denotes the number of isolated lesion regions, and AUC is reported for detecting all DR images combining grades 1–4.

MosMed. MosMed [14] contains human lung CT scans with COVID-19 related findings, as well as some healthy samples. A small subset have been annotated with pixel-wise COVID-19 lesions. CT slices containing COVID-19 lesions are considered as abnormal, ending up with 759 slices. A total of 2024 normal CT slices are selected and extracted from 254 health samples. For the anomaly detection task on this dataset, 5-fold cross-validation is used for evaluation. All CT images are preprocessed by windowing with a window level of -300 HU and a window width of 1400 HU to focus more on lung tissues [7].

3.2   Evaluation Metric

The anomaly detection performance is evaluated using a commonly-employed metric, namely the area under the curve (AUC) of receiver operating characteristic (ROC), keeping consistent with previous anomaly detection works [10,15,25].

3.3   Ablation Studies on EyeQ

Different Annotated Samples. In this experiment, we only use the original lesion patches with no data augmentation, and evaluate the performance of Aug-Paste with different annotated fundus images of IDRiD. In Fig. 3 and Table A1 of the appendix, we show the results of randomly selecting five different images from IDRiD for lesion extraction. Apparently, the difference in the single annotated anomalous image does not affect the anomaly detection performance of our AugPaste, identifying the robustness of our proposed pipeline. We choose a representative image, idrid_48, as the single annotated fundus image for all subsequent experiments on EyeQ.

Table 1. The impact of different data augmentation operations on EyeQ. DR images of grades 1–4 are all considered as abnormal. Color distortion only adjusts the hue and saturation and does not change brightness.

Color distortion	Flip	Contrast	Rotation	Resize	Brightness	AUC
✓						0.7806
	✓					0.7803
		✓				0.7841
			✓			0.7864
				✓		0.7896
					✓	0.7924
				✓	✓	0.7965
			✓	✓	✓	0.8019
		✓	✓	✓	✓	0.8105
	✓	✓	✓	✓	✓	**0.8126**
✓	✓	✓	✓	✓	✓	0.8053

Different Numbers of Annotated Samples. The influence of different numbers of annotated samples is also investigated (see Table A2 of the appendix). We observe that the more annotated samples, the better the anomaly detection performance, although the difference is not huge and the performance gradually reaches bottleneck. Balancing the anomaly detection performance and the cost of annotating lesions, we still use only one single annotated anomalous image.

Data Augmentation Operations. In this experiment, we fix the randomly resampled lesions and their to-be-pasted positions, and then evaluate the importance of six augmentation operations and their compositions. From the top panel of Table 1, we find that brightness works much better than each of the other five operations. As shown in the bottom panel of Table 1, the composition of five augmentation operations other than color distortion achieves the highest AUC of 0.8126, which is even higher than that from using 10 annotated samples (an AUC of 0.8052). This clearly indicates the importance of data augmentation. We conjecture it is because DR lesions are tightly linked to the color information and color distortion may significantly destroy important lesion-related color information. So we apply a composition of the five augmentation operations, namely Flip, Contrast, Rotation, Resize, and Brightness, in all subsequent experiments.

MixUp Coefficients. After identifying the optimal data augmentation strategy, the impact of different MixUp coefficients is analyzed. As shown in Table 2, four different MixUp coefficients (three fixed and one random) are tested and the random MixUp coefficient $\lambda \sim U(0.5, 0.8)$ achieves the best performance.

Table 2. The impact of different MixUp coefficients on EyeQ. *0 vs 1* means to classify images of grade 0 from images of grade 1 and *0 vs all* means to classify images of grade 0 from images of all other grades (1–4).

MixUp coefficient λ	AUC				
	0 vs 1	0 vs 2	0 vs 3	0 vs 4	0 vs all
w.o. MixUp	0.7174	0.8490	0.9574	0.9536	0.8126
0.8	0.7287	0.8487	0.9558	0.9541	0.8150
0.7	0.7242	0.8455	0.9581	0.9546	0.8177
0.5	0.7135	0.8516	**0.9586**	**0.9631**	0.8096
Random	**0.7348**	**0.8528**	0.9582	0.9607	**0.8216**

Table 3. Performance comparisons on EyeQ and MosMed.

Methods	#Anomalous samples in training	EyeQ					MosMed
		AUC					
		0 vs 1	0 vs 2	0 vs 3	0 vs 4	0 vs all	
Fully Supervised VGG16	1807	0.6257	0.8448	0.9714	0.9846	0.7885	0.9975
f-AnoGAN [22]	0	0.5081	0.4915	0.5259	0.5779	0.5148	0.9004
DREAM [25]	0	0.5825	0.6655	0.7618	0.7373	0.6252	0.9162
DevNet [15]	10	0.5541	0.6530	0.9118	0.9153	0.6301	0.8945
AugPaste w.o. MixUp	1	0.7174	0.8490	0.9574	0.9536	0.8126	0.9441
AugPaste	1	**0.7348**	**0.8528**	**0.9582**	**0.9607**	**0.8216**	**0.9546**

3.4   Comparison with State-of-the-Art

In Table 3, we compare our AugPaste method with state-of-the-art anomaly detection works. As shown in that table, our proposed AugPaste significantly outperforms all unsupervised learning and semi-supervised learning methods under comparison, and even works better than the fully supervised counterpart in detecting DR of grade 1 with an AUC of 0.7348, grade 2 with an AUC of 0.8528, and all 1–4 grades combined with an AUC of 0.8216. Particularly for detecting DR of grade 1, dramatic improvements of AugPaste over other methods are observed: an increase of 0.1893 on AUC over the 10-shot anomaly detection method DevNet [15] and an increase of 0.1091 on AUC over the fully supervised method. DR images of grade 1 contain only MA lesions which are extremely tiny in fundus images, and therefore DR of grade 1 is the most challenging anomaly to detect. However, in our AugPaste, most of the synthesized DR images (80%) contain only MA lesions, forcing the classification CNN to learn the most difficult samples, so as to improve the performance on detecting DR images of grade 1. In Table 3, AugPaste also achieves the best result on MosMed. Statistically significant superiority of AugPaste has been identified from DeLong tests [3] at a p-value of e^{-10}. Visualization results of the two anomaly detection tasks are shown in Fig. A3. These results clearly demonstrate the applicability of Aug-Paste to different anomaly detection tasks involving different types of diseases, different types of lesions, as well as different types of medical images.

4 Conclusion

In this paper, we propose a novel OSAD framework for medical images, the key of which is to synthesize artificial anomalous samples using only one annotated anomalous sample. Different data augmentation and pasting strategies are examined to identify the optimal setting for our proposed AugPaste. Compared with state-of-the-art anomaly detection methods, either under the unsupervised setting or the semi-supervised setting, AugPaste shows superior performance on two medical image datasets, especially in the detection of early-stage DR, which even significantly outperforms its fully-supervised counterpart. It is worth pointing out that our proposed AugPaste pipeline still needs one manually and fully annotated abnormal sample. Potential future explorations include: 1) incorporating automatic lesion detection methods to make AugPaste zero-shot; 2) reducing the amount of annotated lesion pixels to make the pipeline even less labor-intensive.

Acknowledgement. This study was supported by the Shenzhen Basic Research Program (JCYJ20190809120205578); the National Natural Science Foundation of China (62071210); the Shenzhen Science and Technology Program (RCYX20210609103056042); the Shenzhen Basic Research Program (JCYJ20200925153847004); the Shenzhen Science and Technology Innovation Committee (KCXFZ2020122117340001).

References

1. Bergmann, P., Fauser, M., Sattlegger, D., Steger, C.: Uninformed students: student-teacher anomaly detection with discriminative latent embeddings. In: CVPR (2020)
2. Burlina, P., Paul, W., Liu, T.A., Bressler, N.M.: Detecting anomalies in retinal diseases using generative, discriminative, and self-supervised deep learning. JAMA Ophthalmol. **140**(2), 185–189 (2022)
3. DeLong, E.R., DeLong, D.M., Clarke-Pearson, D.L.: Comparing the areas under two or more correlated receiver operating characteristic curves: a nonparametric approach. Biometrics **44**, 837–845 (1988)
4. Fu, H., et al.: Evaluation of retinal image quality assessment networks in different color-spaces. In: Shen, D., et al. (eds.) MICCAI 2019. LNCS, vol. 11764, pp. 48–56. Springer, Cham (2019). https://doi.org/10.1007/978-3-030-32239-7_6

5. Graham, B.: Kaggle diabetic retinopathy detection competition report. University of Warwick, pp. 24–26 (2015)
6. He, L., Ren, X., Gao, Q., Zhao, X., Yao, B., Chao, Y.: The connected-component labeling problem: a review of state-of-the-art algorithms. Pattern Recogn. **70**, 25–43 (2017)
7. Hong, R., Halama, J., Bova, D., Sethi, A., Emami, B.: Correlation of PET standard uptake value and CT window-level thresholds for target delineation in CT-based radiation treatment planning. Int. J. Radiat. Oncol. Biol. Phys. **67**(3), 720–726 (2007)
8. Huang, Y., Lin, L., Cheng, P., Lyu, J., Tang, X.: Lesion-based contrastive learning for diabetic retinopathy grading from fundus images. In: de Bruijne, M., et al. (eds.) MICCAI 2021. LNCS, vol. 12902, pp. 113–123. Springer, Cham (2021). https://doi.org/10.1007/978-3-030-87196-3_11
9. Kaggle diabetic retinopathy detection competition. https://www.kaggle.com/c/diabetic-retinopathy-detection
10. Li, C.L., Sohn, K., Yoon, J., Pfister, T.: CutPaste: self-supervised learning for anomaly detection and localization. In: CVPR (2021)
11. Li, T., et al.: Applications of deep learning in fundus images: a review. Med. Image Anal. **69**, 101971 (2021)
12. Lin, L., Li, M., Huang, Y., Cheng, P., Xia, H., et al.: The SUSTech-SYSU dataset for automated exudate detection and diabetic retinopathy grading. Sci. Data **7**(1), 1–10 (2020)
13. Litjens, G., et al.: A survey on deep learning in medical image analysis. Med. Image Anal. **42**, 60–88 (2017)
14. Morozov, S.P., Andreychenko, A.E., Pavlov, N.A., Vladzymyrskyy, A.V., Ledikhova, N.V., et al.: MosMedData: chest CT scans with Covid-19 related findings dataset. arXiv preprint (2020). arXiv:2005.06465
15. Pang, G., Ding, C., Shen, C., Hengel, A.V.D.: Explainable deep few-shot anomaly detection with deviation networks. arXiv preprint (2021). arXiv:2108.00462
16. Pang, G., Shen, C., Cao, L., Hengel, A.V.D.: Deep learning for anomaly detection: a review. ACM Comput. Surv. (CSUR) **54**(2), 1–38 (2021)
17. Perera, P.: OCGAN: one-class novelty detection using GANs with constrained latent representations. In: CVPR (2019)
18. Porwal, P., et al.: Indian diabetic retinopathy image dataset (IDRID): a database for diabetic retinopathy screening research. Data **3**(3), 25 (2018)
19. Quellec, G., Lamard, M., Conze, P.H., Massin, P., Cochener, B.: Automatic detection of rare pathologies in fundus photographs using few-shot learning. Med. Image Anal. **61**, 101660 (2020)
20. Ren, J., et al.: Likelihood ratios for out-of-distribution detection. In: Advances in Neural Information Processing Systems, vol. 32 (2019)
21. Salehi, M., Sadjadi, N., Baselizadeh, S., Rohban, M.H., Rabiee, H.R.: Multiresolution knowledge distillation for anomaly detection. In: CVPR (2021)
22. Schlegl, T., Seeböck, P., Waldstein, S.M., Langs, G., Schmidt-Erfurth, U.: f-AnoGAN: fast unsupervised anomaly detection with generative adversarial networks. Med. Image Anal. **54**, 30–44 (2019)
23. Tian, Yu., Maicas, G., Pu, L.Z.C.T., Singh, R., Verjans, J.W., Carneiro, G.: Few-shot anomaly detection for polyp frames from colonoscopy. In: Martel, A.L., et al. (eds.) MICCAI 2020. LNCS, vol. 12266, pp. 274–284. Springer, Cham (2020). https://doi.org/10.1007/978-3-030-59725-2_27
24. Zavrtanik, V., Kristan, M., Skočaj, D.: Reconstruction by inpainting for visual anomaly detection. Pattern Recogn. **112**, 107706 (2021)

25. Zavrtanik, V., Kristan, M., Skočaj, D.: DRAEM-A discriminatively trained reconstruction embedding for surface anomaly detection. In: CVPR (2021)
26. Zhang, H., Cisse, M., Dauphin, Y.N., Lopez-Paz, D.: mixup: beyond empirical risk minimization. In: ICLR (2018)
27. Zhou, K., et al.: Encoding structure-texture relation with P-net for anomaly detection in retinal images. In: Vedaldi, A., Bischof, H., Brox, T., Frahm, J.-M. (eds.) ECCV 2020. LNCS, vol. 12365, pp. 360–377. Springer, Cham (2020). https://doi.org/10.1007/978-3-030-58565-5_22

Analysing Optical Coherence Tomography Angiography of Mid-Life Persons at Risk of Developing Alzheimer's Disease Later in Life

Darwon Rashid[1]([✉]), Ylenia Giarratano[1], Charlene Hamid[2],
Tom MacGillivray[2,3], Graciela Muniz Terrera[2,6], Craig Ritchie[3,4],
Baljean Dhillon[3], and Miguel O. Bernabeu[1,5]

[1] Centre for Medical Informatics, Usher Institute, The University of Edinburgh, Edinburgh, UK
d.rashid@sms.ed.ac.uk, miguel.bernabeu@ed.ac.uk
[2] Edinburgh Clinical Research Facility and Edinburgh Imaging, University of Edinburgh, Edinburgh, UK
[3] Centre for Clinical Brain Sciences, University of Edinburgh, Edinburgh, UK
[4] Edinburgh Dementia Prevention, University of Edinburgh, Edinburgh, UK
[5] Bayes Centre, University of Edinburgh, Edinburgh, UK
[6] Department of Social Medicine, Ohio University, Athens, OH, USA

Abstract. Cerebrovascular changes associated with Alzheimer's disease (AD) can occur years before the onset of symptoms. Studies have suggested that changes in the retina may act as a surrogate for cerebrovascular changes in the brain, hence the retina might be a source of biomarkers for declining vascular brain health. Optical Coherence Tomography Angiography (OCTA) is a promising retinal imaging modality that has been increasingly used to investigate cerebrovascular diseases in this context. However, the potential clinical translation of advances for early AD detection is still being explored. In this study, we used OCTA retinal phenotypes to investigate differences between participants with and without a high genetic risk characterization of Apoliproprotein E4 (APOE4), and between participants with and without a family history of dementia. Furthermore, we investigated whether there is a difference in OCTA retinal phenotypes between participants with and without a high CAIDE (Cardiovascular Risk Factors, Aging, and Dementia score). This investigation explored retinal phenotypes (from OCTA) both cross-sectionally and longitudinally (2 years follow-up) using participants at mid-life from the PREVENT cohort and our findings suggest that there are retinal vascular changes captured in OCTA images between control and participants at risk of developing AD.

Keywords: OCTA imaging · Retinal vascular phenotype · Preclinical Alzheimer's disease · Longitudinal

Supplementary Information The online version contains supplementary material available at https://doi.org/10.1007/978-3-031-16525-2_2.

1   Introduction

Alzheimer's disease (AD) is the most common sub-type of dementia (around 80% of all dementia cases), and as of present, there is no definitive treatment [22]. AD is commonly diagnosed in the late phase when irreversible damage has occurred. Vascular changes in the brain related to AD are thought to start decades before symptoms manifest [4]. Quantifiable metrics for identifying these early changes would help increase the accuracy of assessing an individual's risk of developing the disease and allow for the monitoring of high-risk asymptomatic people as well as providing the means for new trials for intervention and treatment [13].

Current state-of-the-art diagnostic modalities related to AD include the quantification of cerebrospinal fluid and amyloid beta in brain tissue using magnetic resonance imaging, positron emission tomography, and other neuroimaging modalities [3,12,15]. Although, these technologies have shown success in establishing biomarkers for the identification and monitoring of symptomatic AD, they are limited by cost, invasiveness, evaluation time, and specialist requirements. Furthermore, these biomarkers have not been able to reliably identify AD in its early stages [14].

The retina and brain are part of the central nervous system, sharing embryological origins. Optical coherence tomography angiography (OCTA) is a non-invasive retinal imaging modality that captures the capillary level microvasculature within the retina in high resolution. The non-invasive nature of OCTA has pushed this technology to act as an investigation tool for tracking retinal vascular changes that are linked to retinal and brain diseases.

Among these applications, OCTA has shown considerable potential in providing insight, in particular diseases that are known to have a vascular component. Studies have highlighted retinal biomarkers that may mirror the cerebrovascular changes in symptomatic AD [11,28]. If OCTA can be used to track the progression of AD through to AD dementia [5,28], then it could also be potentially used to detect microvascular changes in the retina decades before AD symptoms manifest. Recent studies have started investigating potential associations between OCTA retinal phenotypes and preclinical AD. Van De Kreeke JA *et al.* reported an increase of retinal vessel density in participants at a high risk for developing AD [26]. A study by Elahi *et al.* reported a decrease of retinal vessel area density and vessel skeleton density in risk participants carrying Apolipoprotein E ϵ4 gene (APOE4) [6]. Details about APOE4 and how it is associated with a higher risk of developing AD has been previously described [17]. Another study by Ma *et al.* reported lower perfused density in APOE4 carriers [19]. Finally, O'Bryhim *et al.* found an increase of the FAZ area in risk participants with a positive biomarker for developing AD [20].

Old age is the greatest risk factor of developing AD [10]. Therefore, it is important to investigate retinal microvascular changes occurring in a cohort at mid-life, however the general limitation of the aforementioned studies is tied to the age of their cohort. Even though they are preclinical AD studies, the mean age of the cohorts are more than 60 years of age with an age variability of more than 30 years. Furthermore, there is a need for more longitudinal studies to investigate the evolution of the candidate OCTA retinal phenotypes throughout preclinical AD for there are currently only two longitudinal studies available [19,21].

In this study, we are interested in exploring the microvascular changes in the retina of mid-life participants at risk of developing AD later in life. The aim is to identify OCTA retinal phenotypes that show a difference between control and participants at risk for developing AD. We conducted this investigation across three different risk groups from a single cohort study. The first risk group being participants with and without known APOE4. The second risk group being participants with and without known family history of dementia (FH). Finally, the last risk group being participants with a high and a low Cardiovascular Risk Factors, Aging, and Dementia (CAIDE) score. Details about the CAIDE score and how it is derived has been previously described [7,16]. We conducted cross-sectional and longitudinal (2 year follow-up) analyses on all three risk groups.

2   Methodology

Dataset. We examined the participants of the PREVENT-Dementia cohort study. Details about this cohort can be found in [24,27]. This is a multi-site longitudinal study based in the UK and Ireland. The cohort recruits participants who are classified as cognitively healthy in the age range of 40–59. Participants with available FH status, APOE4 status, and CAIDE score were included in this study. OCTA scans at baseline and at a 2 year follow-up were acquired. Not all baseline participants had a 2 year follow-up visit. Participants with any ocular disease or history of ocular surgery were excluded for this study. Participants underwent extensive cognitive tests, and age, sex, blood pressure (BP), and body mass index (BMI) were recorded.

Image Processing. Images of both eyes were acquired using the RTVue XR Avanti (Optovue, Inc., Fremont, CA. USA) OCTA device [23]. Scans of the superficial and deep capillary plexuses with 3×3 mm^2 field of view were included in this study. For each image, the OCTA device provides a quality index (QI) that was used to identify poor quality scans. Images with a QI ≤ 6 were discarded from the analyses [1]. Good quality scans were binarized using a U-Net architecture and the vasculature was modeled as a graph to extract retinal measurements as described in [8]. Retinal measurements were divided into eight categories: basic graph-metrics, foveal avascular zone (FAZ) metrics, vessel tortuosity metrics, graphlets metrics, random-walks metrics, binary tree metrics, intercapillary space metrics, and flow metrics. Measurements were calculated in each region of interest, temporal (T), nasal (N), inferior (I), superior (S), foveal (F), and in the whole image (W). Distributions were summarised by reporting mean, median, standard deviation, kurtosis, and skewness. Our methodology has been previously described and can be found in [9]. Figure 1 provides a high-level overview of the OCTA retinal pipeline for this study. Image processing was performed using MATLAB R2020b (version 9.9), whereas vascular network modeling and retinal measurements were implemented in Python 3.6.9.

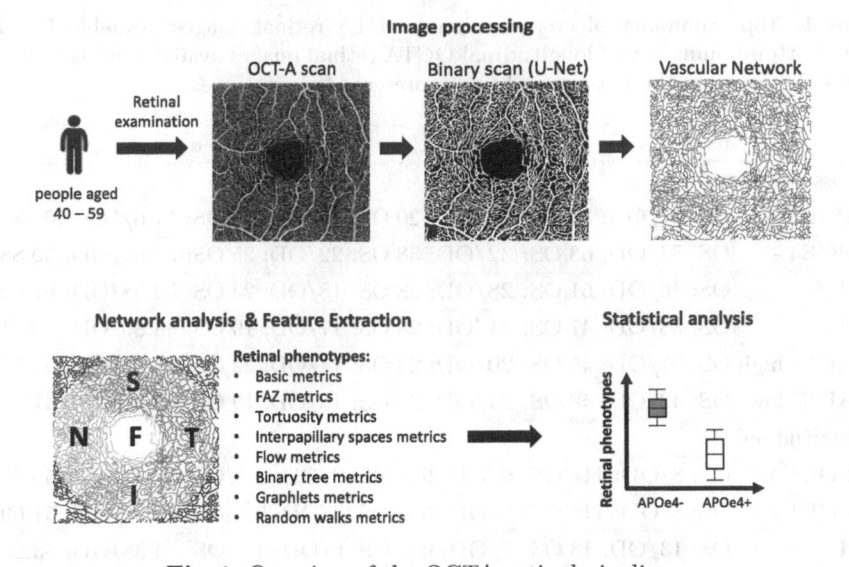

Fig. 1. Overview of the OCTA retinal pipeline.

Statistical Analysis. The two analyses in this study investigated whether any of the retinal OCTA phenotypes showed evidence of difference between control and risk participants cross-sectionally and longitudinally in each respective risk group (APOE4 +/-, FH +/-, CAIDE score high/low). For both the cross-sectional and longitudinal analyses, we used multivariate analysis corrected for possible confounding factors with the CAIDE risk group being the exception. The confounding factors for this study are age, sex, body mass index (BMI), and blood pressure (BP). These have already been accounted for in the derivation of the CAIDE score.

For the APOE4 and FH risk groups, we fitted a linear model using confounding factors, age, sex, BMI, and BP and the risk status (APOE4 +/-, FH +/-) as predictors and the retinal phenotype as the independent variable. For the CAIDE risk group, our only predictor was the risk status (APOE4 +/-, FH +/-). Since we have 620 different retinal phenotypes, we fitted the model on each different retinal phenotype independently and we extracted p-values and coefficients from each model.

Given the amount of retinal phenotypes available, we used false discovery rate (FDR) as a correction method to adjust the p-values [2]. We applied FDR at a category level. The categories are sufficiently different amongst themselves to be considered independent, while within each category, phenotypes tend to be closely related. The resulting p-values that were statistically still significant after being adjusted for correction were reported.

When it comes to the longitudinal analysis, the process is the same with one exception. The first step was to generate delta scores, variables describing the amount of change in the retinal phenotype between baseline and follow-up. After computing the delta scores, the rest of the investigation follows the same

Table 1. Top: Summary of cross-sectional OCTA retinal images available for this study. Bottom: Summary of longitudinal OCTA retinal images available for this study. Note: OS represents the left eye and OD represents the right eye.

Groups	n	n-female	n-male	μ-age
Cross-sectional				
APOE4 +	OS: 31/OD: 36	OS: 18/OD: 20	OS: 13/OD: 16	OS: 51.6/OD: 50.88
APOE4 -	OS: 54/OD: 63	OS: 32/OD: 38	OS: 22/OD: 25	OS: 50.64/OD: 50.88
FH +	OS: 46/OD: 51	OS: 28/OD: 28	OS: 18/OD: 23	OS: 52.58/OD: 51.82
FH -	OS: 38/OD: 47	OS: 21/OD: 28	OS: 17/OD: 19	OS: 48.86/OD: 49.91
CAIDE high	OS: 37/OD: 45	OS: 20/OD: 23	OS: 17/OD: 22	OS: 55.05/OD: 55.17
CAIDE low	OS: 42/OD: 48	OS: 24/OD: 29	OS: 18/OD: 19	OS: 46.95/OD: 47.10
Longitudinal				
APOE4 +	OS: 8/OD: 11	OS: 6/OD: 9	OS: 2/OD: 2	OS: 53.88/OD: 50.09
APOE4 -	OS: 8/OD: 11	OS: 5/OD: 6	OS: 3/OD: 5	OS: 50.50/OD: 51.09
FH +	OS: 13/OD: 13	OS: 7/OD: 9	OS: 6/OD: 4	OS: 54.38/OD: 53.23
FH -	OS: 3/OD: 8	OS: 2/OD: 5	OS: 1/OD: 3	OS: 44.66/OD: 47.87
CAIDE high	OS: 6/OD: 7	OS: 2/OD: 4	OS: 4/OD: 3	OS: 57.66/OD: 57.0
CAIDE low	OS: 9/OD: 13	OS: 7/OD: 9	OS: 3/OD: 4	OS: 47.22/OD: 47.61

methodology as the cross-sectional analysis. All analyses were conducted for each eye of the participants independently, left (OS) and right (OD) eyes respectively. Table 1 summarizes the data available for this study.

3 Results

3.1 Vessel Tortuosity Decreases in Risk Groups

Ninety-nine participants were included at baseline in the APOE4 risk group (OS: 85, OD: 99) and twenty-two had a 2 year follow-up (OS: 16, OD: 22). Ninety-eight participants were included at baseline in the FH risk group (OS: 84, OD: 98) and twenty-one had a 2 year follow-up (OS: 16, OD: 21). Ninety-three participants were included at baseline in the CAIDE risk group (OS: 79, OD: 93) and twenty had a 2 year follow-up (OS: 15, OD: 20).

There were observed phenotypes that were significantly different between control and risk participants in all three respective risk groups. There was a decrease of vessel tortuosity that is consistent across all three risk groups. Table 1 details more information about the retinal images included in this study.

While there was significant change in vessel tortuosity between control and risk participants across each risk group, the CAIDE risk group has seen more retinal phenotypes being significantly different between control and risk participants. There is almost a one-to-one overlap in the number of retinal phenotypes that are significant across both eyes.

Of note, there was an increase of the FAZ area and acircularity (OD and OS), a decrease of vessel skeleton density (OD and OS), a decrease of branching points (OD and OS), and an increase of mean area of the intercapillary spaces (OD and OS) in the vascular network of participants with a high CAIDE score. Table 2 summarizes the cross-sectional results of each respective risk group. Further cross-sectional significant changes related to the CAIDE risk group can be seen in the supplementary material of this study.

Table 2. Top: The details about each retinal phenotype that is statistically significant after using false discovery rate cross-sectionally (baseline) across each respective risk group. Bottom: The details about each retinal phenotype that is statistically significant after using false discovery rate longitudinally (2 year follow-up) across each respective risk group.

Risk group	Category	Eye	Retinal phenotype	p
Cross-sectional				
APOE4 +/-	Tortuosity	OS	Median vessel curvature (S)	0.012
FH +/-	Tortuosity	OD	Standard deviation vessel tortuosity (I)	0.007
FH +/-	Tortuosity	OD	Kurtosis vessel tortuosity (I)	0.006
FH +/-	Tortuosity	OD	Skewness vessel tortuosity (I)	0.004
CAIDE high/low	FAZ	OD and OS	FAZ area and acircularity	<0.001
CAIDE high/low	Basic-graph	OD and OS	Vessel skeleton density (W)	<0.001
CAIDE high/low	Intercapillary-space	OD and OS	Mean intercapillary space area (W)	<0.001
CAIDE high/low	Basic-graph	OD and OS	Number of branching points (W)	<0.001
CAIDE high/low	Tortuosity	OD and OS	Mean vessel tortuosity (W)	<0.001
Longitudinal				
APOE4 +/-	FAZ	OD	Mean radius	0.047
APOE4 +/-	FAZ	OD	Mean boundary curvature	0.038
APOE4 +/-	Graphlets	OS	Graphlet 3: mean radius (I)	0.042
APOE4 +/-	Intercapillary-space	OS	Skewness circularity (I)	0.035
FH +/-	Random-walk	OD	Standard deviation walk length (S)	0.041
CAIDE high/low	Tortuosity	OD and OS	Mean vessel tortuosity (W)	0.012
CAIDE high/low	Basic-graph	OD and OS	Skeleton density (W)	0.024
CAIDE high/low	Intercapillary-space	OD and OS	Mean intercapillary space area (W)	0.034
CAIDE high/low	Basic-graph	OD and OS	Number branching points (W)	0.021

(F): foveal, (N): nasal, (I): inferior, (T): temporal, (S): superior, (W): whole image.

3.2   Longitudinal Variations of Retinal Features in Risk Groups

Table 2 summarizes the longitudinal results across each risk group. Similar to the cross-sectional results, the CAIDE risk group has seen more significant changes in the retinal phenotypes between control and risk participants. Interestingly, there is a continued decrease of whole (all retinal regions) vessel tortuosity (OD and OS), a decrease in vessel skeleton density (OD and OS), an increase of mean area of intercapillary spaces (OD and OS), and a decrease of branching points (OD and OS) in the vascular network. There was no observed change in the FAZ area and acircularity which was observed cross-sectionally. Further longitudinal significant changes related to the CAIDE risk group can be seen in the supplementary material of this study.

4   Discussion

In this study, we were interested in investigating the hypothesis of microvasculature changes that could occur in the retina of mid-life participants at risk of developing AD. There was an observed decrease in vessel tortuosity across risk participants with a FH (OD), risk participants with a APOE4 status (OS), and risk participants with a high CAIDE score (OD and OS). From a bio-mechanical perspective, vessels that are more tortuous have a higher resistance to blood flow, so they might be carrying less flow. This is in line with Poiseuille's law, which states that the resistance to flow of a vessel is a function of its length (amongst several other parameters) [25].

A cross-sectional study by Van De Kreeke JA *et al.* reported an increase of retinal vessel density amongst risk participants for AD when compared to controls [26]. The study enrolled 124 participants with a mean age of 68.6 years (monozygotic twins, 75 twin pairs and 15 incomplete twin pairs) as part of its cohort study. We are not able to compare the results by Van De Kreeke JA *et al.* to our results for we do not compute the vessel density. A study by Elahi *et al.* compared the OCTA retinal phenotypes of vessel area density (VAD) and vessel skeleton density (VSD) between 24 APOE4 carriers (mean age of 72 years) and 51 APOE4 non-carriers (mean age of 75 years) at baseline [6]. The authors reported lower VAD and VSD in APOE4 carriers than in APOE4 non-carriers. We have also reported lower VSD in APOE4 carriers both cross-sectionally and longitudinally.

Another cross-sectional study enrolled 30 participants (16 biomarker-negative and 14 biomarker-positive for preclinical AD, mean age of 74.5 years, age ranging 62–92 years) [20]. Their definition of a risk participant for AD is different from ours. The study determines a participant as a high risk for developing AD based on clinically validated biomarkers measuring amyloid burden within the central nervous system using positron emission tomography (PET). This means it is not directly comparable to our study for we identify a risk participant for developing AD based on either their APOE4 status, FH status, or CAIDE score. The authors reported an increase of the FAZ area in the biomarker-positive group. We also have reported an increase of the FAZ area cross-sectionally, but only in our

CAIDE high risk group. A limitation of their study is not including the exclusion of any vascular diseases that could affect the results of their analysis.

Furthermore, the same authors investigated a follow-up of 3 years from the initial scanning of participants [21]. The participants at follow-up consisted of 11 biomarker negative and 9 biomarker positive for risk of developing AD with a mean age of 75.21 years and the authors reported an increase of the FAZ area in the biomarker positive group. We have reported a change of FAZ-based phenotypes at a 2-year follow up across the APOE4 (OD) and CAIDE (OD and OS) risk groups, but not an increase of the FAZ area. The FAZ-based phenotypes that are different between control and risk participants in the CAIDE risk group (longitudinally) can be viewed in the supplementary material for this study.

A more recent study investigated alterations with OCTA retinal phenotypes between control and risk participants for developing AD both cross-sectionally and longitudinally [19]. The cross-sectional results report that APOE4 carriers had lower perfused density. Perfusion density is the only OCTA retinal phenotype common between our studies. Our equivalent retinal phenotype to perfusion density is VSD and we also reported a decrease of VSD, but in participants with a high CAIDE score (OD and OS). The study enrolled 218 individuals with normal cognition that were aged more than 55 years (mean age of 70.55) with APOE4 status (98 APOE4 carriers and 120 non-carriers). For the longitudinal part of their study, the participants consisted of 71 APOE4 carriers and 78 non-carriers. Their longitudinal results showed continued lower perfusion density (at 2 years follow-up) in the APOE4 carriers. We also reported a continued decrease in VSD in participants with a high CAIDE score (OD and OS) longitudinally. A caveat is that the study did not adjust for multiple comparisons, stating that the nature of the study was exploratory. The authors say that any statistically significant findings would vanish once adjusted for multiple comparisons. We were able to report statistically significant findings after adjusting for multiple comparisons across all three risk groups.

A major strength of our study is the age of the PREVENT cohort. The mean age of each previously mentioned study is above 60 years of age, while the oldest participant in the PREVENT cohort can be a maximum of 59 years of age (mean age is of 51.2 years). In addition, the age variability of other participants is more than 20 years of age, while for PREVENT, the age variability is of 20 years only. This strong inclusion criteria positions the PREVENT cohort as a reliable and robust source of data for investigating the validation of candidate and common OCTA retinal phenotypes as potential biomarkers for tracking preclinical AD [18].

Furthermore, we have reported changes in OCTA retinal phenotypes between control and risk participants that have not been reported on in the literature to our knowledge.

5   Conclusion

In conclusion, we were able to demonstrate microvascular alterations in the retina of asymptomatic participants who are at risk of developing AD. At baseline, there is decreased parafoveal vessel tortuosity in risk participants who carry APOE4 (OS), in risk participants with a FH (OD), and in risk participants with a high CAIDE score (OD and OS). In addition to alterations in vessel tortuosity, we reported changes on FAZ, intercapillary spaces, and further significant changes in OCTA retinal phenotypes between control and risk participants in the CAIDE risk group. At a 2 year follow-up, the majority of the results are consistent with the cross-sectional findings. In addition, further changes in OCTA retinal phenotypes were found between control and risk participants in all three risk groups.

Acknowledgment. DR was supported by a Medical Research Council Precision Medicine Doctoral Training Programme scholarship (MR/N013166/1)

References

1. Ali, N., et al.: Clinical validation of the RTVue optical coherence tomography angiography image quality indicators. Clin. Exp. Ophthalmol. **48**(2), 192–203 (2020)
2. Benjamini, Y., Hochberg, Y.: Controlling the false discovery rate: a practical and powerful approach to multiple testing. J. Roy. Stat. Soc.: Ser. B (Methodol.) **57**(1), 289–300 (1995)
3. Blennow, K., Mattsson, N., Schöll, M., Hansson, O., Zetterberg, H.: Amyloid biomarkers in Alzheimer's disease. Trends Pharmacol. Sci. **36**(5), 297–309 (2015)
4. Cortes-Canteli, M., Iadecola, C.: Alzheimer's disease and vascular aging: JACC focus seminar. J. Am. Coll. Cardiol. **75**(8), 942–951 (2020)
5. Criscuolo, C., et al.: Assessment of retinal vascular network in amnestic mild cognitive impairment by optical coherence tomography angiography. PLoS ONE **15**(6), e0233975 (2020)
6. Elahi, F.M., et al.: Retinal imaging demonstrates reduced capillary density in clinically unimpaired APOE ε4 gene carriers. Alzheimer's Dement. Diagn. Assess. Dis. Monit. **13**(1), e12181
7. Exalto, L.G., Quesenberry, C.P., Barnes, D., Kivipelto, M., Biessels, G.J., Whitmer, R.A.: Midlife risk score for the prediction of dementia four decades later. Alzheimer's Dement. **10**(5), 562–570 (2014)
8. Giarratano, Y., et al.: Automated segmentation of optical coherence tomography angiography images: benchmark data and clinically relevant metrics. Transl. Vis. Sci. Technol. **9**(13), 5 (2020)
9. Giarratano, Y., et al.: A framework for the discovery of retinal biomarkers in optical coherence tomography angiography (OCTA). In: Fu, H., Garvin, M.K., MacGillivray, T., Xu, Y., Zheng, Y. (eds.) OMIA 2020. LNCS, vol. 12069, pp. 155–164. Springer, Cham (2020). https://doi.org/10.1007/978-3-030-63419-3_16
10. Guerreiro, R., Bras, J.: The age factor in Alzheimer's disease. Genome Med. **7**(1), 1–3 (2015)
11. Hui, J., Zhao, Y., Yu, S., Liu, J., Chiu, K., Wang, Y.: Detection of retinal changes with optical coherence tomography angiography in mild cognitive impairment and Alzheimer's disease patients: a meta-analysis. PLoS ONE **16**(8), e0255362 (2021)

12. Jack, C.R., et al.: A/T/N: an unbiased descriptive classification scheme for Alzheimer disease biomarkers. Neurology **87**(5), 539–547 (2016)
13. Jack Jr., C.R., et al.: NIA-AA research framework: toward a biological definition of Alzheimer's disease. Alzheimer's Dement. **14**(4), 535–562 (2018)
14. Janeiro, M.H., et al.: Biomarkers in Alzheimer's disease. Adv. Lab. Med./Avances en Medicina de Laboratorio **2**(1), 27–37 (2021)
15. Khoury, R., Ghossoub, E.: Diagnostic biomarkers of Alzheimer's disease: a state-of-the-art review. Biomark. Neuropsychiatry **1**, 100005 (2019)
16. Kivipelto, M., Ngandu, T., Laatikainen, T., Winblad, B., Soininen, H., Tuomilehto, J.: Risk score for the prediction of dementia risk in 20 years among middle aged people: a longitudinal, population-based study. Lancet Neurol. **5**(9), 735–741 (2006)
17. Liu, C.C., Kanekiyo, T., Xu, H., Bu, G.: Apolipoprotein E and Alzheimer disease: risk, mechanisms and therapy. Nat. Rev. Neurol. **9**(2), 106–118 (2013)
18. López-Cuenca, I., et al.: The value of oct and octa as potential biomarkers for preclinical Alzheimer's disease: a review study. Life **11**(7), 712 (2021)
19. Ma, J.P., et al.: Longitudinal analysis of the retina and choroid in cognitively normal individuals at higher genetic risk of Alzheimer disease. Ophthalmol. Retina **6**, 607–619 (2022)
20. O'Bryhim, B.E., Apte, R.S., Kung, N., Coble, D., Van Stavern, G.P.: Association of preclinical Alzheimer disease with optical coherence tomographic angiography findings. JAMA Ophthalmol. **136**(11), 1242–1248 (2018)
21. O'Bryhim, B.E., Lin, J.B., Van Stavern, G.P., Apte, R.S.: OCT angiography findings in preclinical Alzheimer's disease: 3-year follow-up. Ophthalmology **128**(10), 1489–1491 (2021)
22. Prince, M., Bryce, R., Albanese, E., Wimo, A., Ribeiro, W., Ferri, C.P.: The global prevalence of dementia: a systematic review and metaanalysis. Alzheimer's Dement. **9**(1), 63–75 (2013)
23. Rifai, O.M., et al.: The application of optical coherence tomography angiography in Alzheimer's disease: a systematic review. Alzheimer's Dement. Diagn. Assess. Dis. Monit. **13**(1), e12149 (2021)
24. Ritchie, C.W., Ritchie, K.: The prevent study: a prospective cohort study to identify mid-life biomarkers of late-onset Alzheimer's disease. BMJ Open **2**(6), e001893 (2012)
25. Secomb, T.W.: Blood flow in the microcirculation. Annu. Rev. Fluid Mech. **49**, 443–461 (2017)
26. Van De Kreeke, J.A., et al.: Optical coherence tomography angiography in preclinical Alzheimer's disease. Br. J. Ophthalmol. **104**(2), 157–161 (2020)
27. Wiseman, S.J., et al.: Measuring axial length of the eye from magnetic resonance brain imaging. BMC Ophthalmol. **22**(1), 1–9 (2022)
28. Yoon, S.P., et al.: Retinal microvascular and neurodegenerative changes in Alzheimer's disease and mild cognitive impairment compared with control participants. Ophthalmol. Retina **3**(6), 489–499 (2019)

Feature Representation Learning for Robust Retinal Disease Detection from Optical Coherence Tomography Images

Sharif Amit Kamran[1(✉)], Khondker Fariha Hossain[1], Alireza Tavakkoli[1], Stewart Lee Zuckerbrod[2], and Salah A. Baker[3]

[1] Department of Computer Science and Engineering, University of Nevada, Reno, NV, USA
skamran@nevada.unr.edu
[2] Houston Eye Associates, Houston, TX, USA
[3] School of Medicine, University of Nevada, Reno, NV, USA

Abstract. Ophthalmic images may contain identical-looking pathologies that can cause failure in automated techniques to distinguish different retinal degenerative diseases. Additionally, reliance on large annotated datasets and lack of knowledge distillation can restrict ML-based clinical support systems' deployment in real-world environments. To improve the robustness and transferability of knowledge, an enhanced feature-learning module is required to extract meaningful spatial representations from the retinal subspace. Such a module, if used effectively, can detect unique disease traits and differentiate the severity of such retinal degenerative pathologies. In this work, we propose a robust disease detection architecture with three learning heads, i) A supervised encoder for retinal disease classification, ii) An unsupervised decoder for the reconstruction of disease-specific spatial information, and iii) A novel representation learning module for learning the similarity between encoder-decoder feature and enhancing the accuracy of the model. Our experimental results on two publicly available OCT datasets illustrate that the proposed model outperforms existing state-of-the-art models in terms of accuracy, interpretability, and robustness for out-of-distribution retinal disease detection.

Keywords: Retinal degeneration · SD-OCT · Deep learning · Optical coherence tomography · Representation learning

1   Introduction

Diabetes affects up to 10.2% of the population globally, and it is projected to grow to 783 million people by 2045 [26]. With its prevalence, one-third of every diabetic patient develops Diabetic Retinopathy [27]. As the disease progresses, it can lead to Diabetic Macular Edema (DME), which is caused by damaged blood vessels which leak fluid and cause swelling, resulting in blurry vision. DME is a leading cause of vision loss among the working-age population of most developed countries [14] and affects approximately 750,000 people in the US. Even though, significant advancements in the anti-VEGF (vascular endothelial growth factor) therapy has provided patients with

B. Antony et al. (Eds.): OMIA 2022, LNCS 13576, pp. 22–32, 2022.
https://doi.org/10.1007/978-3-031-16525-2_3

treatment options that can delay the progression of the degeneration [15], without early detection of this disease can result in permanent vision loss.

Optical Coherence Tomography (OCT) is an imaging procedure used where back-scattered light is projected for capturing and analyzing the sub-retinal layers and any deformities, aneurysms, or fluid build-up [24]. OCT images are manually examined by expert ophthalmologists to diagnose any underlying retinal degenerative diseases. Hence, miscategorization of diseases can happen due to human error while perform-ing the differential diagnosis. The underlying reason is the stark similarity between DME and other retinal degenerative neuro-ocular diseases such as Age-related Mac-ular Degeneration (AMD), choroidal neovascularization (CNV), or Drusen [31]. For instance, in wet-AMD leaky blood vessels grow under the retina and cause blurry vision similar to DME. On the other hand, in choroidal neovascularization (CNV), which is a late stage of AMD, new blood vessels grow from the Bruch membrane (BM) into the subretinal pigment epithelium (sub-RPE). Experts usually encounter problems while differentiating between DME and AMD.

Recently, with the advent of deep learning, many automated systems have been deployed for the early detection of retinal degenerative diseases. Also, these architec-tures are trained and tested on the same data distribution and resulting in high prediction accuracy in their respective tasks. However, if applied to the out-of-distribution datasets, the model fails to capture intrinsic features to accurately classify the underlying degen-erative condition. So, the robustness and knowledge distillation of such systems are contentious. To address this problem, we propose a novel supervised-unsupervised rep-resentation learning module that can improve the accuracy of any retinal disease clas-sification model on unseen data distribution. Moreover, this module can be attached to any pre-trained supervised image classification models. Our extensive qualitative and quantitative experiments illustrate the proposed module's interpretability, robustness, and knowledge transferability.

2   Related Work

Many image processing techniques have been proposed to diagnose retinal degener-ative diseases One proposed method is to segment, fuse and delineate multiple reti-nal boundaries to detect anomalies and diseases from Retinal OCT images [3]. Graph cuts and region-based delineation methods have also been proposed to detect differ-ent abnormalities and degeneration in the retinal subspace [28] and for diagnosing the thickness of the choroidal folds and neovascularization [1,18]. Early approaches identi-fied Diabetic Macular Edema (DME) with 75–80% sensitivity score [4,20]. In contrast, segmentation-based approaches can help diagnose underlying causes of liquid buildup in the subretinal layers by detecting irregular retinal features and comparing the dif-ferences between healthy and the degenerated retinal tissue [13,16,19]. Even though segmentation approaches have shown success, it results in severe inaccuracies when applied to OCT images acquired from different OCT acquisition systems [7].

Deep convolutional neural networks (DCNNs) have recently received state-of-the-art results in identifying different retinal degenerative diseases [12]. For example, Fang et al. incorporated CNNs with graph search to simultaneously segment retinal layer boundaries and detect degeneration for patients having Age-related Macular Edema [5]. On the other hand, Xu et al. proposed a Dual-stage framework that utilizes CNNs to segment retinal pigment epithelium detachment [30]. Kamran et al. proposed a novel deep learning architecture called OpticNet-71 that achieved state-of-the-art accuracy in two OCT image benchmarks for identifying DME, AMD, CNV, etc. [8]. Subsequent works have also utilized MobileNet-v2 [17], MobileNet-v3 [29] and VGG16 [11,25] for retinal disease classification. Despite achieving high accuracy in their respective benchmarks, most of these architectures do not converge and lack robustness and knowledge transferability when evaluated on an out-of-distribution dataset, as reported in [9]. To alleviate this, the authors in [9] proposed a joint-attention network with a supervised classifier and unsupervised image reconstruction module. Adopting an adaptive loss function, the model achieved 1.8–9.0% improvement over three baseline state-of-the-art models, namely ResNet-50, MobileNet-v2, and OpticNet-71 on an out-of-distribution dataset. However, the model can perform poorly due to adaptive learning prioritizing image reconstruction over disease classification. Moreover, due to using non-learnable upsampling layers in the image reconstruction module, the model does not retain intrinsic features, hampering overall accuracy and robustness.

We propose a novel robust feature representation learning (RFRL) network that can be incorporated into any deep classification architecture for robust out-of-distribution retinal disease detection. Our module consists of 1) a supervised learning head for classifying diseases, 2) an unsupervised decoder head for disease-specific spatial image reconstruction, and 3) a novel representation learning head for finding similar features robustly from the encoder and decoder of the architecture. Furthermore, the proposed representation learning head incorporates a novel multi-stage feature similarity loss to boost the model's accuracy on out-of-distribution samples. Our experiments confirm that the proposed RFRL network incorporated into baseline and state-of-the-art architectures significantly improves accuracy, sensitivity, and specificity for OOD datasets. Furthermore, we qualitatively evaluate its interpretability using GradCAM [22] and GradCAMv2 [2] to prove its clinical significance. Expert ophthalmologists can leverage this module to improve disease detection from OCT b-scans on OOD datasets and avoid sub-par performance.

3 Methodology

3.1 Robust Feature Learning Architecture

An image classification architecture consists of an encoder module with multiple learnable convolution layers (top left in Fig. 1) and a supervised downstream classification head with global average pooling and dense layers (bottom left in Fig. 1). In addition, we propose an unsupervised decoder head (top right in Fig. 1) for image reconstruction and a feature representation learning head between the encoder and decoder (bottom right in Fig. 1) to be incorporated with the architecture. The objective of the unsupervised module is to reconstruct the original image and learn its intrinsic spatial features. Moreover, we use skip-connections to retain disease-specific and domain-invariant spatial features that help in overall classification performance.

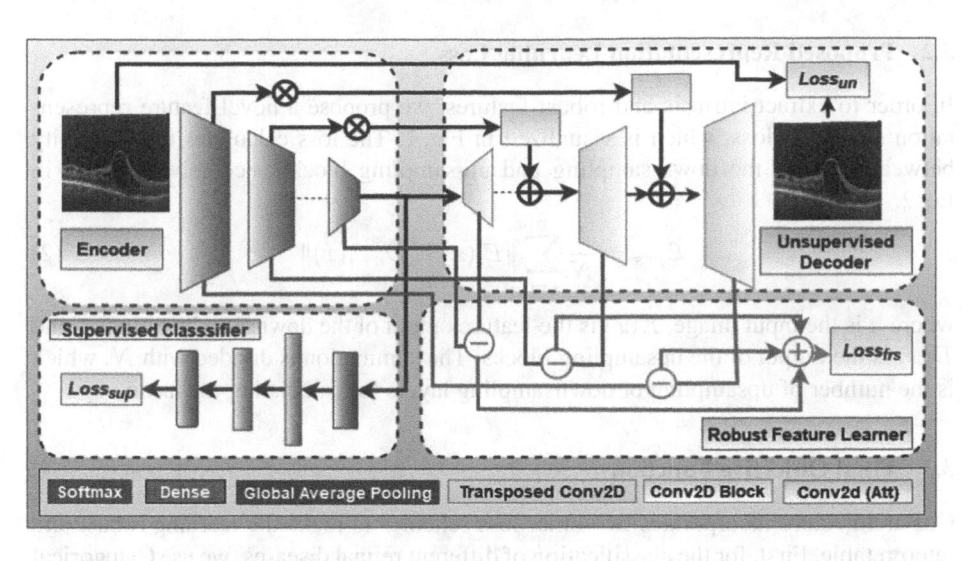

Fig. 1. RFRL-network consisting of (1) Encoder, (2) Unsupervised Decoder, (3) Robust Feature Learner and (4) Supervised Classifier. The unsupervised decoder incorporates mean-squared-error (MSE), supervised classifier utilizes cross-entropy loss and the robust feature learner adopts our novel Feature Representation Similarity (FRS) loss.

Joint-Attention Network [9] incorporated non-learnable bilinear upsampling layers in their unsupervised decoder. As a result, the spatial feature information was insufficient to reconstruct the original image with disease pathology. However, their experiment illustrated an improved overall accuracy over the baseline methods. To further improve upon this, we propose learnable transposed convolution layers for upsampling in our unsupervised decoder, as shown in Fig. 1. The transposed convolution consists of kernel size, $k = 3$, and stride, $s = 2$. Consequently, our method can retain class-specific and domain-independent spatial salient information, an essential missing feature in the low performance of the traditional encoder-based architectures in practice.

The improved decoder utilizes a mean-squared-error loss to learn original image features in an unsupervised manner without any ground truth or class labels. Outputs from each downsampling block in the encoder module are connected with each upsampling block in the decoder module with a skip connection. A convolution layer is used as an attention mechanism and element-wise summation of features between encoder and decoder module, as illustrated in Fig. 1. The output of the decoder can thus be defined by the Eq. (1):

$$O_{recon} = E_0 \otimes A_n \oplus D_n(\cdots E_{n-2} \otimes A_2 \oplus D_1(E_{n-1} \otimes A_1 \oplus D_0(E_n \otimes A_0))) \quad (1)$$

where, $E_0, E_1, ... E_n$ are the output of each of the downsampling blocks, while $D_0, D_1, .. D_n$ symbolise the transposed convolution layers of the decoder. $A_0, A_1, ..., A_n$ are the convolution operations of attention skip-connections for maintaining the same depth as the output of the corresponding up-sampling layer for element-wise summing.

3.2 Proposed Representation Learning Loss

In order to extract intrinsic and robust features, we propose a novel feature representation similarity loss, which is visualized in Fig. 1. The loss calculates the similarity between each of the down-sampling and up-sampling blocks successively, given in Eq. 2.

$$\mathcal{L}_{frs} = \frac{1}{N} \sum_{i=0}^{n} \| E_i(x) - D_{n-i}(x) \| \tag{2}$$

where x is the input image, $E(x)$ is the feature output of the downsampling blocks, and $D(x)$ is the output of the upsampling blocks. The summation is divided with N, which is the number of upsampling or downsampling layers for calculating the mean.

3.3 Final Objective Function

Our architecture incorporates two other loss schemes to make the learning robust and interpretable. First, for the classification of different retinal diseases, we use Categorical cross-entropy in the supervised classifier given by $\mathcal{L}_{sup}$ equation in Eq. (3). Secondly, for calculating the difference between real and reconstructed images, we use Mean-Squared Error (MSE) loss in the unsupervised decoder given by the $\mathcal{L}_{un}$ in Eq. (4).

$$\mathcal{L}_{sup} = -\sum_{i=1}^{c} y_i \log(y_i') \tag{3}$$

$$\mathcal{L}_{un} = \frac{1}{M} \sum_{i}^{M} (x_i - x_i')^2 \tag{4}$$

Here, in Eq. 3, y_i signifies the ground truth label, y_i' symbolizes predicted output, c is for the number of disease categories. In Eq. 4, x_i is the input image, x_i' is the reconstructed output image, and M is the number of pixels in the image.

By combining Eq. 2, Eq. 3 and Eq. 4, we create our final objective function given in Eq. 5.

$$\mathcal{L} = \mathcal{L}_{sup} + \mathcal{L}_{un} + \mathcal{L}_{frs} \tag{5}$$

Unlike the Joint-attention-Network [9] we do not utilize any weights to prioritize one or more of these losses. Instead, equal priority is given to all of them for robust feature learning and improved accuracy, sensitivity, and specificity.

4   Experiments

4.1 Data-Set Processing

We evaluate our proposed architecture models on two separate data-sets, **Srinivasan2014** [24] and **OCT2017** [10]. The **Srinivasan2014** dataset comprises 3,231 images, out of which 2,916 are for training and 5-fold cross-validation, and 315 are for testing. It has three categories of images, Normal, AMD, and DME. The model with

Table 1. Test results on in-distribution Srinivasan2014 [24] Dataset

Architectures	Year	Accuracy		Specificity		Sensitivity	
ResNet50-v1 [23]	2018	94.92		97.46		94.92	
OpticNet-71 [8]	2019	100.00		100.00		100.00	
MobileNet-v2 [9,17]	2020	97.46		98.73		97.46	
VGG16 [11,25]	2021	99.04		99.52		99.04	
MobileNet-v3 [29]	2022	83.80		91.90		87.61	
Joint-Attention-Network ResNet50-v1 [9]	2020	100	↑5.08	100.00	↑2.54	100.00	↑5.08
Joint-Attention-Network OpticNet-71 [9]	2020	99.68	↓0.32	99.84	↓0.16	99.68	↓0.32
Joint-Attention-Network MobileNet-v2 [9]	2020	99.36	↑1.90	99.68	↑0.95	99.36	↑1.90
RFRL-Network ResNet50-v1	2022	100	↑5.08	100.00	↑2.54	100.00	↑5.08
RFRL-Network OpticNet-71	2022	100.0	(−)	100.0	(−)	100.0	(−)
RFRL-Network MobileNet-v2	2022	99.68	↑ 2.22	99.84	↑ 1.11	99.52	↑ 2.06
RFRL-Network VGG16	2022	99.68	↑ 0.64	99.84	↑ 0.32	99.52	↑ 0.64
RFRL-Network MobileNet-v3	2022	99.36	↑ 15.56	99.68	↑ 7.78	99.52	↑ 11.91

the best validation result on the **Srinivasan2014** dataset was used for further testing on the out-of-distribution (OOD) second dataset, i.e., **OCT2017**. The OCT2017 consists of four distinct categories of 1000 test images. We take 250 cases of Normal and DME (in total, 500 samples) for OOD testing. All images for training and testing were resized to $224 \times 224 \times 3$ resolution. Moreover, we incorporated random data augmentation techniques such as horizontal flip, rotation, zoom, width, and height shift for the training set.

4.2 Hyper-parameter Tuning

For training baseline methods and RFRL-Networks, we used Adam optimizer. Moreover, it was the same for both the supervised classifier and the unsupervised decoder. The initial learning rate, $lr = 0.0001$. We utilized a mini-batch of $b = 4$ and trained all methods for 50 epochs. We reduced the learning rate by 0.1 if the validation loss did not decrease for six epochs. The code repository is provided in this link.

4.3 Performance Metrics

We used three standard metrics for calculating the Accuracy, Sensitivity (True Positive Rate) and Specificity (True Negative Rate). The metrics are calculated as follows, Accuracy $= \frac{1}{N} \sum \frac{TP+TN}{TP+TN+FN+FP}$, Sensitivity $= \frac{1}{K} \sum \frac{TP}{TP+FN}$, and Specificity $= \frac{1}{K} \sum \frac{TN}{TN+FP}$.

4.4   Quantitative Evaluation

We worked with five baseline architectures across two distinct data sets to evaluate our model's initial performance. Each of these methods have already been incorporated for retinal disease classification from OCT B-scans [8,17,23,25,29], out of which OpticNet-71 [8] has achieved state-of-the-art result on OCT2017 [10] and Srinavasan2014 [24] datasets. Subramaniam et al. proposed an architecture based on VGG16 [25] which achieved superior results on seven different pathologies, namely, AMD, CNV, DRUSEN, DMR, DR, MH, and CSR. Quite recently, Wang et al. proposed a model based on MobileNet-v3 [29] which achieved scores on par with Optic-Net on the OCT2017 dataset. For a fair comparison, we trained these five models from scratch on the **Srinivasan2014** dataset with 5-fold cross validation. After choosing the best model, we tested on the data distribution familiar to the architecture, which is the **Srinivasan2014** test set of 315 images. We then train, validate and test in the same manner with our proposed RFRL-network on the same data distribution. The quantitative comparison is given in Table 1. As it can be seen, our method's performance

Table 2. Test results on out-of-distribution OCT2017 [10] dataset

Architectures	Year	Accuracy		Specificity		Sensitivity	
ResNet50-v1 [6]	2018	83.40	↓11.52	89.40	↓8.06	83.40	↓11.52
OpticNet-71 [8]	2019	74.40	↓25.60	85.60	↓14.40	74.40	↓25.60
MobileNet-v2 [21]	2020	93.80	↓3.66	96.70	↓2.03	93.80	↓3.66
VGG16 [11,25]	2021	92.40	↓6.64	95.13	↓4.39	92.40	↓6.64
MobileNet-v3 [29]	2022	71.60	↓12.20	85.50	↓6.40	71.60	↓16.01
Joint-Attention-Network ResNet50-v1 [9]	2020	92.40	↑9.0	95.00	↑5.6	92.40	↑9.0
Joint-Attention-Network OpticNet-71 [9]	2020	77.40	↑3.0	89.00	↑3.4	77.40	↑3.0
Joint-Attention-Network MobileNet-v2 [9]	2020	95.60	↑1.8	97.1	↑0.4	95.60	↑1.8
RFRL-Network ResNet50-v1	2022	96.40	↑13.0	97.67	↑8.27	96.40	↑13.0
RFRL-Network OpticNet-71	2022	77.60	↑3.2	86.20	↑0.6	77.60	↑3.2
RFRL-Network MobileNet-v2	2022	95.80	↑2.0	95.80	↓0.9	95.80	↑2.0
RFRL-Network VGG16	2022	96.80	↑4.4	97.93	↑4.8	96.80	↑4.4
RFRL-Network MobileNet-v3	2022	74.60	↑3.0	84.06	↓1.44	74.60	↑3.0

for the five models exceeds the baseline scores. Moreover, Joint-Attention-Network [9] also supersedes the baseline methods; however, both our methods for OpticNet-71 and MobileNet-v2 achieve better scores. For our next benchmark, we test the models on the out-of-distribution test set to evaluate their robustness and knowledge transferability. We use the 500 test images with Normal and DME categories from the **OCT2017** data-set for this evaluation. As illustrated in Table 2, our model retains intrinsic spatial information that helps it achieve higher accuracy than the baseline methods and Joint-Attention-Networks. It should be noted that none of the **OCT2017** images were used for training or validating the models. The most significant improvement is seen in ResNet50-v1, with a 4.0% increase in accuracy over Joint-Attention-Network. Also, there was a slight specificity drop for MobileNet architectures. Still, it is negligible, as correctly classifying diseases (sensitivity) is more important than misclassifying patients without conditions (specificity). We only report test results for ResNet50-v1, OpticNet-71, MobileNet-v2 versions of the Joint-attention-network [9] as these were provided in the literature. Nonetheless, the proposed RFRL-network retains more robust and intrinsic features across different methods and evaluation settings.

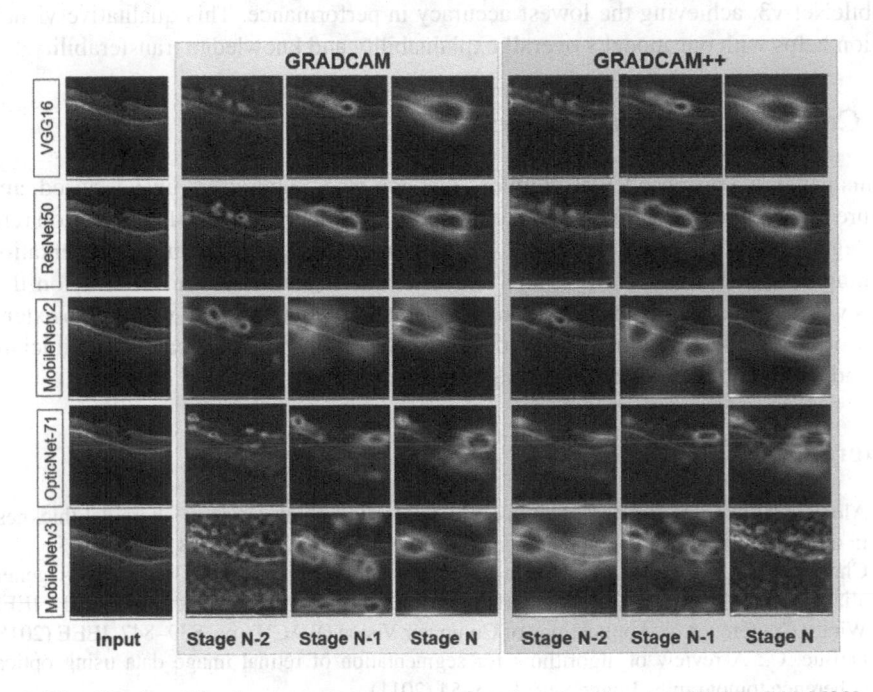

Fig. 2. Visualization of back-propagated gradient activation signals using GRAD-CAM [22] and GRAD-CAM++ [2] on five different RFRL network. Here, Stage N is the last layer of the encoder, the Stage N-1 and Stage N-2 are preceding layers.

4.5 Qualitative Evaluation

For producing "visual explanations" for judgments made by our CNN architectures for accurate classification, we use GRAD-CAM [22] and GRAD-CAM++ [2]. These methods use back-propagated gradients to visualize essential regions of the images of a specific layer, amplified for the classification decision's maximum probability. In Fig. 2, we illustrate the differences in activations of three stages of the encoder layer for five of our methods on a DME image from OCT2017 [10] dataset. Stage N is the last convolution layer before the global average pooling, so it does not have any skip-connection with the unsupervised decoder. However, Stage N-1 and Stage N-2 are the previous encoder layers with attention skip-connections. Additionally, they are utilized for Feature Representation Similarity loss, $\mathcal{L}_{frs}$. From Fig. 2, row 1–2, it is apparent that VGG16 and ResNet50-v1 got activated signals in regions with fluid buildup and hard exudates, explaining the identification of DME in different stages of the encoder. However, in rows 4–5, Optic-Net-71 and MobileNet-v3 got fewer activated signals and activations in the unimportant region, which helped classify the image as DME. The visualization also follows similar trends to standard metrics, where VGG16 achieves the highest to MobileNet-v3, achieving the lowest accuracy in performance. This qualitative visualization helps with our model's overall explainability and knowledge transferability.

5 Conclusion and Future Work

In this paper, we propose RFRL-network that combines supervised, unsupervised, and feature representation learning to make the robust classifiers for out-of-distribution retinal degeneration detection. Moreover, by incorporating a novel feature representation learning loss, our architecture retains intrinsic and essential feature information that helps with knowledge transferability and explainability. In the future, we wish to extend our work to identifying other retinal degenerative conditions. This can help clinicians in conducting complex differential diagnoses.

References

1. Alonso-Caneiro, D., Read, S., Collins, M.: Automatic segmentation of choroidal thickness in optical coherence tomography. Biomed. Opt. Express **4**(12), 2795–2812 (2013)
2. Chattopadhay, A., Sarkar, A., Howlader, P., Balasubramanian, V.N.: Grad-Cam++: generalized gradient-based visual explanations for deep convolutional networks. In: 2018 IEEE Winter Conference on Applications of Computer Vision (WACV), pp. 839–847. IEEE (2018)
3. DeBuc, C.: A review of algorithms for segmentation of retinal image data using optical coherence tomography. Image Seg. **1**, 15–54 (2011)
4. Ege, B.: Screening for diabetic retinopathy using computer based image analysis and statistical classification. Comput. Methods Programs Biomed. **62**(3), 165–175 (2000)
5. Fang, L., Cunefare, D., Wang, C., Guymer, R.H., Li, S., Farsiu, S.: Automatic segmentation of nine retinal layer boundaries in oct images of non-exudative AMD patients using deep learning and graph search. Biomed. Opt. Express **8**(5), 2732–2744 (2017)
6. He, K., Zhang, X., Ren, S., Sun, J.: Deep residual learning for image recognition. In: Proceedings of the IEEE Conference on Computer Vision and Pattern Recognition, pp. 770–778 (2016)

7. Kafieh, R., Rabbani, H., Kermani, S.: A review of algorithms for segmentation of optical coherence tomography from retina. J. Med. Sig. Sens. **3**(1), 45 (2013)
8. Kamran, S.A., Saha, S., Sabbir, A.S., Tavakkoli, A.: Optic-Net: a novel convolutional neural network for diagnosis of retinal diseases from optical tomography images. In: IEEE International Conference on Machine Learning and Applications, pp. 964–971 (2019)
9. Kamran, S.A., Tavakkoli, A., Zuckerbrod, S.L.: Improving robustness using joint attention network for detecting retinal degeneration from optical coherence tomography images. In: 2020 IEEE International Conference On Image Processing (ICIP), pp. 2476–2480. IEEE (2020)
10. Kermany, D.S., et al.: Identifying medical diagnoses and treatable diseases by image-based deep learning. Cell **172**(5), 1122–1131 (2018)
11. Kim, J., Tran, L.: Retinal disease classification from oct images using deep learning algorithms. In: 2021 IEEE Conference on Computational Intelligence in Bioinformatics and Computational Biology (CIBCB), pp. 1–6. IEEE (2021)
12. Lee, C.S., Baughman, D.M., Lee, A.Y.: Deep learning is effective for classifying normal versus age-related macular degeneration OCT images. Ophthalmol. Retina **1**(4), 322–327 (2017)
13. Lee, K., Niemeijer, M., Garvin, M.K., Kwon, Y.H., Sonka, M., Abramoff, M.D.: Segmentation of the optic disc in 3-D OCT scans of the optic nerve head. IEEE Trans. Med. Imaging **29**(1), 159–168 (2010)
14. Lee, R., Wong, T.Y., Sabanayagam, C.: Epidemiology of diabetic retinopathy, diabetic macular edema and related vision loss. Eye Vis. **2**(1), 1–25 (2015)
15. Lim, L.S., Mitchell, P., Seddon, J.M., Holz, F.G., Wong, T.Y.: Age-related macular degeneration. Lancet **379**(9827), 1728–1738 (2012)
16. MeindertNiemeijer, X.C., Lee, L.Z.K., Abràmoff, M.D., Sonka, M.: 3D segmentation of fluid-associated abnormalities in retinal OCT: probability constrained graph-search-graph-cut. IEEE Trans. Med. Imaging **31**(8), 1521–1531 (2012)
17. Nugroho, H.A., Nurfauzi, R.: Convolutional neural network for classifying retinal diseases from OCT2017 dataset. In: 2021 4th International Conference on Information and Communications Technology (ICOIACT), pp. 295–298. IEEE (2021)
18. Philip, A.M., et al.: Choroidal thickness maps from spectral domain and swept source optical coherence tomography: algorithmic versus ground truth annotation. Br. J. Ophthalmol. **100**(10), 1372–1376 (2016)
19. Quellec, G., Lee, K., Dolejsi, M., Garvin, M.K., Abramoff, M.D., Sonka, M.: Three-dimensional analysis of retinal layer texture: identification of fluid-filled regions in SD-OCT of the macula. IEEE Trans. Med. Imaging **29**(6), 1321–1330 (2010)
20. Sánchez, C.I., Hornero, R., Lopez, M., Poza, J.: Retinal image analysis to detect and quantify lesions associated with diabetic retinopathy. In: The 26th Annual International Conference of the IEEE Engineering in Medicine and Biology Society, pp. 1624–1627 (2004)
21. Sandler, M., Howard, A., Zhu, M., Zhmoginov, A., Chen, L.C.: MobileNetV2: inverted residuals and linear bottlenecks. In: Proceedings of the IEEE Conference on Computer Vision and Pattern Recognition, pp. 4510–4520 (2018)
22. Selvaraju, R.R., Cogswell, M., Das, A., Vedantam, R., Parikh, D., Batra, D.: Grad-CAM: visual explanations from deep networks via gradient-based localization. In: Proceedings of the IEEE International Conference on Computer Vision, pp. 618–626 (2017)
23. Serener, A., Serte, S.: Dry and wet age-related macular degeneration classification using OCT images and deep learning. In: 2019 Scientific Meeting on Electrical-Electronics & Biomedical Engineering and Computer Science (EBBT), pp. 1–4. IEEE (2019)
24. Srinivasan, P.P., et al.: Fully automated detection of diabetic macular edema and dry age-related macular degeneration from optical coherence tomography images. Biomed Opt. Express **5**(10), 3568–3577 (2014)

25. Subramanian, M., Shanmugavadivel, K., Naren, O.S., Premkumar, K., Rankish, K.: Classification of retinal oct images using deep learning. In: 2022 International Conference on Computer Communication and Informatics (ICCCI), pp. 1–7. IEEE (2022)

26. Sun, H., et al.: IDF diabetes atlas: global, regional and country-level diabetes prevalence estimates for 2021 and projections for 2045. Diabetes Res. Clin. Pract. **183**, 109119 (2022)

27. Ting, D.S.W., Cheung, G.C.M., Wong, T.Y.: Diabetic retinopathy: global prevalence, major risk factors, screening practices and public health challenges: a review. Clin. Exp. Ophthalmol. **44**(4), 260–277 (2016)

28. Vermeer, K., Van derSchoot, J., Lemij, H., DeBoer, J.: Automated segmentation by pixel classification of retinal layers in ophthalmic OCT images. Biomed Opt. Express **2**(6), 1743–1756 (2011)

29. Wang, X., Gu, Y.: Classification of macular abnormalities using a lightweight CNN-SVM framework. Meas. Sci. Technol. **33**(6) (2022)

30. Xu, Y., et al.: Dual-stage deep learning framework for pigment epithelium detachment segmentation in polypoidal choroidal vasculopathy. Biomed Opt. Express **8**(9), 4061–4076 (2017)

31. Yau, J.W., et al.: Global prevalence and major risk factors of diabetic retinopathy. Diab. Care **35**(3), 556–564 (2012)

GUNet: A GCN-CNN Hybrid Model for Retinal Vessel Segmentation by Learning Graphical Structures

Yishuo Zhang and Albert C. S. Chung[✉]

Department of Computer Science and Engineering,
Hong Kong University of Science and Technology, Sai Kung, Hong Kong
ys.zhang@connect.ust.hk, achung@cse.ust.hk

Abstract. In the retinal vessel segmentation task, maintaining graphical structures of vessels is important for the following analysis steps. However, this task is challenging due to the tiny structures of vessels and bad image quality. Existing methods based on Convolutional Neural Networks (CNNs) can capture local appearances from the regular image grid but are limited to learning high-level features from graphical structures. Motivated by Graph Convolution Networks (GCNs) which capture information on graphs, we propose a novel GCN-CNN hybrid U-shaped model, namely GUNet, which is capable of extracting graphical information of vessels. The hybrid model inherits both merits of CNNs and GCNs. The convolutional blocks extract basic feature representations from local appearances while the GCN blocks learn high-level long-range graphical features along vessels at a deep level. To obtain graphs which effectively represent vessels, we constructed graphs based on the preliminary vessel skeleton segmentation followed by a Hessian filter for vessel enhancement. GUNet takes raw images and corresponding graphs as input and can be trained in an end-to-end manner. The proposed method is evaluated on two fundus photography datasets (STARE and CHASE) and one Scanning Laser Ophthalmoscopy (SLO) dataset (IOSTAR). We conduct experiments to demonstrate that the GCNs module brings significant benefits in terms of graphical similarity and further leads to better overall performances. GUNet also achieves competitive performances compared with state-of-the-art methods.

Keywords: Retinal vessel segmentation · Convolutional Neural Networks · Graph Convolutional Networks · Graphical structure

1 Introduction

Retinal vessel segmentation is the first step for retinal vessel analysis which is commonly applied in both research and clinical communities. The vasculature has a graph-like structure which can be a shape prior during segmentation. Leaning graphical structures of vessels can not only improve the segmentation

B. Antony et al. (Eds.): OMIA 2022, LNCS 13576, pp. 33–42, 2022.
https://doi.org/10.1007/978-3-031-16525-2_4

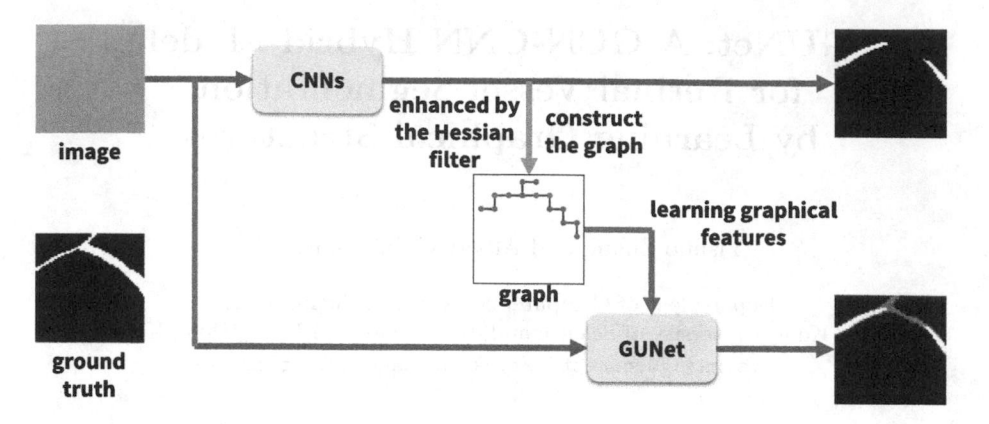

Fig. 1. Learning graphical structures of vessels.

accuracy but also benefit the following analysis steps. However, it is challenging to obtain accurate vessel segmentation with good graphical structures. On the one hand, the tiny structures of vessels and other objects increase the difficulty of detecting vessels; on the other hand, existing imaging modalities, such as fundus photography and scanning laser ophthalmoscopy, suffer from poor image quality and low contrast which affect accuracy in segmentation (Fig. 1).

In recent years, Convolutional Neural Networks (CNNs) based methods [3, 12,13,21,22,26] have been proposed for retinal vessel segmentation and achieved promising results. However, due to the instinct of convolution, CNNs are good at learning local appearances on regular image grids but fail to utilize graphical patterns of vessels. Motivated by Graph Convolutional Networks (GCNs) [10,19], some works attempt to capture features on graphs and learn graphical features in segmentation tasks [9,17,18,24]. However, learning the graphical structures of vessels in the retinal vessel segmentation task has not been fully explored. Existing CNNs or GCNs based methods also focus on pixel-wise performances and pay less attention to evaluating the graphical similarity of vessels.

In this paper, we further develop GCN-based methods for retinal vessel segmentation. To exploit the graphical structures of vessels, we first represent vessels by graphs. The graphs are constructed based on the preliminary vessel skeleton segmentation followed by a Hassian filter to enhance vessels. Our proposed GCN-CNN hybrid model, namely GUNet, takes image patches and corresponding graphs as input and can be trained in an end-to-end manner. In the GUNet model, the GCNs module which contains a series of graph convolution layers is placed at the deep level of the U-shaped structure. GUNet inherits the merits of CNNs and GCNs, which jointly exploits features from both the image grid and graphical structures of vessels. Convolutional blocks extract rich basic feature representations at low levels while the GCNs module captures high-level graphical information. After GCNs amend features maps based on extracted graphical features, the CNNs decoder produces final predictions. In the experiments, we evaluated the proposed method on three benchmarking datasets in two imaging

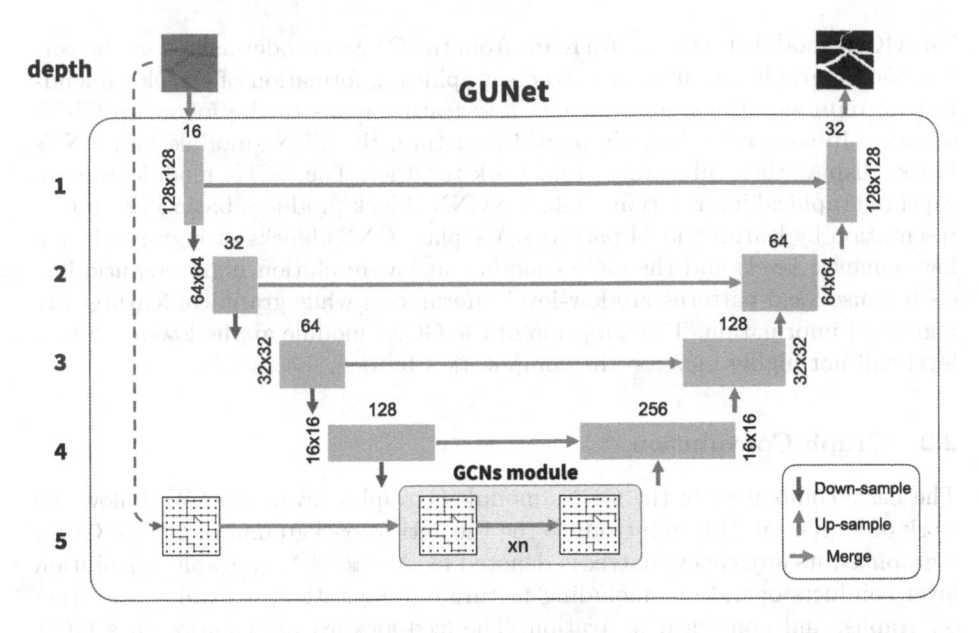

Fig. 2. Overview of GUNet.

modalities. The introduction of the GCNs module yields a significant boost on graphical similarity as well as overall performance. Our proposed method also achieved competitive performance compared with state-of-the-art methods.

2 Method

2.1 GUNet

GUNet is a U-shaped GCN-CNN hybrid model. The U-shaped structure shares the similar idea with UNet [16], as illustrated in Fig. 2. It consists of an encoder and a decoder. The encoder extracts features from multiple resolutions while the decoder produces the final segmentation. The skip connections link corresponding blocks at two sides, helping the decoder reconstruct spatial information. To increase the learning capacity of CNNs, we adopt the densely connected convolutional [7] block as the basic component in the encoder and the decoder. Each convolutional block contains two densely connected convolutional layers. Each convolutional layer uses 3×3 convolutional kernel, followed by a Batch Normalization layer and a ReLU layer. The design of dense connections effectively enables the reuse of features and helps gradient back-propagation. We adopt the max-pooling layer for down-sample and the transposed convolution layer for up-sampling.

At the deep level between the encoder and the decoder, the convolutional block is replaced by the GCNs module, which consists of several GCN layers.

The GCNs module takes feature maps from the CNNs encoder as well as the corresponding graphs as input. It extracts graphical information of vessels, amends feature representations, and outputs new feature maps to the follow-up CNNs decoder. In such a GCN-CNN hybrid structure, the GCNs module and CNNs blocks display their advantages and work together. The GCNs module aims to capture graphical information while the CNNs block produces basic feature representation by learning local patterns. We place CNNs blocks at high-resolution low-semantic levels and the GCNs module at low-resolution high-semantic levels because local patterns are low-level information while graphical features are high-level information. The adoption of the GCNs module at the low-resolution level will not highly increase the computation burden.

2.2   Graph Convolution

The basic component of the GCNs module is graph convolution. We follow the work of Kipf et al. [10] to introduce the theoretical background of GCNs. Given a graph $\mathbf{G}$, its adjacency matrix is denoted by $\mathbf{A} \in \mathbb{R}^{N \times N}$. A graph convolution layer conducts operations including feature representation, feature aggregation on graphs, and non-linear activation. The feed-forward propagation in a GCN layer is conducted as

$$\mathbf{H}^{l+1} = \sigma\left(\hat{\mathbf{A}}\mathbf{H}^l\mathbf{W}^l\right), \tag{1}$$

where $\mathbf{H}^l$ are the hidden features of the lth layer; $\hat{\mathbf{A}} = \hat{\mathbf{D}}^{-1/2}\left(\mathbf{A} + \mathbf{I}\right)\hat{\mathbf{D}}^{-1/2}$ is the re-normalization of the adjacency matrix, and $\hat{\mathbf{D}}$ is the corresponding degree matrix of $\mathbf{A} + \mathbf{I}$; $\sigma\left(\cdot\right)$ is a non-linear function, e.g., the ReLU function; and $\mathbf{W}^l$ is the learnable matrix in the lth layer.

Several GCN layers can be stacked to obtain more capacity for learning complicated features. In this work, the GCNs module contains four GCN layers and no convolutional layer. The residual connection is added to each GCN layer to enable a deeper structure.

2.3   Graph Construction

We construct graphs for each image before training GUNet. The ground truth is not available for constructing graphs, therefore, we need to construct graphs from raw images. As the graphs are used at low-resolution levels, the widths of vessels are not necessary information. Therefore, we construct graphs based on vessel skeletons. The process of constructing graphs is illustrated in Fig. 3.

We train a simple U-Net model to produce the preliminary vessel skeleton segmentation. To fully detect vessels, we adopt the Hessian filter [1] to enhance the preliminary vessel skeleton segmentation results. One advantage of producing vessel skeletons instead of vessels is that we can simplify the searching process for the kernel size inside the Hessian filter. A fixed kernel size can handle all vessel skeletons, which can be determined by parameter searching based on the quality of results. Then, a thinning operation is performed to obtain vessel skeletons.

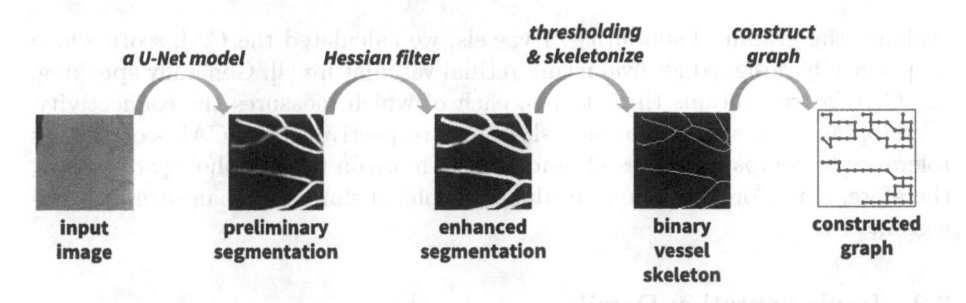

Fig. 3. The process of constructing graphs.

On a high-resolution dataset, we can further train the model to produce dilated vessel skeletons and choose a larger kernel inside the Hessian filter for robustness. After we obtain vessel skeletons, we down-sampled them to fit the resolutions of the GCNs module inside GUNet. Finally, we construct graphs based on the obtained vessel skeletons.

The graphs follow these three rules: (1) All pixels are included in the graph. (2) Pixels on the vessel skeletons are linked to their direct neighbours if their neighbours are also located on the vessel skeletons. (3) Pixels not on the vessel skeletons remain isolated. We can obtain graphs with a fixed number of nodes, which makes it easy to implement as tensor calculation. We omit the isolated pixels in Fig. 3 for better visualization.

3   Experiments

3.1   Datasets and Evaluation Metrics

We evaluated the proposed method on three benchmark datasets in two imaging modalities. Two fundus photography datasets include the STARE[1] [6] and the CHASE dataset[2] [2]. The STARE dataset [6] contains 20 fundus photographs with a resolution of 700 × 605. The CHASE dataset contains 28 images with a resolution of 960 × 999. Following the setting in previous works [5,8], the first 10/20 images in the STARE/CHASE dataset are used for training and the remaining 10/8 images are used for testing. We only evaluated pixels inside the FOV (Field of View). The Scanning Laser Ophthalmoscopy (SLO) image dataset is the IOSTAR [25] dataset. It contains 30 SLO images with a high resolution of 1024 × 1024. Following [20], the first 20 images are used for training and the remaining 10 images are used for testing. During training, one image is excluded from the training set as the evaluation set for hyper-parameters searching.

We report Accuracy (Acc), Area Under the ROC Curve (AUC), and Dice score (Dice) as evaluation metrics to reflect the pixel-wise performances. Due to the severe imbalance, the pixel-wise metrics can not show obvious gaps. To

---

[1] https://cecas.clemson.edu/~ahoover/stare/.

[2] https://blogs.kingston.ac.uk/retinal/chasedb1/.

evaluate the graphical similarity of vessels, we calculated the CAL score which is specifically designed for evaluating retinal vasculature [4]. Generally speaking, the CAL score contains three terms, each of which measures the connectivity, overlapping area, and overlapping skeletons, respectively. The CAL score allows tolerance to compare two vessels and focuses more on the morphology of vessels, therefore, it is more suitable to evaluate graphical similarity than regular pixel-wise metrics.

3.2 Implementation Details

The proposed method has been implemented under the PyTorch framework. All experiments were conducted on one NVIDIA GeForce GTX 1080Ti GPU and each took 2–4 h for training. We used AdamW algorithm with a learning rate of 0.0001 and a weight decay rate of 0.0005.

Regarding image pre-processing, each fundus image has been converted to a grayscale image. For training, we randomly sampled 1000 patches from each image. For testing, we used a sliding window with a stride of 16 to sample patches. The final result for the whole image was achieved by aggregating the predictions of local image patches. We performed image flipping and image rotation for data augmentation.

4 Results

4.1 Experiments on Fundus Photography

Ablation Study. We first conducted ablation experiments on the STARE and CHASE datasets to study the effect of the GCNs module. We report the Dice score to reflect pixel-wise performance and the CAL score to reflect graphical similarity in Table 1. P-values are calculated by paired t-tests between GUNet and the compared model in terms of the CAL scores. $p < 0.05$ indicated a significant improvement over the compared model.

The baseline model is a UNet model with densely connected convolution blocks. Compared with the baseline model, GUNet yielded a 2.96%/0.9% higher CAL score on the STARE/CHASE dataset. It showed that applying the GCN module brings a boost in terms of graphical similarity and verified the effectiveness of the proposed GCN-CNN hybrid structure.

Moreover, we consider a special case where all edges in graphs are removed. According to Eq. 1, graph convolutional layers will degenerate to linear layers. The model yields a CAL score of 79.79%/76.67% on the STARE/CHASE dataset, which shows less gain compared to the results by using normally constructed graphs. It verified that graphical connections bring benefits to the model. In another experiment, we omitted the Hessian filter and constructed graphs with vessels not enhanced. The quality of constructed graphs become worse and it yielded a CAL score of 81.03%/78.12% on the STARE/CHASE dataset, worse than the normal setting. It showed that the Hessian filter can detect more vessels and obtain better graphs.

Table 1. Ablation experiments on the STARE and CHASE dataset.

Model	STARE			CHASE		
	Dice (%)	CAL (%)	p-value	Dice (%)	CAL (%)	p-value
Baseline	81.42	78.77	0.0092	81.17	77.87	0.0163
GUNet w/o edges	81.90	79.78	0.0109	81.03	76.67	0.0018
GUNet w/o Hessian	82.01	81.03	0.0245	81.36	78.12	0.0425
GUNet	**82.55**	**81.73**	-	**81.51**	**78.77**	–

Comparison with State-of-the-Art Methods. We have further compared the performance of the proposed method with the state-of-the-art methods, reported in Table 2. We list results from previous papers as well as our reimplemented models. The re-implemented models are variations of UNet, including UNet [16], UNet++ [27], Attention UNet [15], DUNet [8], and CSNet [14]. The numbers of parameters in the compared models are roughly close. For sake of fairness, all of the compared methods used the same evaluation settings.

In terms of graphical similarity of vessels, GUNet achieved the highest CAL score among compared models. All $p < 0.05$ indicated significant improvements over the compared models. It verified the advantage of GUNet, which is maintaining good graphical structures of vessels. In terms of the pixel-wise performances, GUNet yielded an accuracy of 96.62% and an AUC of 98.70% on the STARE dataset; an accuracy of 96.74% and an AUC of 98.72% on the CHASE dataset. It showed competitive performances compared with the state-of-the-art methods on two benchmarking datasets.

Table 2. Comparisons with state-of-the-art methods on the STARE and CHASE dataset. The CAL score reflects graphical similarity. GUNet achieves a significantly improved CAL score.

Methods	STARE					CHASE				
	Acc (%)	AUC (%)	Dice (%)	CAL (%)	p-value	Acc (%)	AUC (%)	Dice (%)	CAL (%)	p-value
Yan et al. [23]	96.12	98.01	–	–	–	96.10	97.81	–	–	–
Shin et al. [17]	93.78	98.77	–	–	–	93.73	98.30	–	–	–
Guo et al. [5]	96.60	98.72	83.62	–	–	96.27	98.40	79.83	–	–
Jin et al. [8]	96.41	98.32	81.43	–	–	96.10	98.04	78.83	–	–
UNet [16]	96.43	98.46	81.36	78.62	0.0007	96.59	98.63	79.81	72.68	0.0008
UNet++ [27]	96.43	98.45	81.74	78.31	0.0007	96.64	98.66	80.50	74.96	0.0018
AttUNet [15]	96.27	98.42	80.69	76.70	0.0002	96.64	98.66	80.52	75.00	0.0027
CSNet [14]	96.54	98.62	82.34	80.43	0.0419	96.51	98.57	79.11	71.17	0.0001
GUNet	**96.62**	**98.70**	82.55	**81.73**	–	**96.74**	**98.72**	**81.51**	**78.77**	–

4.2   Experiments on SLO Images

On the IOSTAR dataset, we compared GUNet with methods in previous papers [11,20] as well as our reimplemented models. As shown in Table 3, GUNet achieves better performances compared with other models in terms of both graphical similarity and pixel-wise scores. The last column gives p-values of paired t-tests between the CAL score of the compared model and GUNet. All $p < 0.05$ demonstrate that GUNet performs significantly better than other compared models.

Table 3. Performance comparisons on the IOSTAR dataset. GUNet achieves a significantly improved CAL score.

Method	#Paras	Acc (%)	AUC (%)	Dice (%)	CAL (%)	p-value
Li et al. [11]	–	95.44	96.23	–	–	–
UNet [16]	7.8M	96.08	98.30	78.61	77.02	0.0001
UNet++ [27]	9.2M	96.11	98.34	79.67	77.54	0.0001
AttUNet [15]	8.7M	96.24	98.56	79.70	80.74	0.0144
CSNet [14]	8.9M	96.27	98.55	79.84	79.87	0.0018
GUNet	12.24M	**96.41**	**98.72**	**81.09**	**82.06**	–

4.3 Visualization

We visualize several cases from the STARE dataset. In Fig. 4, pixels in red denote false positives while pixels in blue denote false negatives. The baseline model UNet fails to segment tiny structures and tail ends of vessels. Compared to the baseline model UNet, GUNet gives more precise vessel segmentation with better morphology and graphical structures, which verified the effectiveness of the GCNs module in GUNet.

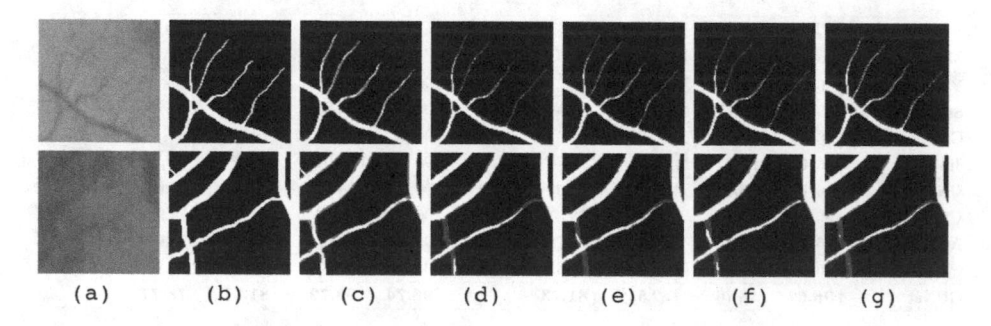

(a)   (b)   (c)   (d)   (e)   (f)   (g)

Fig. 4. Visualization for vessel segmentation (in colour). Red denotes false positives while blue denotes false negatives. (a) original image; (b) ground truth; (c) GUNet; (d) UNet; (e) UNet++; (f) Attention UNet; (g) CSNet. (Color figure online)

5   Conclusion

In this paper, we have proposed a novel U-shaped GCN-CNN hybrid model to deal with the retinal vessel segmentation task. GCNs are adopted to extract information on the graphical structure of vessels, which benefits the overall performance of vessel segmentation. Experiments show that the proposed method achieves competitive performances on three public datasets compared with the state-of-the-art methods. The further research direction can be unifying all steps into an end-to-end model.

References

1. Frangi, A.F., Niessen, W.J., Vincken, K.L., Viergever, M.A.: Multiscale vessel enhancement filtering. In: Wells, W.M., Colchester, A., Delp, S. (eds.) MICCAI 1998. LNCS, vol. 1496, pp. 130–137. Springer, Heidelberg (1998). https://doi.org/10.1007/BFb0056195
2. Fraz, M.M., et al.: An ensemble classification-based approach applied to retinal blood vessel segmentation. IEEE Trans. Biomed. Eng. **59**(9), 2538–2548 (2012)
3. Fu, H., Xu, Y., Wong, D.W.K., Liu, J.: Retinal vessel segmentation via deep learning network and fully-connected conditional random fields. In: 2016 IEEE 13th International Symposium on Biomedical Imaging (ISBI), pp. 698–701. IEEE (2016)
4. Gegúndez-Arias, M.E., Aquino, A., Bravo, J.M., Marín, D.: A function for quality evaluation of retinal vessel segmentations. IEEE Trans. Med. Imaging **31**(2), 231–239 (2011)
5. Guo, S., Wang, K., Kang, H., Zhang, Y., Gao, Y., Li, T.: BTS-DSN: deeply supervised neural network with short connections for retinal vessel segmentation. Int. J. Med. Informatics **126**, 105–113 (2019)
6. Hoover, A., Kouznetsova, V., Goldbaum, M.: Locating blood vessels in retinal images by piecewise threshold probing of a matched filter response. IEEE Trans. Med. Imaging **19**(3), 203–210 (2000)
7. Huang, G., Liu, Z., Van Der Maaten, L., Weinberger, K.Q.: Densely connected convolutional networks. In: Proceedings of the IEEE Conference on Computer Vision and Pattern Recognition, pp. 4700–4708 (2017)
8. Jin, Q., Meng, Z., Pham, T.D., Chen, Q., Wei, L., Su, R.: DUNet: a deformable network for retinal vessel segmentation. Knowl. Based Syst. **178**, 149–162 (2019)
9. Garcia-Uceda Juarez, A., Selvan, R., Saghir, Z., de Bruijne, M.: A joint 3D UNet-graph neural network-based method for airway segmentation from chest CTs. In: Suk, H.-I., Liu, M., Yan, P., Lian, C. (eds.) MLMI 2019. LNCS, vol. 11861, pp. 583–591. Springer, Cham (2019). https://doi.org/10.1007/978-3-030-32692-0_67
10. Kipf, T.N., Welling, M.: Semi-supervised classification with graph convolutional networks. arXiv preprint arXiv:1609.02907 (2016)
11. Li, X., Jiang, Y., Li, M., Yin, S.: Lightweight attention convolutional neural network for retinal vessel image segmentation. IEEE Trans. Industr. Inf. **17**(3), 1958–1967 (2020)
12. Liskowski, P., Krawiec, K.: Segmenting retinal blood vessels with deep neural networks. IEEE Trans. Med. Imaging **35**(11), 2369–2380 (2016)
13. Maninis, K.-K., Pont-Tuset, J., Arbeláez, P., Van Gool, L.: Deep retinal image understanding. In: Ourselin, S., Joskowicz, L., Sabuncu, M.R., Unal, G., Wells, W. (eds.) MICCAI 2016. LNCS, vol. 9901, pp. 140–148. Springer, Cham (2016). https://doi.org/10.1007/978-3-319-46723-8_17

14. Mou, L., et al.: CS-Net: channel and spatial attention network for curvilinear structure segmentation. In: Shen, D., et al. (eds.) MICCAI 2019. LNCS, vol. 11764, pp. 721–730. Springer, Cham (2019). https://doi.org/10.1007/978-3-030-32239-7_80

15. Oktay, O., et al.: Attention U-Net: learning where to look for the pancreas. arXiv preprint arXiv:1804.03999 (2018)

16. Ronneberger, O., Fischer, P., Brox, T.: U-Net: convolutional networks for biomedical image segmentation. In: Navab, N., Hornegger, J., Wells, W.M., Frangi, A.F. (eds.) MICCAI 2015. LNCS, vol. 9351, pp. 234–241. Springer, Cham (2015). https://doi.org/10.1007/978-3-319-24574-4_28

17. Shin, S.Y., Lee, S., Yun, I.D., Lee, K.M.: Deep vessel segmentation by learning graphical connectivity. Med. Image Anal. 58, 101556 (2019)

18. Shit, S., et al.: clDice-a novel topology-preserving loss function for tubular structure segmentation. In: Proceedings of the IEEE/CVF Conference on Computer Vision and Pattern Recognition, pp. 16560–16569 (2021)

19. Veličković, P., Cucurull, G., Casanova, A., Romero, A., Lio, P., Bengio, Y.: Graph attention networks. arXiv preprint arXiv:1710.10903 (2017)

20. Wang, D., Haytham, A., Pottenburgh, J., Saeedi, O., Tao, Y.: Hard attention net for automatic retinal vessel segmentation. IEEE J. Biomed. Health Inform. 24(12), 3384–3396 (2020)

21. Wu, Y., Xia, Y., Song, Y., Zhang, Y., Cai, W.: Multiscale network followed network model for retinal vessel segmentation. In: Frangi, A.F., Schnabel, J.A., Davatzikos, C., Alberola-López, C., Fichtinger, G. (eds.) MICCAI 2018. LNCS, vol. 11071, pp. 119–126. Springer, Cham (2018). https://doi.org/10.1007/978-3-030-00934-2_14

22. Wu, Y., Xia, Y., Song, Y., Zhang, Y., Cai, W.: NFN+: a novel network followed network for retinal vessel segmentation. Neural Netw. 126, 153–162 (2020)

23. Yan, Z., Yang, X., Cheng, K.T.: Joint segment-level and pixel-wise losses for deep learning based retinal vessel segmentation. IEEE Trans. Biomed. Eng. 65(9), 1912–1923 (2018)

24. Zhai, Z., et al.: Linking convolutional neural networks with graph convolutional networks: application in pulmonary artery-vein separation. In: Zhang, D., Zhou, L., Jie, B., Liu, M. (eds.) GLMI 2019. LNCS, vol. 11849, pp. 36–43. Springer, Cham (2019). https://doi.org/10.1007/978-3-030-35817-4_5

25. Zhang, J., Dashtbozorg, B., Bekkers, E., Pluim, J.P., Duits, R., ter Haar Romeny, B.M.: Robust retinal vessel segmentation via locally adaptive derivative frames in orientation scores. IEEE Trans. Med. Imaging 35(12), 2631–2644 (2016)

26. Zhang, Y., Chung, A.C.S.: Deep supervision with additional labels for retinal vessel segmentation task. In: Frangi, A.F., Schnabel, J.A., Davatzikos, C., Alberola-López, C., Fichtinger, G. (eds.) MICCAI 2018. LNCS, vol. 11071, pp. 83–91. Springer, Cham (2018). https://doi.org/10.1007/978-3-030-00934-2_10

27. Zhou, Z., Rahman Siddiquee, M.M., Tajbakhsh, N., Liang, J.: UNet++: a nested U-Net architecture for medical image segmentation. In: Stoyanov, D., et al. (eds.) DLMIA/ML-CDS -2018. LNCS, vol. 11045, pp. 3–11. Springer, Cham (2018). https://doi.org/10.1007/978-3-030-00889-5_1

Detection of Diabetic Retinopathy Using Longitudinal Self-supervised Learning

Rachid Zeghlache[1,2(✉)], Pierre-Henri Conze[1,3], Mostafa El Habib Daho[1,2],
Ramin Tadayoni[5], Pascal Massin[5], Béatrice Cochener[1,2,4], Gwenolé Quellec[1],
and Mathieu Lamard[1,2]

[1] LaTIM UMR 1101, Inserm, Brest, France
rachid.zeghlache@univ-brest.fr
[2] University of Western Brittany, Brest, France
[3] IMT Atlantique, Brest, France
[4] Ophtalmology Department, CHRU Brest, Brest, France
[5] Lariboisière Hospital, AP-HP, Paris, France

Abstract. Longitudinal imaging is able to capture both static anatomical structures and dynamic changes in disease progression towards earlier and better patient-specific pathology management. However, conventional approaches for detecting diabetic retinopathy (DR) rarely take advantage of longitudinal information to improve DR analysis. In this work, we investigate the benefit of exploiting self-supervised learning with a longitudinal nature for DR diagnosis purposes. We compare different longitudinal self-supervised learning (LSSL) methods to model the disease progression from longitudinal retinal color fundus photographs (CFP) to detect early DR severity changes using a pair of consecutive exams. The experiments were conducted on a longitudinal DR screening dataset with or without those trained encoders (LSSL) acting as a longitudinal pretext task. Results achieve an AUC of 0.875 for the baseline (model trained from scratch) and an AUC of 0.96 (95% CI: 0.9593–0.9655 DeLong test) with a p-value <2.2e–16 on early fusion using a simple ResNet alike architecture with frozen LSSL weights, suggesting that the LSSL latent space enables to encode the dynamic of DR progression.

Keywords: Diabetic retinopathy · Deep learning · Self-supervised learning · Longitudinal analysis · Computer-aided diagnosis

1 Introduction

According to the International Diabetes Federation, the number of people affected by diabetes is expected to reach 700 million by 2045 [14]. Diabetic retinopathy (DR) affects over one-third of this population and is the leading cause of vision loss worldwide [8]. This happens when the retinal blood vessels are damaged by high blood sugar levels, causing swelling and leakage. In fundus retina images, lesions appear as leaking blood and fluids. Red and bright lesions

---

The original version of this chapter was revised: an error in the title of the paper was corrected. The correction to this chapter is available at
https://doi.org/10.1007/978-3-031-16525-2_21

are the type of lesions that can be commonly identified during DR screening. The blindness incidence can be reduced if the DR is detected at an early stage. In clinical routine, color fundus photographs (CFP) are employed to identify the morphological changes of the retina by examining the presence of retinal lesions such as microaneurysms, hemorrhages, and soft or hard exudates. The international clinical DR severity scale includes no apparent DR, mild non-proliferative diabetic retinopathy (NPDR), moderate NPDR, severe NPDR, and proliferative diabetic retinopathy (PDR), labeled as grades 0, 1, 2, 3, (illustrated in Fig. 1) and 4. NPDR (grades 1, 2, 3) corresponds to the early-to-middle stage of DR and deals with a progressive microvascular disease characterized by small vessel damages and occlusions. PDR (grade 4) corresponds to the period of potential visual loss which is often due to a massive hemorrhage. Early identification and adequate treatment, particularly in the mild to moderate stage of NPDR, may slow the progression of DR, consequently preventing the establishment of diabetes-related visual impairments and blindness.

In the past years, deep learning has achieved great success in medical image analysis. Many supervised learning techniques based on convolutional neural networks have been proposed to tackle the automated DR grading task [4,10,11]. Nevertheless, these approaches rarely take advantage of longitudinal information. In this direction, Yan et al. [17] proposed to exploit a Siamese network with different pre-training and fusion schemes to detect the early stage of RD using longitudinal pairs of CFP acquired from the same patient. Further, self-supervised learning (SSL) held great promise as it can learn robust high-level representations by training on pretext tasks [1] before solving a supervised downstream task. Current self-supervised models are largely based on contrastive learning [3,6]. However, the choice of the pretext task to learn a good representation is not straightforward, and the application of contrastive learning to medical images is relatively limited. To tackle this, a self-supervised framework using lesion-based contrastive learning was employed for automated diabetic retinopathy (DR) grading [5].

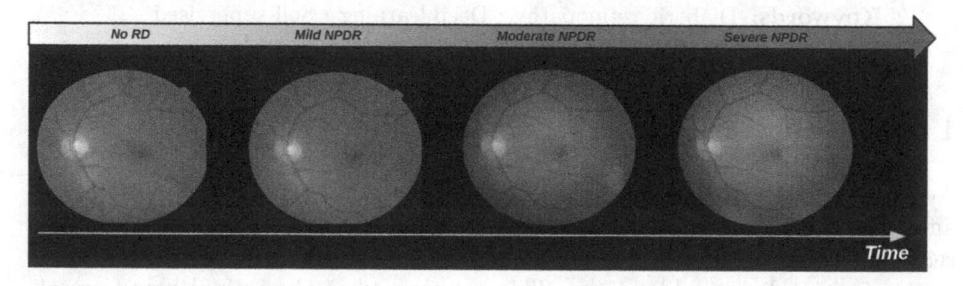

Fig. 1: Evolution from no DR to severe NPDR for a patient in OPHDIAT [7] dataset.

More recently, a new pretext task has appeared for classification purposes in a longitudinal context. Rivail et al. [12] proposed a longitudinal self-supervised learning Siamese model trained to predict the time interval between two consecutive longitudinal retinal optical coherence tomography (OCT) acquisitions and thus capturing the disease progression. Yang et al. [18] proposed an auto-encoder named LSSL that takes two consecutive longitudinal scans as inputs. They added to the classic reconstruction term a time alignment term that forces the topology of the latent space to change in the direction of longitudinal changes. An extension of such principle was provided in [9]. To reach a smooth trajectory field, a dynamic graph in each training batch was computed to define a neighborhood in the latent space for each subject. The graph then connects nearby subjects and enforces their progression directions to be maximally aligned.

In this regard, we aim to use LSSL approaches to capture the disease progression to predict the change between no DR/mild NPDR (grade 0 or 1) and more severe DR (grade ≥ 2) through two consecutive follow-ups. To this end, we explore three methods incorporating current and prior examinations. Finally, a comprehensive evaluation is conducted by comparing these pipelines on the OPHDIAT dataset [7]. To the best of our knowledge, this work is the first to automatically assess the early DR severity changes between consecutive images using self-supervised learning applied in a longitudinal context.

2   Methods

In this work, we study the use of different longitudinal pretext tasks. We use the encoders trained with those pretext tasks as feature extractors embedded with longitudinal information. The aim is to predict the severity grade change from normal/mild NPDR to more severe DR between a pair of follow-up CFP images. Let $\mathcal{X}$ be the set of subject-specific image pairs for the collection of all CFP images. $\mathcal{X}$ contains all (x^t, x^s) that are from the same subject with x^t scanned before x^s. These image pairs are then provided as inputs to an auto-encoder (AE) structure (Fig. 2c). The latent representations generated by the encoder are denoted by $z^t = F(x^t)$ and $z^s = F(x^s)$ where F is the encoder. From this encoder, we can define the $\Delta z = (z^s - z^t)$ trajectory vector and then formulate $\Delta z^{(t,s)} = (z^s - z^t)/\Delta t^{(t,s)}$ as the normalized trajectory vector where $\Delta t^{(t,s)}$ is the time interval between the two acquisitions. The decoder H uses the latent representation to reconstruct the input images such that $\tilde{x}^t = H(z^t)$ and $\tilde{x}^s = H(z^s)$. $\mathbf{E}$ denotes the expected value. In what follows, three longitudinal self-supervised learning schemes are further described.

2.1   Longitudinal Siamese

The Siamese network takes the two image pairs (x^t, x^s). These images are encoded into a compact representation (z^t, z^s) by the encoder network, F. A feed forward neural network (denoted G) then predicts $\Delta t^{(t,s)}$, the time interval between the pair of CFP images (Fig. 2a). The regression model is trained by minimizing the following L2 loss: $\| G(z^t, z^s) - \Delta t^{(t,s)} \|_2^2$.

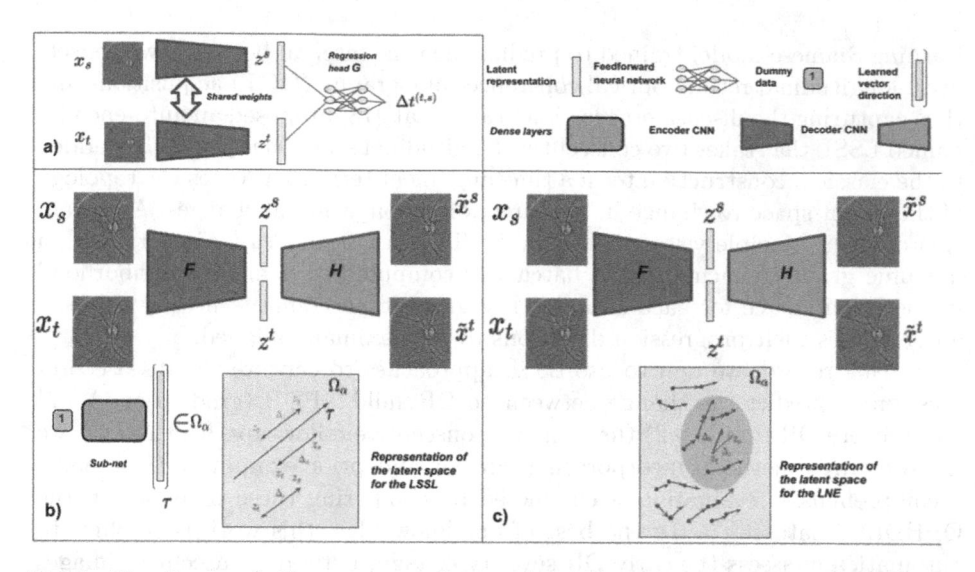

Fig. 2: The figure a) illustrates to longitudinal Siamese and takes as inputs a pair of consecutive images and predict the time between the examinations. The figure b) represents the longitudinal self-supervised learning which is composed of two independent modules, an AE and dense layers. The AE takes as input the pair of consecutive images and reconstruct the image pairs while the dense layer maps a dummy vector to the direction vector τ. The figure c) corresponds to the LNE, and takes as input the consecutive pairs and build a dynamic graph to align in a neighborhood the subject-specific trajectory vector (Δz) and the pooled trajectory vector (Δh) that represents the local progression direction in latent space (green circle). (Color figure online)

2.2   Longitudinal Self-supervised Learning

The longitudinal self-supervised learning (LSSL) exploits a standard AE. The AE is trained with a loss that forces the trajectory vector Δz to be aligned with a direction that could rely in the latent space of the AE called τ. This direction is learned through a sub-network composed of single dense layers which map a dummy data into a vector $\tau \in \Omega_\alpha$, the dimension of the latent space. The high-level representation of the network is illustrated in Fig. 2b. Enforcing the AE to respect this constraint is equivalent to encouraging $\cos(\Delta z, \tau)$ to be close to 1, i.e. a zero-angle between τ and the direction of progression in the representation space.

Objective Function.

$$\mathbf{E}_{(x^t,x^s)\sim\mathcal{X}} \left(\lambda_{rec} \cdot \| x^t - \tilde{x}^t \|_2^2 + \| x^s - \tilde{x}^s \|_2^2 - \lambda_{dir} \cdot \cos(\Delta z, \tau) \right) \tag{1}$$

2.3   Longitudinal Neighbourhood Embedding

Longitudinal neighborhood embedding (LNE) is based on the LSSL framework. The main difference is that a directed graph $\mathcal{G}$ is built in each training batch. A pair of sample (x_t, x_s) serves as a node in the graph with node representation Δz. For each node i, Euclidean distances to other nodes $j \neq i$ are computed by $D_{i,j} = \| z_i^t - z_j^t \|_2$. The neighbour size (N_{nb}) is the closest nodes of node i form its 1-hop neighbourhood $\mathcal{N}_i$ with edges connected to i. The adjacency matrix A for the directed graph $(\mathcal{G})$ is then defined as:

$$A_{i,j} := \begin{cases} exp(-\frac{D_{i,j}^2}{2\sigma_i^2}) & j \in \mathcal{N}_i \\ 0, & j \notin \mathcal{N}_i \end{cases}.$$

$$\text{with } \sigma_i := max(D_{i,j\in\mathcal{N}_i}) - min(D_{i,j\in\mathcal{N}_i})$$

This matrix regularizes each node's representation by a longitudinal neighbourhood embedding Δh pooled from the neighbours' representations. The neighborhood embedding for a node i is computed by:

$$\Delta h_i := \sum_{j\in\mathcal{N}_i} A_{i,j} O_{i,j}^{-1} \Delta z_j,$$

where O is the out-degree matrix of graph $\mathcal{G}$, a diagonal matrix that describes the sum of the weights for outgoing edges at each node. They define $\theta_{\langle\Delta z,\Delta h\rangle}$ the angle between Δz and Δh, and only incite $\cos(\theta_{\langle\Delta z,\Delta h\rangle}) = 1$, i.e., a zero-angle between the subject-specific trajectory vector and the pooled trajectory vector that represents the local progression direction in the latent space (Fig. 2c).

Objective Function.

$$\mathbf{E}_{(x^t,x^s)\sim\mathcal{X}} \left(\lambda_{rec} \cdot \| x^t - \tilde{x}^t \|_2^2 + \| x^s - \tilde{x}^s \|_2^2 - \lambda_{dir} \cdot \cos(\theta_{\langle\Delta z,\Delta h\rangle}) \right) \qquad (2)$$

3   Dataset

The proposed models were trained and evaluated on OPHDIAT [7], a large CFP database collected from the Ophthalmology Diabetes Telemedicine network consisting of examinations acquired from 101,383 patients between 2004 and 2017. Within 763,848 interpreted CFP images 673,017 are assigned with a DR severity grade, the others being non-gradable. Image sizes vary from 1440×960 to 3504×2336 pixels. Each examination has at least two images for each eye. Each subject had 2 to 16 scans with an average of 2.99 scans spanning an average time interval of 2.23 years. The age range of the patients is from 9 to 91.

Image Pair Selection. The majority of patients from the OPHDIAT database have multiple images with different fields of view for both eyes. To facilitate the pairing, we propose to select a single image per eye for each examination: we select the one that best characterizes the DR severity grade, as detailed hereafter. For this purpose, we train a standard classifier using the complete dataset that predicts the DR severity grade (5 grades). During the first epoch, we randomly select one image per eye and per examination for the full dataset. After the end of the first epoch with the learned weights of the model, for each image present in every examination, we select the image that gives the highest classification probability. We repeat this process until the selected images by the model converge to a fixed set of images per examination. From the set of selected images, we construct consecutive pairs for each patient and finally obtain 100,033 pairs of images from 26,483 patients. Only 6,690 (6.7%) pairs have severity grade changes from grade 0 or 1 to grade ≥ 2 against 93,343 (93.3%) pairs with severity changes that lie between grades 0 and 1. The resulting dataset exhibits the following proportions in gender (Male 52%, Female 48%) and diabetes type (type 2 69%, type 1 31%). This dataset was further divided into training (60%), validation (20%), and test (20%) based on subjects, i.e., images of a single subject belonged to the same split and in a way that preserves the same proportions of examples in each class as observed in the original dataset.

Image pre-processing. Image registration is a fundamental pre-processing step for longitudinal analysis [15]. Therefore, using an affine transformation, we first conducted a registration step to align x_t to x_s. Images are then adaptively cropped to the width of the field of view (i.e., the eye area in the CPF image) and then resized to 256×256. A Gaussian filter estimates the background in each color channel to attenuate the strong intensity variations among the dataset which is then subtracted from the image. Finally, the field of view is eroded by 5% to eliminate illumination artifacts around the edges. During the training, random resized crops ([0.96, 1.0] as scale range and [0.95, 1.05] as aspect ratio range) are applied for data augmentation purposes.

4   Experiments and Results

Implementation Details. As it was conducted in [9,18], we constructed a standard AE for all the compared methods to focus only on the presented methodology and make a fair comparison between approaches, with the hope that using advanced AE structures could lead to better encoding and generalization. In our basic architecture, we employed a stack of n pre-activated residual blocks, where n determines the depth of that scale for the encoder. In each res-block, the residual feature map was calculated using a series of three 3×3 convolutions, the first of which always halves the number of the feature maps employed at the present scale, such that the residual representations live on a lower-dimensional manifold. Our encoder comprises five levels; the first four levels are composed of two residual blocks, and the latter only one residual block. This provides a latent representation of size $64 \times 4 \times 4$. The employed decoder is a reverse structure of the encoder. The different networks were trained for 100 epochs by the AdamW optimizer with a learning rate of 5×10^{-4}, OneCycleLR as scheduler and a weight decay of 10^{-5}, using an A6000 GPU with the PyTorch framework. The regularization weights were set to $\lambda_{dir} = 1.0$ and $\lambda_{rec} = 5.0$. A batch size of 64 was used for all models, and a neighbour size $N_{nb} = 5$ and $\Delta z^{(t,s)}$ were used for the LNE, as in the original paper [9].

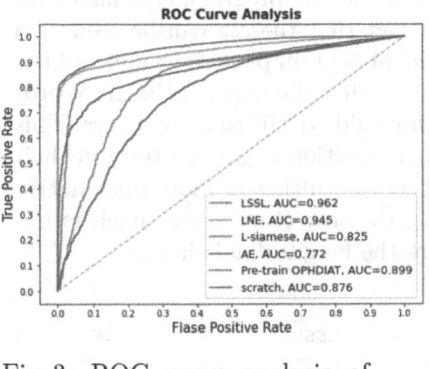

Fig. 3: ROC curve analysis of the compared methods

Table 1: Comparison of the approach on the early change detection with the frozen encoder.

Model	AUC (95% CI)	Acc
No pretrain	0.8758 (0.8688–0.883)	0.8379
Pre-train on OPHDIAT	0.8994 (0.8921–0.9068)	0.8289
AE	0.7724 (0.7583–0.7866)	0.5599
L-siamese [12]	0.8253 (0.8127–0.838)	0.9354
LSSL [18]	**0.9624** (0.9593–0.9655)	0.8871
LNE [9]	**0.9448** (0.9412–0.9486)	0.8646

4.1 Comparison of the Approaches on the Early Change Detection

We evaluate the LSSL encoders on detecting the severity grade change from normal/mild NPDR to more severe DR between a pair of follow-up CFP images. The classifier was constructed as the concatenation of the learned backbone (feature extractor) and a multi-layer perceptron (MLP). The MLP consists of two fully connected layers of dimensions 1024 and 64 with LeakyReLU activation followed by a last single perceptron. Receiving the flattened representation of the trajectory vector Δz, the MLP predicts a score between 0 and 1. We compared the area under the receiver operating characteristics curve (AUC) and the accuracy (Acc) in Table 1 for different pre-training strategies (from scratch, trained on LSSL methods, encoder from a standard AE). We also pre-trained on the OPHDIAT dateset (classification of the DR severity grade) to compare the LSSL pre-training strategies with a conventional pre-training method. The statistical significance was estimated using DeLong's t-test [13] to analyze and compare ROC curves. The results in Table 1 and Fig. 3 show the clear superiority of the LSSL encoder, with a statistical significance p-value $<2.2e–16$. Due to class imbalance, the Longitudinal-siamese (L-siamese) have a high Acc while exhibiting a lower AUC than the baseline (trained from scratch).

4.2 Norm of Trajectory Vector Analyze

We constructed different histograms in Fig. 4 representing the mean value of the norm of the trajectory vector with respect to both diabetes type and progression type. According to Fig. 4, only the models with the direction alignment loss term are able to capture the change detection in the DR relative to the longitudinal representation. Therefore, we observe in the histogram that the trajectory vector (Δz) is able to dissociate the two types of diabetes (t-test p-value <0.01) and change detection (t-test p-value <0.01). For the diabetes type, a specific study

[2] about the OPHDIAT dataset indicates that the DR progression is faster for patients with type 1 diabetes. Based on the fact that the Δz can be seen as a relative speed, this observation agrees with the histogram plot of the mean of the Δz norm represented in Fig. 4. We also observed that the norm of the Δz vector is lower for the normal stage of the DR than for mild NPDR to more severe. This was expected because only the methods with a direction alignment term in their objective explicitly modeled longitudinal effects, resulting in more informative Δz. This also implies that simply computing the trajectory vector itself is not enough to force the representation to capture the longitudinal change.

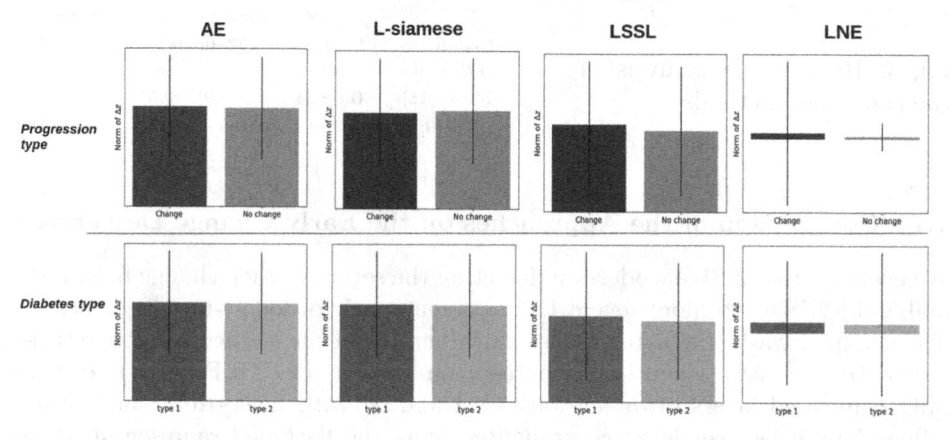

Fig. 4: Mean of the trajectory vector norm for the different self-supervised method used

5   Discussion

We applied different LSSL techniques to encode diabetic retinopathy (DR) progression. The accuracy boost, relative to a network trained from scratch or transferred from conventional tasks, demonstrates that longitudinal pre-trained self-supervised representation learns clinically meaningful information. Concerning the limitations of the LSSL methods, we first observe that the models with no time alignment loss perform poorly and provide no evidence of disease progression encoding. Also, we report for the LNE that the normalized trajectory vector for some pairs, that have a large time between examinations, is almost all zeros, which results in a non-informative representation. This could explain the difference between the LSSL and LNE prediction performances. Moreover, during the LSSL and the LNE training, we often faced a plateau with the direction loss alignment. Therefore, we also claim that intensive work should be done regarding the choice of the hyperparameters : constant weights for the losses, latent space size (Ω_α), neighbour size (N_{nb}). The results concerning quantifying the encoding of the disease progression from the models trained with a time direction alignment are encouraging but not totally clear. As it was mentioned in [16], one limitation of the LSSL approach pretains to the cosine loss (direction alignment term from Eqs. (1,2) used to encode the longitudinal progression in a specific direction in the latent space and learned while training. The loss only focuses on the correlation with the disease progression timeline but not disentanglement of the disease progression itself. Therefore, a more in-depth analysis of the latent space is required to evaluate if the trajectory vector could be used to find a specific progression trajectory according to patient characteristics (diabetes types, age, DR severity). The pairing and the registration are critical steps in the longitudinal study. As it was previously mentioned, by using a better registration method and exploiting different fusion schemes and backbone architectures, we could get enriched latent representation and, thus, hopefully, better results. Also, the frozen encoders could be transferred to other types of longitudinal problems. In summary, LSSL techniques are quite promising: preliminary results are encouraging, and we expect further improvements.

Acknowledgements. The work takes place in the framework of the ANR RHU project Evired. This work benefits from State aid managed by the French National Research Agency under "Investissement d'Avenir" program bearing the reference ANR-18-RHUS-0008

References

1. Albelwi, S.: Survey on self-supervised learning: auxiliary pretext tasks and contrastive learning methods in imaging. Entropy **24**(4) (2022). https://doi.org/10.3390/e24040551, https://www.mdpi.com/1099-4300/24/4/551
2. Chamard, C., et al.: Ten-year incidence and assessment of safe screening intervals for diabetic retinopathy: the OPHDIAT study. Br. J. Ophthalmol. **105**(3), 432–439 (2020). https://doi.org/10.1136/bjophthalmol-2020-316030
3. Chen, T., Kornblith, S., Norouzi, M., Hinton, G.: A simple framework for contrastive learning of visual representations (2020). https://doi.org/10.48550/ARXIV.2002.05709, https://arxiv.org/abs/2002.05709
4. Gayathri, S., Gopi, V.P., Palanisamy, P.: A lightweight CNN for diabetic retinopathy classification from fundus images. Biomed. Signal Process. Control **62**, 102115 (2020)
5. Huang, Y., Lin, L., Cheng, P., Lyu, J., Tang, X.: Lesion-based contrastive learning for diabetic retinopathy grading from fundus images (2021). https://doi.org/10.48550/ARXIV.2107.08274, https://arxiv.org/abs/2107.08274
6. Liu, X., et al.: Self-supervised learning: generative or contrastive. arXiv preprint arXiv:2006.08218 vol. 1, no. 2 (2020)
7. Massin, P., et al.: Ophdiat: a telemedical network screening system for diabetic retinopathy in the Île-de-france. Diab. Metab. **34**, 227–34 (2008). https://doi.org/10.1016/j.diabet.2007.12.006
8. Ogurtsova, K., et al.: IDF diabetes atlas: global estimates for the prevalence of diabetes for 2015 and 2040. Diab. Res. Clin. Pract. **128**, 40–50 (2017)

9. Ouyang, J., et al.: Self-supervised longitudinal neighbourhood embedding. In: de Bruijne, M., et al. (eds.) MICCAI 2021. LNCS, vol. 12902, pp. 80–89. Springer, Cham (2021). https://doi.org/10.1007/978-3-030-87196-3_8

10. Pratt, H., Coenen, F., Broadbent, D.M., Harding, S.P., Zheng, Y.: Convolutional neural networks for diabetic retinopathy. Procedia Comput. Sci. **90**, 200–205 (2016). https://doi.org/10.1016/j.procs.2016.07.014, https://www.sciencedirect.com/science/article/pii/S1877050916311929, 20th Conference on Medical Image Understanding and Analysis (MIUA 2016)

11. Quellec, G., Charrière, K., Boudi, Y., Cochener, B., Lamard, M.: Deep image mining for diabetic retinopathy screening. Med. Image Anal.**39**, 178–193 (2017). https://doi.org/10.1016/j.media.2017.04.012, https://www.sciencedirect.com/science/article/pii/S136184151730066X

12. Rivail, A., et al.: Modeling disease progression in retinal OCTs with longitudinal self-supervised learning. In: Rekik, I., Adeli, E., Park, S.H. (eds.) PRIME 2019. LNCS, vol. 11843, pp. 44–52. Springer, Cham (2019). https://doi.org/10.1007/978-3-030-32281-6_5

13. Robin, X., et al.: pROC: an open-source package for r and s to analyze and compare ROC curves. BMC Bioinf. **12**(1) (2011). https://doi.org/10.1186/1471-2105-12-77

14. Saeedi, P., et al.: Global and regional diabetes prevalence estimates for 2019 and projections for 2030 and 2045: results from the international diabetes federation diabetes atlas, 9th edn. Diab. Res. Clin. Pract. **157**, 107843 (2019). https://doi.org/10.1016/j.diabres.2019.107843

15. Saha, S.K., Xiao, D., Bhuiyan, A., Wong, T.Y., Kanagasingam, Y.: Color fundus image registration techniques and applications for automated analysis of diabetic retinopathy progression: a review. Biomed. Sig. Process. Control **47**, 288–302 (2019). https://doi.org/10.1016/j.bspc.2018.08.034

16. Vernhet, P., Durrleman, S.: Longitudinal self-supervision to disentangle inter-patient variability, pp. 231–241 (2021). https://doi.org/10.1007/978-3-030-87196-3

17. Yan, Y., et al.: Longitudinal detection of diabetic retinopathy early severity grade changes using deep learning. In: Fu, H., Garvin, M.K., MacGillivray, T., Xu, Y., Zheng, Y. (eds.) OMIA 2021. LNCS, vol. 12970, pp. 11–20. Springer, Cham (2021). https://doi.org/10.1007/978-3-030-87000-3_2

18. Zhao, Q., Liu, Z., Adeli, E., Pohl, K.M.: Longitudinal self-supervised learning. Med. Image Anal. **71** (2021). https://doi.org/10.1016/j.media.2021.102051

Multimodal Information Fusion for Glaucoma and Diabetic Retinopathy Classification

Yihao Li[1,2](✉), Mostafa El Habib Daho[1,2], Pierre-Henri Conze[1,3],
Hassan Al Hajj[1,2], Sophie Bonnin[4], Hugang Ren[5], Niranchana Manivannan[5],
Stephanie Magazzeni[5], Ramin Tadayoni[6], Béatrice Cochener[1,2,7],
Mathieu Lamard[1,2], and Gwenolé Quellec[1]

[1] LaTIM UMR 1101, Inserm, Brest, France
Yihao.Li@etudiant.univ-brest.fr
[2] University of Western Brittany, Brest, France
[3] IMT Atlantique, Brest, France
[4] Ophthalmology Department, Rothschild Foundation Hospital, Paris, France
[5] Carl Zeiss Meditec Inc, Dublin, CA, USA
[6] Ophthalmology Department, Lariboisière Hospital, AP-HP, Paris, France
[7] Ophthalmology Department, CHRU Brest, Brest, France

Abstract. Multimodal information is frequently available in medical tasks. By combining information from multiple sources, clinicians are able to make more accurate judgments. In recent years, multiple imaging techniques have been used in clinical practice for retinal analysis: 2D fundus photographs, 3D optical coherence tomography (OCT) and 3D OCT angiography, etc. Our paper investigates three multimodal information fusion strategies based on deep learning to solve retinal analysis tasks: early fusion, intermediate fusion, and hierarchical fusion. The commonly used early and intermediate fusion are simple but do not fully exploit the complementary information between modalities. We developed a hierarchical fusion approach that focuses on combining features across multiple dimensions of the network, as well as exploring the correlation between modalities. These approaches were applied to glaucoma and diabetic retinopathy classification, using the public GAMMA dataset (fundus photographs and OCT) and a private dataset of PLEX®Elite 9000 (Carl Zeis Meditec Inc.) OCT angiography acquisitions, respectively. Our hierarchical fusion method performed the best in both cases and paved the way for better clinical diagnosis.

Keywords: Glaucoma classification · Diabetic retinopathy classification · Multimodal information fusion · Deep learning · Computer-aided diagnosis

1 Introduction

Glaucoma and diabetic retinopathy (DR) are two of the leading causes of blindness and visual impairment in the world. The glaucomatous neurodegeneration

B. Antony et al. (Eds.): OMIA 2022, LNCS 13576, pp. 53–62, 2022.
https://doi.org/10.1007/978-3-031-16525-2_6

causes a disconnection between the retina and the brain, resulting in irreversible blindness. By 2040, around 111.8 million people are expected to suffer from glaucoma [17]. The DR mutilates the retinal blood vessels of diabetic patients. Diabetic retinopathy consists of two major types: non-proliferative diabetic retinopathy (NPDR) and proliferative diabetic retinopathy (PDR) [13]. By 2030, there will be 454 million DR patients worldwide [15].

In recent years, algorithms for diagnosing glaucoma and DR have emerged with the development of deep learning and improved computer equipments. Fundus photography and optical coherence tomography (OCT) are the two most cost-effective screening tools for glaucoma and DR [18]. For two-dimensional fundus photographs, powerful convolutional neural networks (CNN) such as ResNet or GoogleNet Inception models, were used to achieve pathology detection [1,10,16]. It should be noted that 2D fundus data are more accessible than other modalities, so data-sets are generally larger, and thus, models can be trained more efficiently. OCT data are more sensitive to structural pathological features. Both 3D-CNN networks and 2D-CNN networks operating on 2D slices, were used to achieve feature extraction from OCT volumes [2,11,12]. In addition, optical coherence tomography angiography (OCTA) is a new, non-invasive imaging technique that generates volumetric angiography images in seconds. It can display both structural and blood flow information [4]. The effectiveness of CNN networks in classifying DR using OCTA data was also demonstrated [14].

All the previous algorithms are usually based on information from only one modality. However, multi-modality screening is often recommended to reach a more accurate and reliable diagnosis [18]. This is why multimodal algorithms are needed in ophthalmic pathology diagnosis.

This paper presents three fusion algorithms for multimodal data in ophthalmology: early, intermediate and hierarchical fusion. They enable the fusion of 2D and 3D modal data. Specifically, the innovative hierarchical fusion algorithm we developed (Fig. 1) achieves excellent glaucoma and DR classification results.

2   Methods

This section will explore three approaches to multimodal fusion in ophthalmology: early fusion, intermediate fusion, and hierarchical fusion. We will examine the challenges of applying different fusion methods to ophthalmic data and the structural aspects of our network.

2.1   Early Fusion

In early fusion, also called input-level fusion, data from different modalities are fed into a classification network as different channels [21]. Specifically, multimodality images are fused channel by channel to form multi-channel inputs. Then, a classification network is trained to learn a fused feature representation from these inputs. Many of today's medical fusion strategies use early fusion [5,9].

Let $X \times Y \times Z$ denote the size of the 3D volumes in voxels. In the early-fusion solution, the 2D images are resized to $X \times Y$ pixels and duplicated Z times, to form a $X \times Y \times Z$ voxel channel. Feature extraction from the multimodal input of size $C \times X \times Y \times Z$, where C denotes the number of channels, is then performed using a 3D-CNN network. In addition, the alignment of different modalities is crucial to early fusion.

Early fusion is a simple method, but it is not very effective due to the semantic gap between the modalities of ophthalmic data. For example, fundus photographs give an overall en-face view of the retina, in 2D and OCT volumes provide structural information about the retina in 3D. However, there is a significant gap between these two modalities regarding the equipment used to capture them, imaging methods, and data information. In particular, when we convert 2D data into 3D volumes, we cannot guarantee that the modalities are accurately aligned.

2.2 Intermediate Fusion

In contrast with early fusion, intermediate fusion does not assume spatially aligned modalities. Instead, each modality data is used as an input to a single classification branch, and the outputs from each branch are integrated to produce a final result [7,19]. The intermediate fusion strategy fuses features before the final decision layer. In contrast, late fusion fuses the decision results, ignoring any correlation between the different modalities [3].

As we use different independent branches to extract feature information from each modality, we do not need to consider the consistency of the input data. Using different 2D and 3D CNN branches to extract different features for 2D and 3D data is possible.

Intermediate fusion is a simple yet effective method for feature fusion. The method effectively bridges the significant gaps between different modalities in ophthalmology (2D fundus images and 3D OCT or OCTA volumes). In particular, most participants in Task1 of the GAMMA Challenge employed this method to classify glaucoma and achieved good results [18]. Nevertheless, as intermediate fusion is a mere concatenation of high-dimensional features, the correlation information inevitably gets lost, adversely impacting classification performance.

2.3 Hierarchical Fusion

In this work, we have extended the network structure of intermediate fusion to address its shortcomings. Like intermediate fusion, hierarchical fusion works by using each modality image as an input of a single classification branch, then fusing these learned individual feature representations in the deeper layers of the network. However, unlike intermediate fusion, an additional branch performs feature fusion at different scales. A decision layer is then applied to the fused result to obtain the final label [20].

Fusion between modality-specific features of different dimensions in a network structure is challenging. Prior studies have generally focused on simpler problems. For example, the fused modalities are all 3D data of the same size in

[6]. In that case, multimodal features always have the same shape at each scale, so feature fusion can be easily achieved through concatenation. For ophthalmic data, the size and dimensionality of the features are modality-dependent: 3D tensors for 2D images and 4D tensors for 3D images.

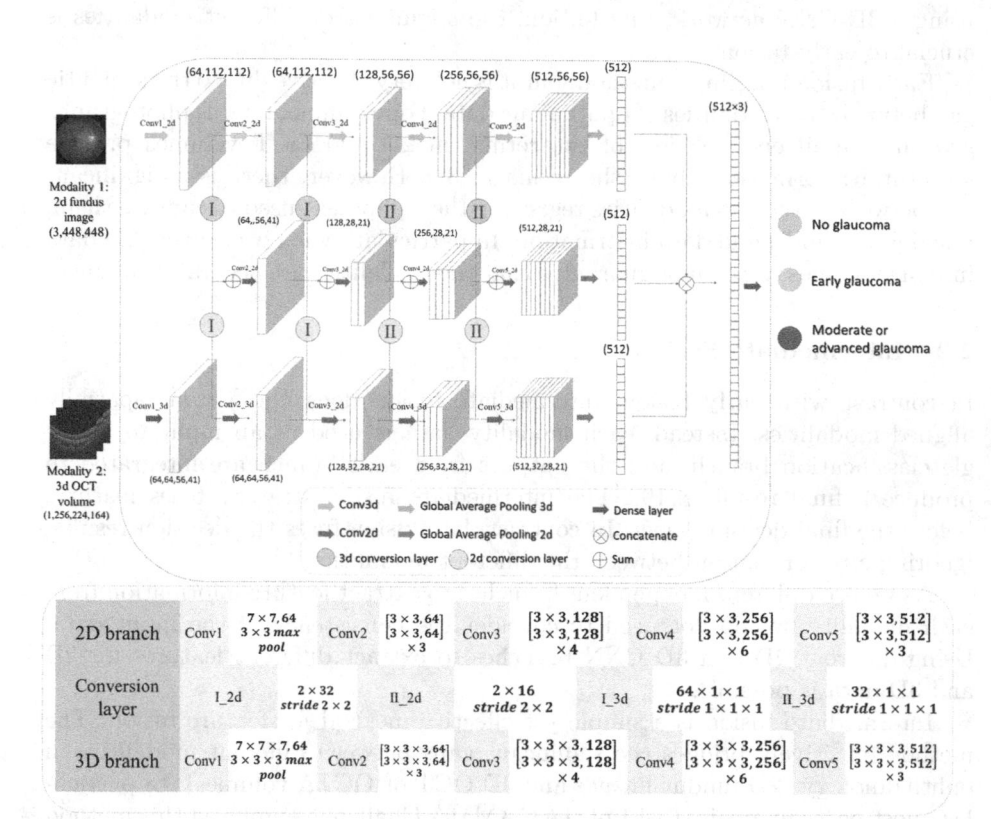

Fig. 1. Proposed hierarchical fusion configuration, illustrated using 2D and 3D ResNet34, for glaucoma classification from 2D fundus photography and 3D OCT. I and II are different types of conversion layers, and their configurations are shown in the list.

A solution is proposed hereafter and illustrated in Fig. 1. Two CNN branches are used to extract features from a multichannel 2D image and a multichannel 3D volume, respectively. Furthermore, we use a third fusion branch to achieve feature fusion at different scales. Since the dimensional features are of different dimensions and sizes, we use additional conversion convolutional layers to harmonize their shape before concatenating them. In these conversion convolution layers, the parameters are calculated according to the size of the modality-specific features.

$$F_{3D}\left(C \times Z_{3D} \times X_{3D} \times Y_{3D}\right) \Longrightarrow F'_{3D}\left(C \times 1 \times X_{3D} \times Y_{3D}\right)$$
$$F_{2D}\left(C \times X_{2D} \times Y_{2D}\right) \longrightarrow F'_{2D}\left(C \times X_{3D} \times Y_{3D}\right)$$

where F is feature of modality, X, Y, Z, C represent the length, width, depth, and number of channels of the features. $\Longrightarrow$ and $\longrightarrow$ represent the 3D and 2D conversion convolutional layers respectively. The convolution kernel size and stride of 3D conversion convolutional layers are $(Z_{3D} \times 1 \times 1)$ and $(1 \times 1 \times 1)$. For the 2D conversion layer, the stride is set to $(2, 2)$ and the filter size is set to $(X_{2D} - 2[X_{3D} - 1], Y_{2D} - 2[Y_{3D} - 1])$, without padding, to ensure that F'_{2D} matches the size of F'_{3D}. The parameters of each convolutional layer are shown in Fig. 1 for ResNet34.

We also extract the features from the 2D CNN block to reduce the number of parameters of the fusion branch. In the end, the high-dimensional features of the three branches are concatenated, and the classification layer is used to make the final classification.

In addition to the advantages of intermediate fusion, hierarchical fusion also considers features from different scales, enhancing the correlation between different modalities and increasing the accuracy of diagnosis.

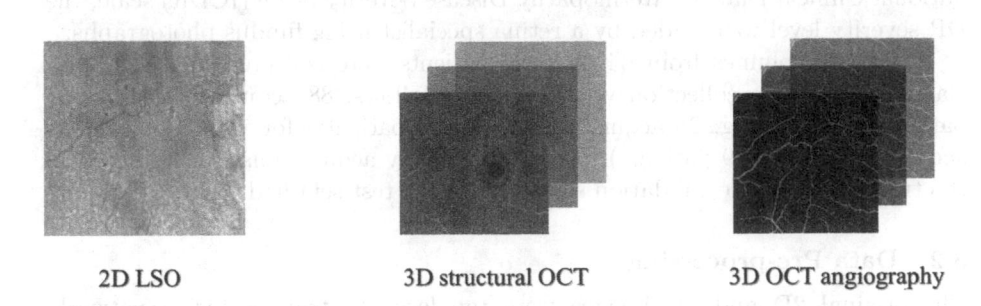

2D LSO   3D structural OCT   3D OCT angiography

Fig. 2. Data from three imaging modalities in the PlexEliteDR dataset.

3   Material and Experiments

We evaluated the proposed method using the public GAMMA challenge dataset for glaucoma classification and a private dataset for proliferative DR (PDR) classification: PlexEliteDR. For the GAMMA dataset, we analyzed clinical data from 2D fundus images, and 3D OCT scans to classify glaucoma into three groups based on visual features: no glaucoma, early glaucoma, and moderate or advanced glaucoma. For the PlexEliteDR dataset, we investigated the fusion of 3 modalities: 3D structural OCT, 3D OCT angiography, and 2D line scanning ophthalmoscope (LSO) for the classification of PDR and NPDR.

3.1 Data

GAMMA Dataset is provided by Sun Yat-sen Ophthalmic Center, Sun Yat-sen University, Guangzhou, China. There are 200 pairs of clinical modality images in the dataset, 100 pairs in the training set, and 100 pairs in the test set. Each pair contains a fundus image and an OCT volume. The OCT volumes were acquired using a Topcon DRI OCT Triton machine. The OCT was centered on the macula and had a 3×3 mm en-face field of view. The Kowa 2000×2992 and Topcon TRC-NW400 cameras were used to acquire fundus images [18].

There are 50 pairs of no glaucoma patients in the training set, 26 pairs of early glaucoma patients, and 24 pairs of moderate or advanced glaucoma patients in the training set. These pairs were divided as follows: 80 pairs for training (41 pairs no glaucoma, 21 pairs early glaucoma, 18 pairs moderate or advanced glaucoma) and 20 pairs for validation (9 pairs no glaucoma, 6 pairs early glaucoma, 5 pairs moderate or advanced glaucoma).

PlexEliteDR Dataset is a private dataset. 3D structural OCT, 3D OCT angiography and 2D LSO data were acquired simultaneously with a Plex®Elite 9000 (Carl Zeiss Meditec Inc. Dublin, California, USA) as Fig. 2. Scanning protocols included 3×3 mm, 6×6 mm, and 15×9 mm. According to the International Clinical Diabetic Retinopathy Disease Severity Scale (ICDR) scale, the DR severity level was graded by a retina specialist using fundus photographs.

151 OCT volumes from 64 diabetic patients were collected for the binary classification. This collection was divided as follows: 88 acquisitions (from 31 patients) for training, 28 acquisitions (from 14 patients) for validation and 35 acquisitions (from 19 patients) for testing. Thirty acquisitions (including 16 in the train set, 5 in the validation set and 9 in the test set) had PDR.

3.2 Data Pre-processing

The original 2D and 3D images were too large to train a fusion network. They were therefore cropped to remove black areas and resized. The following dimensions were used: $X = 224$, $Y = 164$ and $Z = 256$ for GAMMA, $X = Y = Z = 100$ for PlexEliteDR. For intermediate and hierarchical fusion, 2D images could be larger than 3D images: they were resized to 448×448 pixels for GAMMA and 400×400 pixels for PlexEliteDR. Note that 2D and 3D data are not spatially registered in GAMMA; they are only approximately centered on the same anatomical structure (the optic nerve head). All modality are natively registered in PlexEliteDR.

3.3 Implementation Details

Experiments were performed using 2D and 3D versions of ResNet [8] and DenseNet [6]. These networks were used as is, or adapted for each fusion strategy. To augment the data, RandomGamma, GaussianNoise, and flipping were applied for all tests. Gradient descent was performed with the Adam optimizer, which has an initial learning rate of 1e–4, and a weight decay rate of 1e–4.

4   Results

4.1   GAMMA Dataset

We tested the performance of four ResNet networks on the same dataset: ResNet34, ResNet50, ResNet101, and ResNet152. As a standard evaluation metric for the multi-category classification task, Cohen's Kappa was used to evaluate the GAMMA dataset's three-category results.

The best-performing models were selected from the validation set and tested on the 100 pairs test set. The final Kappa results on the test set were computed independently by the PaddlePaddle deep learning platform[1] which is the host platform for the GAMMA challenge.

We tested each modality separately, as well as the three fusion methods, and the results are shown in Table 1.

Table 1. Kappa results of different fusion methods on the GAMMA dataset

Backbone	Single modality (fundus image)	Single modality (OCT)	Early fusion	Intermediate fusion	Hierarchical fusion
ResNet34	0.6997	0.6841	0.6718	0.7547	0.7684
ResNet50	0.6555	0.5952	0.6896	0.7690	**0.8404**
ResNet101	0.6767	0.5794	0.7113	0.7551	0.8255
ResNet152	0.5207	0.4646	0.4642	0.6570	0.7816
Average	0.6382	0.5808	0.6342	0.7340	0.8040

The Kappa results above show that color fundus images outperform OCT volumes when using data from a single modality. In addition, ResNet34 has better performance, possibly because simple features of a single modality are easy to learn. Although, according to the average of different backbones, 0.6382 is still far from a result that can be useful for diagnosis. Thus, single-modality glaucoma classification is very ineffective.

Results for the early fusion were not significantly improved. The reason probably is that fundus and OCT images are not spatially registered in this dataset.

Intermediate fusion is a more suitable fusion algorithm in this case because of the disparity between fundus images and OCT volumes, and the dual feature extraction branch can effectively handle the large differences between modalities. As a result, the performance of intermediate fusion is greatly improved compared to the single-modality scenario. In addition, for ResNet152, we had to reduce the batch size during training to avoid the device from exceeding the memory limit, which is one reason for the poor performance of ResNet152.

The GAMMA challenge also uses intermediate fusion as its baseline [18]. In the official baseline, two convolutional branches are used for intermediate fusion. Based on 3D OCT, retinal thickness is used as a channel for the input of the 2D convolutional branch in the algorithm. By contrast, we utilize 3D convolutional branches to extract 3D OCT features, which allows us to fully utilize the spatial

---

[1] https://aistudio.baidu.com/aistudio/competition/detail/119/0/introduction.

features of 3D data. This is why our Kappa value of 0.734 for intermediate fusion is higher than the official intermediate fusion result of 0.702.

Comparatively to intermediate fusion, hierarchical fusion is able to better exploit correlations between features of different dimensions: the Kappa value increased by 0.0700. These results support the efficiency of our hierarchical fusion.

Specifically, our hierarchical fusion performs very well on ResNet50 and ResNet101. To achieve a higher score in the GAMMA challenge, we selected the models of ResNet50 and ResNet101 for further training. The training and validation sets were re-divided and the checkpoint obtained from the previous test was fine-tuned. Finally, we achieved a Kappa value of 0.8662 for ResNet50 and 0.8745 for ResNet101. For our hierarchical fusion, we improved the final Kappa to 0.8996 by ensembling the predicted values of ResNet50 and ResNet101 models.

4.2   PlexEliteDR Dataset

For the PlexEliteDR dataset, the following backbones were investigated for each method: ResNet50, ResNet101, DenseNet121, and DenseNet169. The Area under the ROC Curve (AUC) was used to assess the binary classification performance (Table 2).

Table 2. Results of different fusion methods on the PlexEliteDR dataset

Method	Backbone	AUC	Sensitivity	Specificity	Improvement
Single modality (Structure)	ResNet101	0.859	0.78	0.77	Baseline
Single modality (Flow)	DenseNet169	0.816	0.78	0.85	−0.043
Single modality (LSO)	DenseNet121	0.662	0.67	0.74	−0.197
Hierarchical fusion	DenseNet121	**0.911**	**0.86**	**0.88**	**+0.052**
Early fusion	DenseNet121	0.865	0.78	0.85	+0.006
Intermediate fusion	DenseNet121	0.744	0.67	0.85	−0.115

Using a single modality, the structure data achieved the best performance: AUC reaches 0.859 using ResNet101 (this is our baseline). Intermediate fusion performed worse than baseline. Unlike the GAMMA dataset, the three modalities are spatially aligned in PlexEliteDR, so the early fusion approach achieves good results. Hierarchical fusion achieves the best results: AUC reaches 0.911 using DenseNet121. The LSO images do not provide very distinct pathological details, compared to fundus images, hence a more limited impact of information fusion.

5   Conclusion

This paper presents three fusion strategies based on deep learning: early fusion, intermediate fusion, and hierarchical fusion. On glaucoma and diabetic retinopathy classification tasks, they clearly outperform classification using a single modality. The novel hierarchical fusion approach is particularly promising, both for glaucoma grading and proliferative DR detection. However, these experiments should be replicated in larger datasets to demonstrate clinically useful detection performance. Additionally, hierarchical fusion is a complex model, and the larger number of parameters requires a robust hardware setup. Larger input sizes are worth testing as hardware evolves.

Acknowledgements. The work takes place in the framework of the ANR RHU project Evired. This work benefits from State aid managed by the French National Research Agency under "Investissement d'Avenir" program bearing the reference ANR-18-RHUS-0008.

References

1. Ahn, J.M., Kim, S., Ahn, K.S., Cho, S.H., Lee, K.B., Kim, U.S.: A deep learning model for the detection of both advanced and early glaucoma using fundus photography. PLoS ONE **13**(11), 1–8 (2018)
2. Asaoka, R.: Using deep learning and transfer learning to accurately diagnose early-onset glaucoma from macular optical coherence tomography images. Am. J. Ophthalmol. **198**, 136–145 (2019)
3. Benzebouchi, N.E., Azizi, N., Ashour, A.S., Dey, N., Sherratt, R.S.: Multi-modal classifier fusion with feature cooperation for glaucoma diagnosis. J. Exp. Theoret. Artif. Intell. **31**(6), 841–874 (2019)
4. de Carlo, T.E., Romano, A., Waheed, N.K., Duker, J.S.: A review of optical coherence tomography angiography (octa). Int. J. Retina Vitreous **1**(1), 5 (2015). https://doi.org/10.1186/s40942-015-0005-8
5. Clèrigues, A., Valverde, S., Bernal, J., Freixenet, J., Oliver, A., Lladó, X.: Acute and sub-acute stroke lesion segmentation from multimodal MRI. Comput. Methods Program. Biomed. **194**, 105521 (2020)
6. Dolz, J., Gopinath, K., Yuan, J., Lombaert, H., Desrosiers, C., Ben Ayed, I.: Hyperdense-net: a hyper-densely connected CNN for multi-modal image segmentation. IEEE Trans. Med. Imaging **38**(5), 1116–1126 (2019). https://doi.org/10.1109/TMI.2018.2878669
7. Gao, X.W., Hui, R., Tian, Z.: Classification of CT brain images based on deep learning networks. Comput. Methods Program. Biomed. **138**, 49–56 (2017)
8. He, K., Zhang, X., Ren, S., Sun, J.: Deep residual learning for image recognition (2015)
9. Isensee, F., Kickingereder, P., Wick, W., Bendszus, M., Maier-Hein, K.H.: Brain tumor segmentation and radiomics survival prediction: contribution to the BRATS 2017 challenge. In: Crimi, A., Bakas, S., Kuijf, H., Menze, B., Reyes, M. (eds.) BrainLes 2017. LNCS, vol. 10670, pp. 287–297. Springer, Cham (2018). https://doi.org/10.1007/978-3-319-75238-9_25
10. Li, F., Liu, Z., Chen, H., Jiang, M., Zhang, X., Wu, Z.: Automatic detection of diabetic retinopathy in retinal fundus photographs based on deep learning algorithm. Transl. Vis. Sci. Technol. **8**(6), 4 (2019)
11. Muhammad, H., et al.: Hybrid deep learning on single wide-field optical coherence tomography scans accurately classifies glaucoma suspects. J. Glaucoma **26**(12), 1086–1094 (2017). https://doi.org/10.1097/IJG.0000000000000765, pMC5716847[pmcid]

12. Perdomo, O., et al.: Classification of diabetes-related retinal diseases using a deep learning approach in optical coherence tomography. Comput. Methods Program. Biomed. **178**, 181–189 (2019)
13. Qummar, S., et al.: A deep learning ensemble approach for diabetic retinopathy detection. IEEE Access **7**, 150530–150539 (2019)
14. Ryu, G., Lee, K., Park, D., Park, S.H., Sagong, M.: A deep learning model for identifying diabetic retinopathy using optical coherence tomography angiography. Sci. Rep. **11**(1), 23024 (2021). https://doi.org/10.1038/s41598-021-02479-6
15. Saeedi, P., et al.: Global and regional diabetes prevalence estimates for 2019 and projections for 2030 and 2045: results from the international diabetes federation diabetes atlas. 9th edition. Diab. Res. Clin. Pract. **157**, 107843 (2019)
16. Shibata, N., et al.: Development of a deep residual learning algorithm to screen for glaucoma from fundus photography. Sci. Rep. **8**(1), 14665 (2018). https://doi.org/10.1038/s41598-018-33013-w
17. Tham, Y.C., Li, X., Wong, T.Y., Quigley, H.A., Aung, T., Cheng, C.Y.: Global prevalence of glaucoma and projections of glaucoma burden through 2040: a systematic review and meta-analysis. Ophthalmology **121**(11), 2081–2090 (2014)
18. Wu, J., et al.: Gamma challenge:glaucoma grading from multi-modality images (2022)
19. Zhang, C., Zhao, J., Niu, J., Li, D.: New convolutional neural network model for screening and diagnosis of mammograms. PLoS ONE **15**(8), 1–20 (2020)
20. Zhang, T., Shi, M.: Multi-modal neuroimaging feature fusion for diagnosis of alzheimer's disease. J. Neurosci. Methods **341**, 108795 (2020)
21. Zhou, T., Ruan, S., Canu, S.: A review: deep learning for medical image segmentation using multi-modality fusion. Array **3–4**, 100004 (2019)

Mapping the Ocular Surface from Monocular Videos with an Application to Dry Eye Disease Grading

Ikram Brahim[1,2,3(✉)], Mathieu Lamard[1,3], Anas-Alexis Benyoussef[1,3,4],
Pierre-Henri Conze[1,5], Béatrice Cochener[1,3,4], Divi Cornec[2,3],
and Gwenolé Quellec[1(✉)]

[1] LaTIM UMR 1101, Inserm, Brest, France
ikrammeki@gmail.com, gwenole.quellec@inserm.fr
[2] LBAI UMR 1227, Inserm, Brest, France
[3] University of Western Brittany, Brest, France
[4] Ophtalmology Department, CHRU Brest, Brest, France
[5] IMT Atlantique, Brest, France

Abstract. With a prevalence of 5 to 50%, Dry Eye Disease (DED) is one of the leading reasons for ophthalmologist consultations. The diagnosis and quantification of DED usually rely on ocular surface analysis through slit-lamp examinations. However, evaluations are subjective and non-reproducible. To improve the diagnosis, we propose to 1) track the ocular surface in 3-D using video recordings acquired during examinations, and 2) grade the severity using registered frames. Our registration method uses unsupervised image-to-depth learning. These methods learn depth from lights and shadows and estimate pose based on depth maps. However, DED examinations undergo unresolved challenges including a moving light source, transparent ocular tissues, etc. To overcome these and estimate the ego-motion, we implement joint CNN architectures with multiple losses incorporating prior known information, namely the shape of the eye, through semantic segmentation as well as sphere fitting. The achieved tracking errors outperform the state-of-the-art, with a mean Euclidean distance as low as 0.48% of the image width on our test set. This registration improves the DED severity classification by a 0.20 AUC difference. The proposed approach is the first to address DED diagnosis with supervision from monocular videos.

Keywords: Dry Eye Disease · Self-supervised learning · Sphere fitting loss

1 Introduction

Dry Eye Disease (DED) is a condition that damages the ocular surface and tear film stability. DED can be traced back to a range of medical disorders, including Sjögren's syndrome, Parkinson, lupus, as well as smoking, contact lens, lasic

B. Antony et al. (Eds.): OMIA 2022, LNCS 13576, pp. 63–72, 2022.
https://doi.org/10.1007/978-3-031-16525-2_7

surgery, or allergies [14]. One of the ways to assess the damaged ocular surface is through the staining [22]. The tear quality and quantity can be measured by the tear break-up time (TBUT), i.e. the interval between an eye blink and a tear break-up. Both ocular surface staining and TBUT have been used clinically for over a century [2]. Algorithms have been proposed to automate the staining (punctate dot grading) [18] and TBUT [17] by analyzing digital slit lamp recordings and using supervised learning. But these tasks are still challenging due to eye motion and the video quality.

One way to help facilitate DED quantification is through image registration, to compensate for eye motion and visualise the full eye. To achieve this goal we take into account multiple camera views and estimate the camera motion between them in an unsupervised manner using artificial intelligence (AI). The proposed method "SiGMoid: Semantic & geometric monocular visual odometry", learns how to predict both depth and egomotion, which allows for image registration. This method improves automated DED classification compared to a baseline.

Related works: Structure from motion (SfM) is a complex problem in computer vision, whose aim is to reconstruct a 3D structure from a set of images. SfM uses images with different viewpoints in order to reconstruct a scene. More specifically, visual odometry (VO) is recovering the motion of a calibrated camera. This requires both camera motion estimation as well as inferred depth. The techniques differ in terms of what information is available as input [1]. Focusing on monocular visual odometry, the latest and most promising methods are Deep VO [19]. For more precise estimations, this includes learning depth, optical flow, features and egomotion in a self-supervised manner. Unsupervised learning is made possible by a fundamental element, photometric loss, which is the difference between a pixel distorted from the source image, by estimated depth and pose, and the pixel recorded in the target view. Methods presented in [4,5,23] take advantage of structures and semantic segmentation for unsupervised monocular learning of depth and egomotion. Semantic image segmentation assigns a class to each pixel to indicate what is being represented. Semantics are used to identify moving objects and allow for robust egomotion estimation. The 3D geometry of the scene is used in [13] for more robust estimation. The method uses a 3D iterative closest point (ICP) loss, without prior shape knowledge, along with the photometric loss. In parallel, another team in [21] explores the use of semantic segmentation of the scene for improvement as a novel 2D loss. They also combine a 3D ICP loss, which is less specific than a sphere fitting loss for our application. Lastly, a self-supervised spatial attention based depth and pose estimation is proposed by [15]. The method is applied for capsule endoscopy images and utilised synthetically generated data.

These methods fall short for our objective because they are heavily driven by color, light disparity and shadows. In our examinations, just like many medical examinations, the source of light is attached to the camera. Light changes resulting from camera motion imply that matched points will have different colors in consecutive images. The resulting color variance is a disturbance and inhibits any learning through photometric loss, used in most methods. We propose a semantic segmentation reconstruction loss that disregards any change in color and ensures semantic constraint. This loss checks if matched points have the same semantic label in consecutive images. It should be noted that, in previous methods, semantic segmentation is only used to mask out moving/disturbing objects. Another limitation of previous methods is that they generally don't take advantage of the known geometry of the scene. In contrast, we propose a shape fitting loss, which penalizes unlikely depth maps, given the patient anatomy. This loss, which also relies on semantic segmentation, is made unique to our application as a sphere fitting loss. It is less complex than an ICP implementation yet influences more specific constraints.

2   Proposed Method

We setup SiGMoid in the framework developed by Google, tested on autonomous driving datasets [5,8,11]. Given the extracted frames from the examination videos, and the camera intrinsic parameters, we want to learn how to transform one frame onto another's coordinate system. It involves learning the depth of each frame and the egomotion between two. Our contributions are two new losses, semantic reconstruction loss and a sphere fitting loss. We first use a previously trained segmentation network (based on Feature Pyramid Networks - FPN [12]), to assign each pixel to the following classes: eyelid, sclera, cornea. All pixels labeled as 'eyelid' are ignored in all training and inference since they have no valuable information for the target applications (TBUT, punctate dot grading). The eyelid also moves with respect to the eyeball, and therefore violates the assumption behind the photometric and semantic losses, and cannot be modeled by a rigid (spherical) shape model. The predicted semantic segmentations are then used for both training and inference. Our framework, detailed below Fig. 1, includes two CNNs (DepthNet and EgomotionNet) joined by the semantic reconstruction and photometric loss, which can be trained jointly (sharing of weights). Although trained jointly, they can be used separately for inference. Depth is inferred by DepthNet using a single image and simultaneously the camera pose is computed from two frames in a sequence. Inputs to the CNNs are: Frames $I : [I_{t-n}, I_t, I_{t+n}]$ and the Semantic Segmentation $S : [S_{t-n}, S_t, S_{t+n}]$ are used for loss calculations.

1. Depth: a fully convolutional encoder-decoder architecture produces a depth map from a single RGB frame.

$$D_i = \theta(I_i), \theta : \mathbb{R}^{(H \times W \times 3)} \rightarrow \mathbb{R}^{(H \times W)} \tag{1}$$

2. Egomotion: a network takes three frames (ex. $[I_{t-n}, I_t, I_{t+n}]$) and predicts transformations simultaneously

$$\psi_E(I_{i-n}, I_i) = (t_{x_1}, t_{y_1}, t_{z_1}, r_{x_1}, r_{y_1}, r_{z_1}) \tag{2}$$

$$\psi_E(I_i, I_{i+n}) = (t_{x_2}, t_{y_2}, t_{z_2}, r_{x_2}, r_{y_2}, r_{z_2}) \tag{3}$$

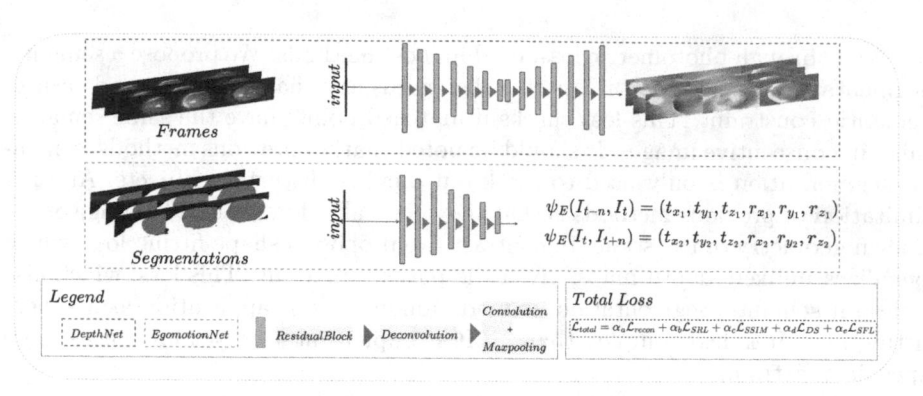

Fig. 1. SiGMoid framework.

The losses used to obtain the warped image, using a differentiable image warping operator $\phi(I_i, D_j, E_{i \to j}) \to \hat{I}_{i \to j}$, make up the total loss for every pair of $\hat{I}_{i \to j} - I_j$, Eq. 4 and are detailed below. The warping operator takes an RGB image I_i , a depth map D_j, and the egomotion $E_{i \to j}$, giving us the reconstructed $\hat{I}_j^{th}$ image.

$$\mathcal{L}_{total} = \alpha_a \mathcal{L}_{SRL} + \alpha_b \mathcal{L}_{recon} + \alpha_c \mathcal{L}_{SSIM} + \alpha_d \mathcal{L}_{DS} + \alpha_e \mathcal{L}_{SFL} \tag{4}$$

Semantic reconstruction loss (SRL) is the main supervision signal.

$$\mathcal{L}_{SRL} = min(\|\hat{S}_{i \to j} - S_j\|) \tag{5}$$

Photometric loss (RECON) is similar to SRL except frames are used as input to compare this reconstructed image $\hat{I}_{i \to j}$ to the next frame I_j [4].

$$\mathcal{L}_{recon} = min(\|\hat{I}_{i \to j} - I_j\|) \tag{6}$$

Structural similarity loss (SSIM) is used to assess the quality of the warping [20]. SSIM combines comparisons of luminance, contrast and structure [20], and we measure this between $\hat{I}_{i \to j}$ and I_j.

$$\mathcal{L}_{SSIM} = 1 - SSIM(\hat{I}_{i \to j}, I_j) \tag{7}$$

$$SSIM(\hat{I}_{i \to j}, I_j) = \frac{(2\mu_{\hat{I}_{i \to j}}\mu_{I_j} + l_1)(2\sigma_{\hat{I}_{i \to j}I_j} + l_2)}{(\mu_{\hat{I}_{i \to j}}^2 + \mu_{I_j}^2 + l_1)(\sigma_{\hat{I}_{i \to j}}^2 + \sigma_{I_j}^2 + l_2)}$$

where $\mu_{\hat{I}_{i \to j}}, \mu_{I_j}$ are the average , $\sigma_{\hat{I}_{i \to j}}^2, \sigma_{I_j}^2$ the variance, and $\sigma_{\hat{I}_{i \to j}I_j}$ covariance of $\hat{I}_{i \to j}, I_j$. $l_1 = (k_1 L)^2$, $l_2 = (k_2 L)^2$, L the dynamic range of the pixel-values, $k_1 = 0.01$, $k_2 = 0.03$.

Depth smoothness (DS) encourages smoothness by penalizing depth discontinuity if the image shows continuity in the same area [7].

$$\mathcal{L}_{DS} = |\nabla_x D_i| e^{-\nabla_x I_i} + |\nabla_y D_i| e^{-\nabla_y I_i} \tag{8}$$

where ∇_x, ∇_y are image gradients in the horizontal and vertical direction, respectively.

Sphere fitting loss (SFL) is implemented for what is estimated to be the eye's shape: two intersecting spheres [16]. A smaller anterior transparent sphere is the cornea and a posterior sphere representing the sclera. In order to implement this loss, we first estimate a depth map, and then using the semantic segmentation, we calculate the sphericity of the two regions: cornea and sclera. As detailed in (13) we first use the segmentations to obtain the depth predictions of either regions. The sphere fitting is then implemented twice for both, the loss is the sum of both errors. We apply a threshold of 0.5 before calculating this loss to ensure either regions are present in the frame. We define our threshold as the count of non zero pixels pertaining to either regions and dividing that by the total number of pixels of the frame. Once a frame's calculated region presence exceeds the threshold, we use the depth estimations for either the corneal or scleral region and convert it to a 3D point cloud projection using the inverse of the intrinsic matrix. We then use the estimated point cloud and apply a least squares sphere fitting. Following the method proposed by Jekel, we are able to determine the best sphere center for the given data points [10]. By rearranging the terms in Eq. 9, we can express the equation in matrix notation and solve for $\vec{c}$ (see Eq. 11). By fitting the n data points x_k, y_k, z_k, we can solve for the centre coordinates of the sphere x_0, y_0, z_0 and the radius r.

$$(x - x_0)^2 + (y - y_0)^2 + (z - z_0)^2 = r^2 \tag{9}$$

$$x^2 + y^2 + z^2 = 2xx_0 + 2yy_0 + 2zz_0 + r^2 - x_0^2 - y_0^2 - z_0^2 \tag{10}$$

$$\vec{f} = A\vec{c} \tag{11}$$

$$\vec{f} = \begin{bmatrix} x_k^2 + y_k^2 + z_k^2 \\ x_{k+1}^2 + y_{k+1}^2 + z_{k+1}^2 \\ \vdots \\ x_n^2 + y_n^2 + z_n^2 \end{bmatrix} \quad A = \begin{bmatrix} 2x_k & 2y_k & 2z_k & 1 \\ 2x_{k+1} & 2y_{k+1} & 2z_{k+1} & 1 \\ \vdots & \vdots & \vdots & \vdots \\ 2x_n & 2y_n & 2z_n & 1 \end{bmatrix} \quad \vec{c} = \begin{bmatrix} x_0 \\ y_0 \\ z_0 \\ r^2 - x_0^2 - y_0^2 - z_0^2 \end{bmatrix} \tag{12}$$

Sphere fitting loss $\mathcal{L}_{SFL}$ is a mean square error (MSE) between the fitted sphere and the data points. The sphericity for each of the corneal and scleral regions have a weight α_e. With both regions fitted to a sphere we then calculate the loss for each pixel p.

$$\mathcal{L}_{SFL} = \mathcal{L}_{cornea_{SFL}} + \mathcal{L}_{sclera_{SFL}} \tag{13}$$

$$\mathcal{L}_{cornea_{SFL}} = \frac{1}{p_c} \sum_{k=1}^{p_c} ((x_{ck} - x_{c0}) - r_c)^2, \mathcal{L}_{sclera_{SFL}} = \frac{1}{p_s} \sum_{k=1}^{p_s} ((x_{sk} - x_{s0}) - r_s)^2 \tag{14}$$

where p_c are pixels, x_{ck} data points, x_{c0} centre coordinate on the corneal surface, r_c the cornea radius and p_s are pixels, x_{sk} data points, x_{s0} centre coordinate on the scleral surface, r_s the estimated sclera radius.

3   Experiments and Results

Dataset. The dataset was collected from slit lamp videos taken during the examination of patients with Sjögren's syndrome (PEPPS study). This is a prospective cohort evaluating the ocular surface damages in patients with Sjögren's syndrome followed at the university hospital of Brest. The videos were recorded using the Haag Streit BQ 900 slit lamp and the camera module CM 900 (resolution 1600×1200, 12 fps, magnification ×10). The ocular surface was analysed after illumination with white light (lissamine green evaluation) followed by cobalt blue light and interposition of a yellow filter (fluorescein evaluation). Our database contains 26 videos from 26 patients.

3.1   SiGMoid

Using our dataset, we conducted several experiments mainly using transfer learning. We used models pre-trained on the Cityscapes dataset (C) [6,8].

Preprocessing. Calibration was performed using Matlab (MathWorks, Natick, MA) with images of a planar checkerboard (8 × 7 squares of 2 × 2 mm). We employed 10 calibration images (pattern placed at different poses). The intrinsic parameters obtained from the calibration were the focal length fx = fy = 3758.9 pixels, and the central points cx = 138.8, cy = 85.4.

To prepare the data we first use our trained FPN model to predict the semantic segmentation for each of the frames. For training we produce three-frame sequences with an interval of $n = 10$ frames. This is a setup we chose given that our videos have 12 frames per second and the motion between consecutive frames is usually small. This resulted in 15,275 three-frame sequences for training.

Evaluation. Unlike existing methods, we do not have access to ground truth depth and odometry. We manually annotated punctate dots (damaged areas) on the surface of the eye, and visible veins on the sclera. To visualise the accuracy of our predictions, we warp a source frame into a target frame and tracked the marked points. By using the equation $p_s \sim K\hat{T}_{t \to s}\hat{D}_t(p_t)K^{-1}p_t$, we project source frame pixels p_s to the target frame p_t. Our evaluation used the inverse warping which first requires the depth map $\hat{D}_t$ prediction of the target frame, and then the egomotion from source to target which also gives us the transformation matrix $\hat{T}_{t \to s}$. Evaluation was performed on a test set of 3 patients with 54 frames. Our test set consists of 126 points on the sclera on vein intersections and punctate dots, 33 points on the cornea of visible punctate dots.

Training Setup. The baseline we used to compare is the implementation of [5], which had to be trained in intervals due to the loss diverging to infinity, as well as the predicted egomotion matrix being non-invertible. Baseline and SiGMoid were trained using a learning rate 0.0002, batch size of 8, SSIM weight 0.15, and depth smoothing weight 0.04 [4]. The baseline L1 reconstruction weight 0.85 and SiGMoid's training setup was using L1 reconstruction weight 0.15, L2 semantic reconstruction loss weight 0.85, sphere fitting weight 10000 (given the very small distances this required a big weight). All models were trained until 200 epochs, with the best model (lowest loss achieved) saved for inference.

Results. Table 1 shows the evaluation results on our test set by different methods. By defining the two novel losses, we are able to stabilise training and avoid the loss diverging and obtain better results. Despite the increase in computation during training via the losses, our inference time remains similar to the baseline. In the following experiments, we preprocessed the data using a frame step $n = 10$. We compared two configurations: SiGMoid no. 3 with only $\mathcal{L}_{SRL}$, SiGMoid no. 4 with both contributions $\mathcal{L}_{SRL}$ and $\mathcal{L}_{SFL}$.

The mean Euclidean distance in pixels is lowest in SiGMoid no. 4 with both CNN inputs being the frames. Our proposed method achieves the lowest error when compared to the baseline. The reconstruction improves in all SiGMoid implementations proving that a simple photometric loss used in [5] is less efficient for our data. We also compute a mean inter-grader error (result no. 5). We asked three graders to re-annotate the test set points giving us an average human error of 4.81 px. We visualise the depth map predictions in Fig. 2.

Table 1. Experiment details and results.

No	Method	Frame step	$\mathcal{L}_{SRL}$	$\mathcal{L}_{SFL}$	Mean Euclidian (px)	Mean Euclidan (%)
1	Casser [5]*	No	–	–	29.08	1.82
2	Casser [5]*	Yes	–	–	27.19	1.70
3	SiGMoid no. 3	Yes	Yes	No	22.48	1.40
4	SiGMoid no. 4	Yes	Yes	Yes	**7.7**	**0.48**
5	Grader errors	NA	NA	NA	4.81	0.30

CNN Inputs → DepthNet : Frames (I), EgomotionNet : Frames (I)
*denotes trained in multiple intervals due to loss divergence → ∞

3.2 DED Diagnosis: Classification

In order to evaluate our proposed method in a diagnostic aspect, we apply it to the automated classification of mild versus severe DED. Mild DED (respectively severe DED) is defined as a corneal Oxford score ≤ 1 (respectively ≥ 2) [3].

Preprocessing. We train the baseline with the raw frames from the videos of the examinations. We compare this with a mosaic from a pair of frames obtained using our registration method and selecting only the frames with a warping error (SRL) less than 5%. This resulted in ≈ 35% of frames being removed.

Training Setup. The training setup was identical for both experiments; learning rate 2e-06, batch size of 64 and using resnet50 as backbone. Due to data scarcity, an additional dataset of 28 videos acquired using a different examination protocol was used as the validation set for our DED classification training.

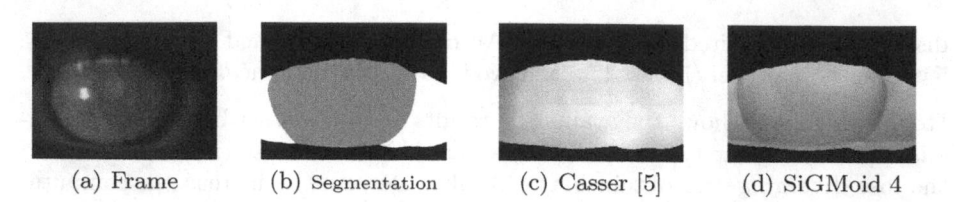

(a) Frame   (b) Segmentation   (c) Casser [5]   (d) SiGMoid 4

Fig. 2. CNN inputs and depth map predictions.

The data was split into ; 35 eyes for the train, 39 for the validation and 14 for the test. All eyes from the same patient were assigned to the same set.

Evaluation. Area under the (receiver operating characteristic) curve (AUC), accuracy (ACC), precision and recall were used as metrics. The validation and test evaluation were performed per eye by using a majority vote for the n frames per patient. As shown in Table 2, the classification improves when using the registered frames obtained using SiGMoid. All metrics improve with a margin of 0.08–0.22 validating the application of our proposed method to DED grading.

Table 2. Classification evaluation results

No	Method	Backbone	AUC	ACC	Precision	Recall
1	Baseline	resnet50 [9]	0.69	0.57	0.73	0.67
2	SiGMoid	resnet50 [9]	**0.89**	**0.79**	**0.81**	**0.83**

4 Discussion and Conclusion

We proposed SiGMoid, a self-supervised image registration algorithm towards DED diagnosis and quantification from slit lamp videos. This is the first use, to our knowledge, of monocular DED examinations in a self-supervised manner for this application. Our results validate that, due to the color/illumination variance present in the examinations, the baseline method is not sufficient. Although both contributions improved our results, we see a more significant improvement from the sphere fitting loss. Our method also has the closest mean euclidean distance to what we considered human error. Additional data acquired from a different acquisition device could enable to robustify our approach. In particular, it could allow us to test how generalizable our method is and also expand it through fine-tuning. Finally, we demonstrated that obtaining an accurate reconstruction is beneficial to the classification of DED grading.

Acknowledgments. This research was supported by funding from the Innovative Medicines Initiative 2 Joint Undertaking (JU) under grant agreement No. 806975. The JU receives support from the European Union's Horizon 2020 research and innovation program and EFPIA. It is also funded in part by The Brittany Region through the ARED doctoral program.

References

1. Aqel, M.O.A., Marhaban, M.H., Saripan, M.I., Ismail, N.B.: Review of visual odometry: types, approaches, challenges, and applications. SpringerPlus **5**(1), 1–26 (2016). https://doi.org/10.1186/s40064-016-3573-7
2. Begley, C., Caffery, B., Chalmers, R., Situ, P., Simpson, T., Nelson, J.D.: Review and analysis of grading scales for ocular surface staining. Ocul. Surf. **17**(2), 208–220 (2019)
3. Bron, A.: Reflections on the tears. Eye **11**(5), 583–602 (1997)
4. Casser, V., Pirk, S., Mahjourian, R., Angelova, A.: Depth prediction without the sensors: leveraging structure for unsupervised learning from monocular videos. In: Thirty-Third AAAI Conference on Artificial Intelligence (AAAI-19) (2019)
5. Casser, V., Pirk, S., Mahjourian, R., Angelova, A.: Unsupervised monocular depth and ego-motion learning with structure and semantics. In: CVPR Workshop on Visual Odometry and Computer Vision Applications Based on Location Cues (VOCVALC) (2019)
6. Cordts, M., et al.: The cityscapes dataset for semantic urban scene understanding. In: Proceedings of the IEEE Conference on Computer Vision and Pattern Recognition, pp. 3213–3223 (2016)
7. Godard, C., Mac Aodha, O., Brostow, G.J.: Unsupervised monocular depth estimation with left-right consistency. In: Proceedings of the IEEE Conference on Computer Vision and Pattern Recognition, pp. 270–279 (2017)
8. Gordon, A., Li, H., Jonschkowski, R., Angelova, A.: Depth from videos in the wild: unsupervised monocular depth learning from unknown cameras. In: Proceedings of the IEEE/CVF International Conference on Computer Vision, pp. 8977–8986 (2019)
9. He, K., Zhang, X., Ren, S., Sun, J.: Deep residual learning for image recognition. In: Proceedings of the IEEE Conference on Computer Vision and Pattern Recognition, pp. 770–778 (2016)
10. Jekel, C.F.: Digital image correlation on steel ball (2016). https://hdl.handle.net/10019.1/98627
11. Li, H., Gordon, A., Zhao, H., Casser, V., Angelova, A.: Unsupervised monocular depth learning in dynamic scenes. arXiv preprint arXiv:2010.16404 (2020)
12. Lin, T.Y., Dollár, P., Girshick, R., He, K., Hariharan, B., Belongie, S.: Feature pyramid networks for object detection. In: Proceedings of the IEEE Conference on Computer Vision and Pattern Recognition, pp. 2117–2125 (2017)
13. Mahjourian, R., Wicke, M., Angelova, A.: Unsupervised learning of depth and ego-motion from monocular video using 3d geometric constraints. In: Proceedings of the IEEE Conference on Computer Vision and Pattern Recognition, pp. 5667–5675 (2018)
14. Manaviat, M.R., Rashidi, M., Afkhami-Ardekani, M., Shoja, M.R.: Prevalence of dry eye syndrome and diabetic retinopathy in type 2 diabetic patients. BMC Ophthalmol. **8**(1), 1–5 (2008)

15. Ozyoruk, K.B., et al.: Endoslam dataset and an unsupervised monocular visual odometry and depth estimation approach for endoscopic videos: endo-sfmlearner (2020)
16. Park, S., Zhang, X., Bulling, A., Hilliges, O.: Learning to find eye region landmarks for remote gaze estimation in unconstrained settings. In: Proceedings of the 2018 ACM Symposium on Eye Tracking Research & Applications, pp. 1–10 (2018)
17. Su, T.Y., Liu, Z.Y., Chen, D.Y.: Tear film break-up time measurement using deep convolutional neural networks for screening dry eye disease. IEEE Sens. J. **18**(16), 6857–6862 (2018)
18. Su, T.Y., Ting, P.J., Chang, S.W., Chen, D.Y.: Superficial punctate keratitis grading for dry eye screening using deep convolutional neural networks. IEEE Sens. J. **20**(3), 1672–1678 (2019)
19. Wang, K., Ma, S., Chen, J., Ren, F., Lu, J.: Approaches challenges and applications for deep visual odometry toward to complicated and emerging areas. IEEE Trans. Cogn. Dev. Syst. **14**(1), 35–49 (2020)
20. Wang, Z., Bovik, A.C., Sheikh, H.R., Simoncelli, E.P.: Image quality assessment: from error visibility to structural similarity. IEEE Trans. Image Process. **13**(4), 600–612 (2004)
21. Wei, X., Feng, J., Zhou, J.: Semantics-driven unsupervised learning for monocular depth and ego-motion estimation. arXiv preprint arXiv:2006.04371 (2020)
22. Wood, S.D., Mian, S.I.: Diagnostic tools for dry eye disease. J. Diagn. Tools Dry Eye Dis., 101–107 (2016)
23. Zhou, T., Brown, M., Snavely, N., Lowe, D.G.: Unsupervised learning of depth and ego-motion from video. In: Proceedings of the IEEE Conference on Computer Vision and Pattern Recognition, pp. 1851–1858 (2017)

Rethinking Retinal Image Quality: Treating Quality Threshold as a Tunable Hyperparameter

Fabian SL Yii[1]([✉]), Raman Dutt[1], Tom MacGillivray[1], Baljean Dhillon[1], Miguel Bernabeu[1], and Niall Strang[2]

[1] University of Edinburgh, Edinburgh, UK
fabian.yii@ed.ac.uk

[2] Glasgow Caledonian University, Glasgow, UK

Abstract. Assuming the robustness of a deep learning model to suboptimal images is a key consideration, we asked if there was any value in including training images of poor quality. In particular, should we treat the (quality) threshold at which a training image is either included or excluded as a tunable hyperparameter? To that end, we systematically examined the effect of including training images of varying quality on the test performance of a DL model in classifying the severity of diabetic retinopathy. We found that there was a unique combination of (categorical) quality labels or a *Goldilocks* (continuous) quality score that gave rise to optimal test performance on either high-quality or suboptimal images. The model trained exclusively on high-quality images yielded worse performance in all test scenarios than that trained on the optimally tuned training set which included images with some level of degradation.

Keywords: Image quality · Tunable hyperparameter · Deep learning

1   Introduction

A common pre-processing step in deep learning (DL) applied to retinal image analysis is to exclude images of sub-optimal quality before training and testing a model for a given downstream task. For instance, Poplin et al. filtered out 12% of 96,082 UK Biobank (UKBB) retinal images of 'poor quality' for a downstream task of predicting different cardiovascular risk factors [14]. Likewise, 12% of UKBB retinal images of 'very poor quality' were excluded in another study aiming to predict refractive error [18]. Lin et al. removed 14,003 retinal images

F. Yii and R. Dutt–Contributed equally to this work. F. Yii is supported by the Medical Research Council [grant number MR/N013166/1].

The original version of this chapter was revised: an error on page 78 was corrected and Electronic Supplementary Material (ESM) was added. The correction to this chapter is available at https://doi.org/10.1007/978-3-031-16525-2_21

Supplementary Information The online version contains supplementary material available at https://doi.org/10.1007/978-3-031-16525-2_8.

that were 'subjectively' deemed to be poor – or if the optic disc and fovea were not present simultaneously – from a total of 35,126 EyePacs images, with a view to training a model to detect referable diabetic retinopathy (DR) [11].

The tacit assumption of removing poor images in the application of DL is that only input images of *relatively high quality* are to be used when a model is deployed in the real world. Such a model will, conceivably, not generalise well to images with some degradation arising from, say, naturally occurring senile eye conditions like cataract, or sub-optimal patient positioning leading to non-uniform illumination. We are therefore drawn to think that *careful* inclusion of images with some appropriate level of degradation may in fact make a model more *versatile*, i.e. robust to a wider distribution of image quality. Indeed, segmentation of retinal sublayers and choroid in optical coherence tomography (OCT) images improves when a DL model is trained on degraded images [9]. Similar observation has been made when classifying non-medical images with DL [3].

But how do we determine if a given training image has an appropriate level of degradation, such that it is high enough to add some useful noise but low enough to not undermine the model? We propose that the image quality threshold, at which we decide if an image should or should not be used for training, can be treated as a *tunable hyperparameter*. Our ultimate goal is to maximise the performance of a trained model on the *unfiltered* test set to simulate real-world distribution of image quality. This is in contrast to studies where the model is trained and tested on *filtered* datasets. While some may argue that a simpler approach is to *apply* various levels and types of image degradation [4], and settle on the level that yields the best test performance, we are of the opinion that such artificial image degradation, e.g. gaussian blur, is not nuanced enough to capture the kind of degradation particular to a retinal image, e.g. areas of under- and over-exposure during acquisition.

The idea that image quality threshold can be treated as a tunable hyperparameter raises the question of whether it should be done on a *categorical* or *continuous* scale. In this regard, it is conceivable that superior outcome (as judged by the test performance of a downstream model trained on the resultant, filtered dataset) is contingent upon one's ability to partition training images based on their quality at as *granular* a level as possible – since this renders any effect of nuanced variation in image quality discernible. Thus, the main objectives of our work are to see if:

- including images of poorer quality in the training set has a positive bearing on the test performance (particularly on the *unfiltered* test set) of a DL model for a downstream task of classifying DR severity. If so, should we treat quality threshold as a tunable hyperparameter?
- tuning the quality threshold on a *continuous* scale offers additional value (more optimal test performance) than tuning on a categorical scale. We hypothesise an increase in test performance (model made more robust) as the training set becomes noisier up to a point before falling.

2   Methods

2.1   Quality Prediction on a Categorical Scale and Continuous Scale

To predict image quality on a categorical scale, we utilised *Multiple Color-space Fusion Network* (MCF-Net), a DL model that achieved a state-of-the-art test accuracy of 91.75% [6]. Briefly, an image is considered *good* if there are no low-quality factors; *usable* if there are some low-quality factors but important features like the optic disc are still clear enough for ophthalmological assessment to be carried out; *reject* if a full assessment is impossible.

Description of the Adapted (regression) Model. To turn the original model into a regression model, we removed the softmax function corresponding to each of the 5 loss functions. Mean absolute error (MAE) was used in place of the original cross-entropy loss function. The output of the adapted model (normalised between 0 and 1) would be *closer to 0 for a high-quality image*. The model achieved an MAE of 0.154 on the test set. More information on the adapted model is available as supplementary material (S1).

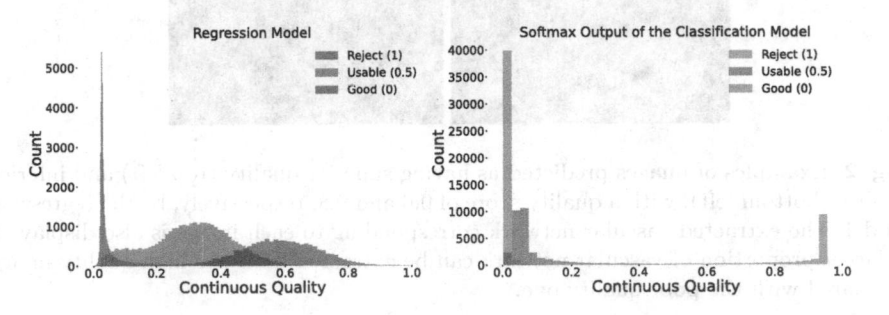

Fig. 1. Distribution of continuous quality scores of the entire *EyePACS* dataset (n = 88,702) as predicted by the regression model (left) and as represented by the softmax output (*Reject* class, i.e. greater value corresponds to poorer quality) of the original classification model (right). Each hue represents a different quality class.

As a baseline approach (owing to its simplicity), we also extracted the softmax output in the final classification layer of the *original* (classification) model. In theory, the softmax output represents the confidence of the model in assigning an input image to a particular class label, e.g. *Reject*, and may therefore be treated as a continuous quality score of some sort. However, the distribution of the quality scores as represented by the softmax output is qualitatively inferior, i.e. as expected, cross-entropy loss function biases softmax output towards the extremums, to those predicted by the regression model (Fig. 1). Tuning the quality filter threshold using the softmax output would conceivably be less granular, e.g. setting the threshold to 0.4 or 0.5 would not make much of a difference to quality distribution, so we settled on the quality scores predicted by the regression model for all experiments.

Validation of the Regression Model. We first extracted the vascular network of 10,044 randomly selected Kaggle EyePACS retinal images using Deformable U-Net [8]. It is widely held that low image quality has a detrimental effect on vessel segmentation [12,16]. As such, one would generally expect a smaller proportion of vascular network to be extracted from poorer images (Fig. 2). In line with this, images predicted as having poorer quality tend to return a smaller proportion of vascular network (Pearson's r = −0.69; $p < 0.001$; see S4).

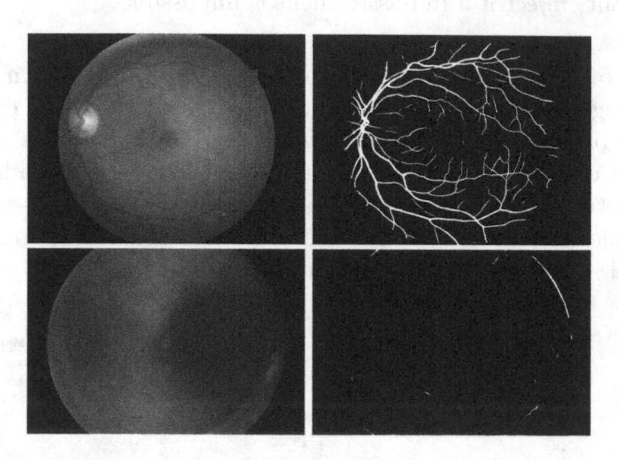

Fig. 2. Examples of images predicted as having superior quality (top left) and inferior quality (bottom left), with a quality score of 0.0 and 0.8, respectively, by the regression model. The extracted vascular network corresponding to each image is also displayed. A larger proportion of vascular network can be extracted from the high-quality image compared with the poor-quality one.

2.2   Effect of Varying Image Quality Threshold

DR is a common diabetic complication that affects the retina. Timely treatments are required to prevent or minimise vision loss when DR progresses to more severe stages, e.g. growth of new, leaky blood vessels. As such, many DL algorithms have been developed over the past few years to classify DR severity, with a view to aiding large-scale DR screening programmes [13]. The Kaggle EyePACS dataset was used in this study to elucidate the effect of varying quality threshold on the downstream DR classification task. Each image is labelled with an integer representing DR severity (ranges from 0 to 4) [20].

We should point out that the overwhelming majority of images graded as having the most advanced stage of DR (level 4) are of **poorer** quality (Fig. 3; refer also to the figure in S2). This naturally leads one to wonder if excluding poorer training images might bias a downstream model against severe DR. The original dataset (n = 88,702) was made up of a training set (40%) and a test set

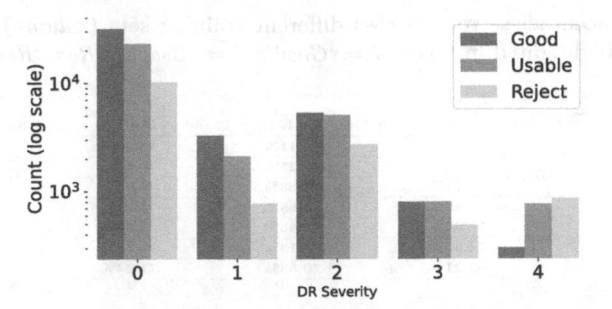

Fig. 3. Frequency of each quality label as predicted by the original MCF-Net across different DR severities. Similar figure using continuous score can be found in S2.

(60%). We used 30% (n = 10,538) of training images to build a separate valida-tion set. Images in each sub-dataset were filtered based on different pre-defined (either categorical or continuous) quality thresholds. A ResNet-50 pre-trained on ImageNet was then fine-tuned (detailed in S3) on the different resultant training sets, before comparing their test performance with one another.

3 Experiments

3.1 Altering Quality Threshold on a Categorical Scale

As shown in Table 1, training the model on the *unfiltered (G+U+R)* training set consistently yielded the highest test accuracy across different combinations of quality labels – including the *unfiltered test set.* That is, using *poorer images* on top of good images (*G+U+R*) gave rise to **optimal** performance on the test set comprised of *exclusively good images* (80.63%), which was even higher than the model trained exclusively on good images (79.08%). This is consistent with observation by Zhou et al. [22] that fine-tuning a model on poor images (origi-nally trained on good images) did not hurt the model's performance on 'clean' data. Our observation therefore challenges conventional wisdom (see conclusion in [4]) that poor training images have undesirable effect on the test performance of a model, which presumably motivates the exclusion of suboptimal images in studies cited in Sect. 1.

One caveat, however, is that the gain in performance accorded by the *G+U+R* training set in all test scenarios *might* arise largely as a result of its sheer size (n = 24,588) [17]. That said, the fact that a model trained on *U+R* – notwithstanding its small size (n = 13,023) – still performs better on all test sets compared with a model trained on the much larger *G+U* training set (n = 20,458), indicates that the observed difference in performance might still be attributable to a *variation in quality distribution* as opposed to the size of the training set.

What gives Rise to the Superior Performance of *G+U+R*? Previous experiments were repeated after applying just *one of* the following conventional

Table 1. Test accuracies (*row*) across different training sets (*column*). Best overall performance is highlighted in bold. G = 'Good'; U = 'Usable'; R = 'Reject'.

Test	Train				
	G+U+R (n = 24,588)	G+U (n = 20,458)	G+R (n = 15,695)	U+R (n = 13,023)	G (n = 11,565)
G+U+R	78.24%	75.29%	76.11%	76.29%	75.72%
G+U	79.26%	76.74%	77.26%	77.34%	77.12%
G+R	78.66%	75.71%	76.63%	76.75%	76.36%
U+R	76.12%	72.49%	73.68%	74.11%	72.73%
G	**80.63%**	78.44%	78.85%	78.75%	79.08%
U	77.48%	74.53%	75.18%	75.48%	74.56%
R	73.25%	68.21%	70.53%	71.24%	68.89%

Table 2. Test accuracies (*row*) across different training sets (*column*), **augmented** such that the resultant number of training images matches that of G+U+R (n = 24,588). G = 'Good'; U = 'Usable'; R = 'Reject'; A = 'Augmentation'.

Test	Train			
	G+U+A (n = 24,458)	G+R+A (n = 24,195)	U+R+A (n = 24,023)	G+A (n = 24,130)
G+U+R	75.28%	74.51%	76.04%	73.80%
G+U	76.68%	75.77%	76.95%	74.93%
G+R	75.70%	75.19%	76.58%	74.65%
U+R	72.57%	71.72%	73.97%	70.95%
G	78.38%	77.66%	78.38%	76.98%
U	74.52%	73.30%	75.09%	72.24%
R	68.47%	68.41%	71.62%	68.23%

augmentation techniques to each randomly chosen training image: random rotation of no greater than 30°, vertical flip, horizontal flip and Gaussian blur. 3 of these 4 techniques were not expected to alter image quality so the quality distribution between the original and augmented datasets could be assumed to be broadly similar. The number of augmented images was predefined such that the size of the resultant training set would be comparable to that of *G+U+R* (n = 24,588), since our primary aim was to increase the size of the smaller training sets while preserving their quality distribution. Any difference in test performance between *G+U+R* could therefore be attributed largely to a variation in quality distribution.

Comparing the test performance of the model trained on *G+U+R* in Table 1 to that of the models trained on the different **augmented** training sets (Table 2), the former model still had a clear edge over all latter models. Importantly, *G+U+R*'s superior performance was evident across all test sets, *including those whose quality distribution differed from itself.* For instance, even after increasing the size of the *U+R* training set from 13,023 to 24,023, its performance on the *U+R* test set (73.97%) still lagged far behind that of the model trained on *G+U+R* (76.12%). The inferior performance of the augmented training sets vis-a-vis *G+U+R* training set in all test scenarios also lends credence to our proposition that conventional augmentations fail to capture the nuanced degradation in, and variation between, naturally acquired retinal images.

On a side note, the paradoxical observation that the *G+A* training set resulted in poorer test performance (e.g. 76.98% on *G* test set) than the *G* training set (79.08% on *G* test set) despite the former's significantly larger size could plausibly be the result of exacerbated class imbalance, which was already severe before augmentation (around 75% of G training images did not have DR). This unreservedly biased the model to level 0 DR (S5). However, it is unclear how augmentation could have worsened class imbalance as training images were randomly augmented with uniform probability. Taken together, our findings can only parsimoniously suggest that the optimally tuned training set does not owe its superior performance to its sheer size.

'Clean' Training Set Biased Model Against Severe DR. To see if training the model on exclusively good images would bias a model against more severe levels of DR (discussed in 2.2), we computed the model's accuracy for classifying images with level 3 and level 4 DR taken from the $G+U$ test set. As hypothesised, training the model on good images alone undermined its ability to classify level 3 DR (15.72%) and level 4 DR (0%) compared with the test performance gained by using the optimally tuned $G+U+R$ training set (36.12% and 24.00%, respectively). Augmenting the smaller training sets also did not improve their performance anywhere near that seen with $G+U+R$. This further justifies our contention against indiscriminate exclusion of poor training images and supports the notion of treating quality threshold as a tunable hyperparameter.

3.2   Altering Quality Threshold on a Continuous Scale

Quality threshold was gradually increased from 0.10 to 1.00, i.e. progressively poorer images are included at each step. All training details, e.g. model, optimiser, learning rate, seed for validation-test split, etc., were identical to previous experiments to allow for a fair comparison of results. The performance of the model trained on each resultant (filtered) training set was assessed based on its accuracy on two different test sets, i.e. *unfiltered* and *'Good'* (based on the original MCF-Net classification) images. As Fig. 4 shows, the performance of the model tends to increase on both test sets with the inclusion of increasingly poorer images in the training set. The performance then peaked at 79.83% and 77.65% on the *'Good'* and *unfiltered* test sets, respectively, when the threshold was set to 0.72, and dropped from that point on.

This observation is consistent with our postulation about the presence of a *Goldilocks* level of image quality. Images beyond this optimal point are of such poor quality that they only serve to undermine the model. In support of this we observed *disproportionately* large changes in test accuracy as the threshold was changed from the optimal point to 1.00 and from 0.66 to the optimal point, i.e. -0.89% and $+1.66\%$, despite relatively small changes in the number of images, i.e. $+497$ and $+529$ (see S6 for full table). Some *'Reject'* images were poorer still and had undesirable effect on test performance. Conversely, poor though those 529 additional images included at the optimal point were, they were beneficial insofar as they helped the model learn some 'usable' noise. As with before, the fact that adding increasingly poorer training images improved the model's performance on *good* images up until the optimal point contradicts conventional

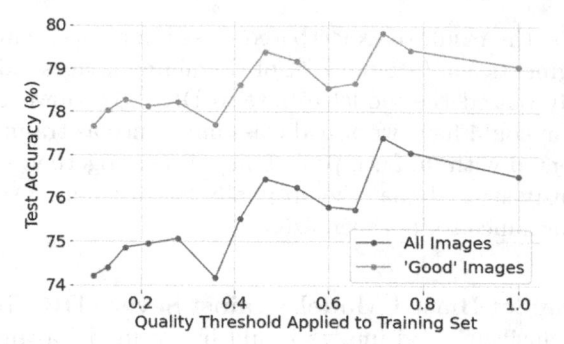

Fig. 4. Classification accuracy of the downstream model trained on different datasets filtered as per varying pre-defined continuous quality thresholds on two different test sets: *unfiltered* (blue) and *'good'* (categorical quality) images (orange). (Color figure online)

wisdom that using exclusively high-quality training images would yield optimal performance on high-quality test images. Taken together, the very presence of this optimal point which lies at some distance from the *expedient* threshold of 1.00 (i.e. inclusion of all images) *further strengthens* our justification that quality threshold can – and should indeed be – treated as a tunable hyperparameter.

3.3   Tuning on a Continuous Scale: Does it Confer *Additional* Value?

When quality threshold was tuned on a three-level categorical scale, the highest classification accuracy on the *unfiltered* and *'Good'* test sets came from the model trained on $G+U+R$, i.e. 78.24% and 80.63%, respectively (Table 1). If tuning the threshold on a *finer* scale had an *additional* benefit, one would expect the accuracy of the model on the same test sets to be even higher. However, the test accuracy from tuning the threshold on a *continuous* scale was in fact slightly lower – 77.40% and 79.83%, respectively (Fig. 4). That said, our results **should not** be construed as evidence against the use of continuous over categorical scale because we had not been able to fully account for the stochastic nature of model training and evaluation, e.g. variation in minibatch images across runs, etc. This is evident if one considers the fact that the test accuracy of the model from the 'continuous' experiments with quality threshold set to 1.00 *did not agree with* its categorical equivalent ($G+U+R$ training images).

4   Discussions and Conclusions

Considering the diminishing returns of increasing network complexity [2,21] and size of training data [17] in the domain of DL, it is apt that we focus our present work on the quality of input images. In particular, we propose – and have provided empirical justification – that image quality threshold should be treated as a *tunable hyperparameter*. There is ample demonstration of the detrimental effect of synthetic image degradation on the performance of DL models trained on 'clean' datasets [1,4,7,9,15,19]. In line with this, natural sources of image degradation have also been shown to reduce the performance of a DL model trained exclusively on high-quality retinal images [21]. Our work is therefore driven by a desire to bring about a paradigm shift away from training a model exclusively on high-quality images to *carefully* curating a training set that also includes some suboptimal images. Indeed, when tested on poorer images (e.g. U test set) – in relation to the G test set – the G training set experienced the largest drop in accuracy among all training sets (Table 1).

To mitigate poor robustness to noise, much work has focused on retraining or fine-tuning an existing model with an augmented dataset – e.g. contrast reduction, Gaussian noise, defocus blur, etc. [5,9,19,22]. While these studies have unequivocally demonstrated an improvement in model's performance, this has only been demonstrated in *synthetically degraded* test images. It remains (largely) unclear how close such augmentations mimic naturally occurring degradation particular to retinal images, and if they can equally help a model generalise to such natural degradation as they are to synthetic degradation. Indeed, our concern is not unfounded because **even** generalisation across different types of *synthetic degradation* - from Gaussian noise to Gaussian blur [5] or from uniform defocus blur to oriented motion blur [19] - is not guaranteed. Our finding that the model trained on the *augmented* G training set did not have better performance on the poorer U test set than the model trained on the *original* G training set therefore *fills the aforementioned gap* by indicating that augmentation has *limited generalisability to naturally occurring degradation*. Our work also sets the scene for a solution centring on tuning the quality threshold for the training set.

Given that the stochastic nature of model training and evaluation has not been fully accounted for in this study, future studies could repeat each set of our experiments multiple times. This would allow one to better elucidate if there is any additional value in tuning the quality threshold on a *continuous* scale. Future work should also carry out a systematic investigation of the generalisability of other (more nuanced) augmentations such as contrast reduction, localised blur, etc. to naturally occurring degradation to help us confidently rule out the benefit of augmentation over inclusion of poor images. Moreover, other DL-based retinal image quality models could be used in addition to MCF-Net to verify the central thesis of this paper. To the best of our knowledge, we are the first to investigate the effect of tuning quality threshold on a downstream task related to retinal pathology. As we focused on DR, future work could make use of other retinal datasets [10], e.g. PALM, to see if similar conclusions apply to other diseases such as age-related macular degeneration.

References

1. Akkoca Gazioğlu, B.S., Kamaşak, M.E.: Effects of objects and image quality on melanoma classification using deep neural networks. Biomed. Sig. Process. Control **67**, 102530 (2021). https://doi.org/10.1016/j.bspc.2021.102530, https://www.sciencedirect.com/science/article/pii/S1746809421001270
2. Canziani, A., Paszke, A., Culurciello, E.: An analysis of deep neural network models for practical applications. CoRR abs/1605.07678 (2016). http://arxiv.org/abs/1605.07678
3. da Costa, G.B.P., Contato, W.A., Nazare, T.S., Neto, J.E.S.B., Ponti, M.: An empirical study on the effects of different types of noise in image classification tasks, September 2016. http://arxiv.org/abs/1609.02781
4. Dodge, S., Karam, L.: Understanding how image quality affects deep neural networks, April 2016. http://arxiv.org/abs/1604.04004
5. Dodge, S.F., Karam, L.J.: Quality resilient deep neural networks. CoRR abs/1703.08119 (2017). http://arxiv.org/abs/1703.08119
6. Fu, H., Wang, B., Shen, J., Cui, S., Xu, Y., Liu, J., Shao, L.: Evaluation of retinal image quality assessment networks in different color-spaces, July 2019. https://doi.org/10.1007/978-3-030-32239-7_6, http://arxiv.org/abs/1907.05345
7. Jeelani, H., Martin, J., Vasquez, F., Salerno, M., Weller, D.S.: Image quality affects deep learning reconstruction of MRI. In: 2018 IEEE 15th International Symposium on Biomedical Imaging (ISBI 2018), pp. 357–360 (2018). https://doi.org/10.1109/ISBI.2018.8363592
8. Jin, Q., Meng, Z., Pham, T.D., Chen, Q., Wei, L., Su, R.: Dunet: a deformable network for retinal vessel segmentation. Knowledge-Based Systems **178**, 149–162 (2019). https://doi.org/10.1016/j.knosys.2019.04.025, http://dx.doi.org/10.1016/j.knosys.2019.04.025
9. Kugelman, J., Alonso-Caneiro, D., Read, S.A., Vincent, S.J., Chen, F.K., Collins, M.J.: Effect of altered oct image quality on deep learning boundary segmentation. IEEE Access **8**, 43537–43553 (2020). https://doi.org/10.1109/ACCESS.2020.2977355
10. Li, T., et al.: Applications of deep learning in fundus images: a review. Med. Image Anal **69**, 101971 (2021). https://doi.org/10.1016/j.media.2021.101971, https://www.sciencedirect.com/science/article/pii/S1361841521000177
11. Lin, G.M., et al.: Transforming retinal photographs to entropy images in deep learning to improve automated detection for diabetic retinopathy. J. Ophthalmol. 2018 (2018). https://doi.org/10.1155/2018/2159702
12. Moccia, S., De Momi, E., El Hadji, S., Mattos, L.S.: Blood vessel segmentation algorithms - review of methods, datasets and evaluation metrics. Comput. Methods Program. Biomed. **158**, 71–91 (2018). https://doi.org/10.1016/j.cmpb.2018.02.001, https://www.sciencedirect.com/science/article/pii/S0169260717313421
13. Ng, W., et al.: Updates in deep learning research in ophthalmology. Clin. Sci. **135**(20), 2357–2376 (2021). https://doi.org/10.1042/CS20210207
14. Poplin, R., et al.: Prediction of cardiovascular risk factors from retinal fundus photographs via deep learning. Nat. Biomed. Eng. **2**, 158–164 (2018). https://doi.org/10.1038/s41551-018-0195-0
15. RichardWebster, B., Anthony, S.E., Scheirer, W.J.: Psyphy: a psychophysics driven evaluation framework for visual recognition. IEEE Trans. Pattern Anal. Mach. Intell. **41**(9), 2280–2286 (2019). https://doi.org/10.1109/TPAMI.2018.2849989

16. Singh, N., Kaur, L.: A survey on blood vessel segmentation methods in retinal images. In: 2015 International Conference on Electronic Design, Computer Networks Automated Verification (EDCAV), pp. 23–28 (2015). https://doi.org/10.1109/EDCAV.2015.7060532
17. Sun, C., Shrivastava, A., Singh, S., Gupta, A.: Revisiting unreasonable effectiveness of data in deep learning era. In: 2017 IEEE International Conference on Computer Vision (ICCV). pp. 843–852 (2017). https://doi.org/10.1109/ICCV.2017.97
18. Varadarajan, A.V., et al.: Deep learning for predicting refractive error from retinal fundus images. Invest. Ophthalmol. Vis. Sci. **59**, 2861–2868 (2018). https://doi.org/10.1167/iovs.18-23887
19. Vasiljevic, I., Chakrabarti, A., Shakhnarovich, G.: Examining the impact of blur on recognition by convolutional networks. CoRR abs/1611.05760 (2016). http://arxiv.org/abs/1611.05760
20. Wilkinson, C.P., et al.: Proposed international clinical diabetic retinopathy and diabetic macular edema disease severity scales. Ophthalmology **110**, 1677–1682 (2003). https://doi.org/10.1016/S0161-6420(03)00475-5
21. Yip, M., et al.: Technical and imaging factors influencing performance of deep learning systems for diabetic retinopathy screening. NPJ Digit. Med. **3** (2020). https://doi.org/10.1038/s41746-020-0247-1
22. Zhou, Y., Song, S., Cheung, N.: On classification of distorted images with deep convolutional neural networks. CoRR abs/1701.01924 (2017). http://arxiv.org/abs/1701.01924

Robust and Efficient Computation of Retinal Fractal Dimension Through Deep Approximation

Justin Engelmann[1(✉)], Ana Villaplana-Velasco[2], Amos Storkey[3], and Miguel O. Bernabeu[2]

[1] CDT Biomedical AI, School of Informatics, University of Edinburgh, Edinburgh, Scotland
justin.engelmann@ed.ac.uk
[2] Centre for Medical Informatics, University of Edinburgh, Edinburgh, Scotland
[3] School of Informatics, University of Edinburgh, Edinburgh, Scotland

Abstract. A retinal trait, or phenotype, summarises a specific aspect of a retinal image in a single number. This can then be used for further analyses, e.g. with statistical methods. However, reducing an aspect of a complex image to a single, meaningful number is challenging. Thus, methods for calculating retinal traits tend to be complex, multi-step pipelines that can only be applied to high quality images. This means that researchers often have to discard substantial portions of the available data. We hypothesise that such pipelines can be approximated with a single, simpler step that can be made robust to common quality issues. We propose Deep Approximation of Retinal Traits (DART) where a deep neural network is used predict the output of an existing pipeline on high quality images from synthetically degraded versions of these images. We demonstrate DART on retinal Fractal Dimension (FD) - a measure of vascular complexity - calculated by VAMPIRE, using retinal images from UK Biobank that previous work identified as high quality. Our method shows very high agreement with $FD^{VAMPIRE}$ on unseen test images (Pearson $r = 0.9572$). Even when those images are severely degraded, DART can still recover an FD estimate that shows good agreement with $FD^{VAMPIRE}$ obtained from the original images (Pearson $r = 0.8817$). This suggests that our method could enable researchers to discard fewer images in the future. Our method can compute FD for over 1,000 img/s using a single GPU. We consider these to be very encouraging initial results and hope to develop this approach into a useful tool for retinal analysis. Code for running DART with the trained model is available on GitHub.

Keywords: Retinal fractal dimension · Deep approximation of retinal traits · Robust retinal image analysis

A. Storkey and M. O. Bernabeu—Equal supervision.

1   Introduction

Retinal fundus images are non-invasive and low-cost. They are important for ophthalmology and also capture a detailed picture of the retinal vasculature. Thus, they can be used for studying and potentially predicting diseases such as diabetes, stroke, hypertension and neurovascular disease [10]. To analyse the relationships between aspects of the retina and other quantities of interest, retinal traits (also called features, parameters or phenotypes) are used as a quantitative description of a specific aspect of the retinal image. Reducing a complex image to a single, meaningful number is necessary to use standard statistical methods yet a challenging task. It is challenging to identify a potentially salient aspect of the retina in the first place and to then design a method that can reliably quantify this aspect. This is further complicated by the large variability in retinal images stemming from idiosyncrasies of the imaged retinas (e.g. due to retinal diseases or rare phenotypes) and image quality (e.g. due to operator inexperience or time pressures in large scale cohort studies). Thus, pipelines for extracting such retinal traits tend to be complex and comprise of multiple steps, and can only be applied to images of sufficient quality.

Poor image quality is a key problem in retinal image analysis. Particularly for large scale studies such as UK Biobank, many images are of poor quality being blurred, obscured, or hazy [9]. Imaging artefacts such as noise, non-uniform illumination or blur can also lead to poor vessel segmentations [12]. Previous work analysing 2,690 UK Biobank participants found that only 60% had an image that could be adequately analysed by VAMPIRE [9]. Two recent large-scale studies using retinal Fractal Dimension (FD) for predicting cardiovascular disease risk discarded 26% [21] and 43% [16] of the images in UK Biobank. Although necessary, this is unfortunate as it leads to lower sample sizes and makes it hard to study rare diseases in particular.

We hypothesise that it is possible to approximate pipelines for calculating retinal traits with a single, simpler step and propose Deep Approximation of Retinal Traits (DART). Figure 1 gives a high-level overview of our approach. DART trains a deep neural network (DNN) to predict the output of an original method (OM) for calculating a retinal trait. We can then train the model to be robust to image quality issues by synthetically degrading the input images during training and asking the DNN model to predict the output of the OM on the original high quality image. The intuition behind this approach is that obtaining a high quality segmentation of the entire retina is a much harder task than describing an aspect of the vasculature like vascular complexity directly. DART offers a segmentation-free way of computing retinal traits related to the vasculature, but can also be applied to any other retinal image analysis method like feature extraction for disease grading or pathology segmentation.

In the present work, we focus on retinal FD, a key retinal trait that has been used to predict cardiovascular disease risk [16,21] and is associated with neurodegeneration and stroke [6]. FD is a mathematical measure of the complexity of a self-similar object. Applied to the retinal vasculature, FD captures how complex and branching it is which in turn might be a proxy for how healthy the

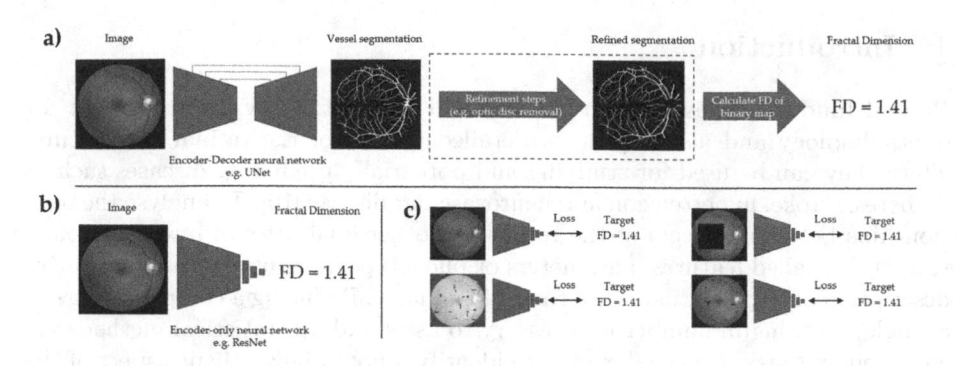

Fig. 1. Overview of our proposed framework. a) A typical pipeline for computing FD: an encoder-decoder neural network for segmentation, potentially some refinement steps like optic disc segmentation and removal, and a method to calculate FD of the segmentation (e.g. box counting or multifractal). b) DART, our proposed approach outputs a deep approximation of FD in a single step using an encoder-only neural network, with drastically reduced complexity. c) We can train our model to be robust to image quality issues by synthetically degrading input images and training our model to minimise the loss between its output and the FD obtained with the original high quality image.

vasculature is. We use FD as calculated by VAMPIRE [15] with the multifractal [14] method as the OM we apply DART to. At minimum, FD^{DART} should have very high agreement with $FD^{VAMPIRE}$ on high quality images so that it can be interpreted in the same way. To be a useful method, it should further be robust to image quality issues and efficient. Robustness would enable researchers to discard fewer images than currently necessary while efficiency allows to conduct analyses at large scale without requiring large compute resources.

2   Deep Approximation of Retinal Traits (DART)

2.1   Motivation and Theory

We hypothesise that it is possible to approximate the entire pipeline of an original method (OM) for calculating a retinal trait in a single, simpler step. We denote the distribution of high quality retinal fundus images as X^{HQ}, where each image x_i has dimensions height H, width W, and channels C. The OM can be interpreted as a function f that maps from the image space to one-dimensional retinal trait space (in our case, FD) $f : \mathbb{R}^{HxWxC} \to \mathbb{R}^1$, i.e. given an image $x_i \in X^{HQ}$ the FD computed by the OM is $FD^{OM} = f(x_i)$. Our goal is to find an alternative function $g : \mathbb{R}^{HxWxC} \to \mathbb{R}^1$ that is both simpler than f and has high agreement with f for all images of sufficient quality that the OM can be used, i.e. for all $x_i \in X^{HQ}$ $f(x_i) \approx g(x_i)$.

Designing such a simpler function by hand would be very challenging. Thus, we use a deep neural network (DNN). DNNs are universal function approximators in theory and very effective for image analysis in practice. We can then find a good approximation of f by simply updating the model parameters θ (weights, biases, normalisation layer parameters) to minimise some differentiable measure of divergence between $f(x_i)$ and $g(x_i)$, e.g. mean squared error.

Accuracy. The output of the OM is fully determined by the given image, so we would expect that very high accuracy can be achieved. This contrasts with other problems, e.g. clincians take into account additional information like symptoms and family history, and might disagree with each other or even themselves if shown the same image multiple times.

Simplicity and Efficiency. Some readers might not perceive DNNs as simple or efficient. However, modern pipelines for retinal image analysis tend to use DNNs for vessel segmentation, so not requiring additional steps implies strictly lower complexity both computationally and in terms of required code. Furthermore, segmentation models tend to have an encoder-decoder structure (e.g. UNet) whereas models for classification/regression only need an encoder and small prediction head, making them more parameter-, memory-, and compute-efficient. Finally, given the widespread adoption of deep learning, the frameworks are very mature and can be very efficiently GPU-accelerated.

Robustness. We hypothesise that there images of lower quality that are such that a) current pipelines would not produce a useful FD number, but b) there is still sufficient information to give an accurate estimate of the FD number we would have obtained on a counterfactual high quality image. For example, in an image with an obstruction, only part of the retina might be visible. Thus, the resulting vessel segmentation map would be poor and the FD of this map would be very different from that of the counterfactual high quality image, yet the visible parts of the retina might contain sufficient information about the vascular complexity of the retina as a whole to recover an accurate estimate of the FD.

As we do not observe counterfactual high quality images or objective ground truth FD values, we artificially degrade high quality images with a degradation function $\text{degrade}(x_i) = x_i^{\text{degarded}}$ and train our model to minimise the difference between the predicted FD for the degraded image and the OM's FD for the high quality image $g_\theta(x_i^{\text{degarded}}) \approx f(x_i)$. If there indeed is sufficient information in the degraded images, then our model should be able to predict the OM's FD from the high quality image reasonably well. However, this is a much harder task than matching the OM on high quality images, as the degradations lose information and for a given degraded image there are multiple possible counterfactual high quality images.

2.2 Implementation

Model and Training. Our model consists of a pretrained ResNet18 [4] backbone that extracts a feature map from the images, followed by spatial average

Table 1. Severity levels for the degradations. Brightness, contrast and gamma changes are independently sampled from the given interval. Dimensions in pixels.

Severity	1	2	3	4	5
Brightness/Contrast/ Gamma	±5%	±10%	±15%	±20%	±25%
Mini Artifacts (holes, height, width)	2–20/1–3/5–8	2–24/1–5/5–12	2–28/1–5/5–16	2–32/1–3/5–20	2–40/1–3/5–24
Square Artifacts (side length)	25	50	75	100	125
Chop Artifacts (% of image removed)	10–15	10–25	10–35	10–45	10–50
Advanced Blur (kernel size, sigma)	3–5/0.2–0.5	3–7/0.2–0.7	3–9/0.2–0.8	3–11/0.2–0.9	3–13/0.2–1.0
Gaussian Noise (variance)	1–10	5–10	5–20	5–25	5–30

pool and a small multi-layer perceptron with a two hidden layers with 128 and 32 units, and a single output. Each hidden layer is followed by a layernorm [1] and GELU [5] activation. No activation is applied to the final output. ResNet is a well-established architecture that has been shown to perform competitively with more recent architectures when using modern training techniques [2,19]. We use Resnet18 as it is the most light-weight member of the Resnet family. We initialise the backbones with pre-trained weights on natural images from Instagram [20]. Those images are very different from retinal images, thus this is merely a minor refinement on random initialisation. We resize images to 224×224 pixels for computational efficiency and lower memory requirements. Apart from standard normalisation using channel-wise ImageNet mean and standard deviations, no further preprocessing is done and all 3 colour channels are kept.

We train our model using a batchsize of 256 to minimise the mean squared error between prediction and target after normalizing the target to zero mean and unit variance, using mean and standard deviation from the training data to avoid data leakage. The model output can then be mapped back to FD range by applying the inverse transformation. We use the AdamW optimiser [8] ($\beta_1 = 0.9, \beta_2 = 0.999$, weight decay of 10^{-6}) and a cosine learning rate schedule [7]. We train for 35 epochs with a linear learning rate warmup from $\eta_{min} = 10^{-5}$ to $\eta_{max} = 10^{-3}$ for 5 epochs, followed by 3 cycles of 10 epochs each. During each cycle, the current epoch learning rate is set according to a cosine schedule, and after each cycle η_{max} is decayed by taking the square root. We apply generic data augmentations (horizontal ($p = 0.5$) and vertical flip ($p = 0.1$), mild affine transformations ($p = 0.15$, rotation by up to $\pm 10°$, shear of up to $\pm 5°$, and scaling by $\pm 5\%$)) as well as the image degradations described in the next section with $p = 0.75$ (sampling all 5 levels uniformly) to the images during training. We used Python 3.9 with PyTorch and timm [18]. Our code for running DART, including the trained model, is available here: https://github. com/justinengelmann/DART_retinal_fractal_dimension.

Synthetic Degradations. We focus on three types of quality issues in retinal images [9,12]: Lighting issues, artifacts/obstructions, and imaging issues. To simulate general lighting issues, we independently change brightness, contrast and gamma of the image. To simulate artifacts/obstructions and severely inconsistent lighting, we introduce one of three artifacts: 1) many smaller rectangular holes placed across the retina, b) a single large square hole, or c) we "chop" off the bottom or top part of the image. The latter is inspired by the observation that in UK Biobank some images only have the top or bottom part properly illuminated. To simulate general imaging issues, we add pixel-wise Gaussian noise and blur the image. Standard isotropic Gaussian blur kernels do not mimic realistic image blur, so we use an advanced anisotropic blurring technique developed for image super-resolution [17] where the standard deviations for both dimensions of the kernel are sampled independently, and the kernel is then rotated and has some noise added before being applied to the image. These synthetic degradations are inspired by common retinal imaging quality issues but do not perfectly mirror them. Our goal here is to test the feasibility of using DART to recover good FD estimates from severely degraded images. Thus, our degradations heavily feature artifcats and blur, both of which remove information from the images. If DART can recover good FD estimates under these challenging conditions, then this would be reason to think that it will also work under more realistic, yet less challenging conditions.

We specify degradation parameters for five levels of severity, shown in Table 1. For a given level, we sample parameters for each image independently from the given ranges. Degradations are applied after images have already been downsized to 224×224. We apply an artifact with $p = 0.2 * s$ where s is the severity. If an image was chosen to have an artifact applied to it, we then choose Mini Artifacts with $p = 0.85$, Square Artifact with $p = 0.10$, and Chop Artifact with $p = 0.05$. Degradations are implemented using the albumentations package [3].

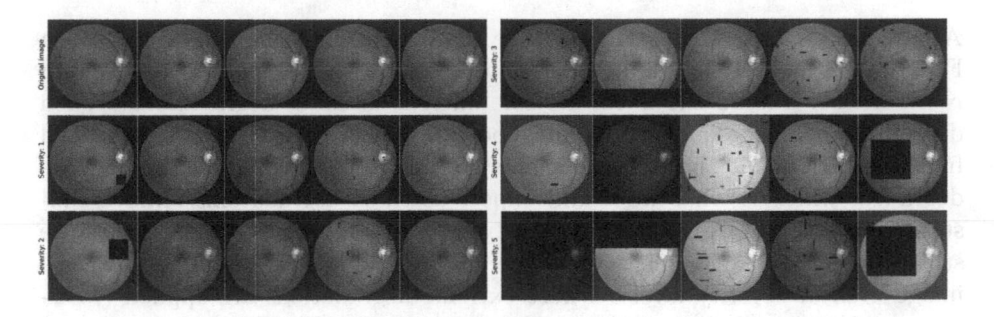

Fig. 2. Random examples of synthetically degraded versions of the same fundus image. Best viewed zoomed in, especially for the advanced blur. UK Biobank asks to only reproduce imaging data where necessary, so we demonstrate the degradations on an image taken from DRIVE [13] which is similar in appearance to those in UK Biobank.

Table 2. Agreement between $FD^{VAMPIRE}$ obtained on high quality images, and FD^{DART} for different levels of degradation measured on 14,907 held-out test set images.

Degradations	R^2	Pearson r (p-value)	Spearman r (p-value)	OLS Regression fit
None	0.9160	0.9572 (0.0000)	0.9561 (0.0000)	$y = 0.01 + 1.00x$
Severity 1	0.8957	0.9467 (0.0000)	0.9446 (0.0000)	$y = 0.01 + 0.99x$
Severity 2	0.8859	0.9414 (0.0000)	0.9396 (0.0000)	$y = 0.01 + 0.99x$
Severity 3	0.8623	0.9287 (0.0000)	0.9282 (0.0000)	$y = 0.00 + 1.00x$
Severity 4	0.8309	0.9116 (0.0000)	0.9103 (0.0000)	$y = 0.01 + 0.99x$
Severity 5	0.7773	0.8817 (0.0000)	0.8840 (0.0000)	$y = 0.02 + 0.99x$

3 Experiments

3.1 Data

We apply our DART framework multi-fractal FD [14] calculated with VAM-PIRE [15]. We use only images from UK Biobank that had been identified as high quality (top 60% of in terms of quality) in a previous study that used FD for cardiovascular disease risk prediction [16]. Thus, for those images $FD^{VAMPIRE}$ should be reliable and can be considered as a reasonable "ground-truth". We randomly split the data into train, validation, and test sets containing 70, 10, and 20% of the participants in UK Biobank, resulting in 52,242/7,478/14,907 images belonging to 32,300/4,614/9,229 participants in each set. We split at the participant level such that no images of the same participant occur in different sets. Images are cropped to square to remove black non-retinal regions and processed at 224×224 as described above.

3.2 Results

Agreement and Robustness. We find very high agreement between $FD^{VAMPIRE}$ and FD^{DART} on the original images with Pearson $r = 0.9572$ and $r^2 = 0.9160$. Table 2 shows results for different levels of degradations. When degrading the images and asking our model to predict the $FD^{VAMPIRE}$ obtained from the high quality image, agreements goes down as the images become more degraded, which is what we would expect as these degradations remove substantial information about the retinal vasculature. However, despite this, we still observe good agreement with the $FD^{VAMPIRE}$ obtained on the original image even at severity level 5 where extreme degradations are applied (Pearson $r = 0.8817$ and $R^2 = 0.7773$). This suggests that DART can recover good estimates of the retinal trait that would have been obtained from a counterfactual high quality image even if the available image has very poor quality. Thus, this might allow for discarding much fewer images than currently necessary.

For comparison, a previous study comparing FD for arteries and veins separately between VAMPIRE and SIVA [11] found very poor agreement between the measures of the two tools ($R^2 = 0.139$ and $R^2 = 0.168$ for arteries and

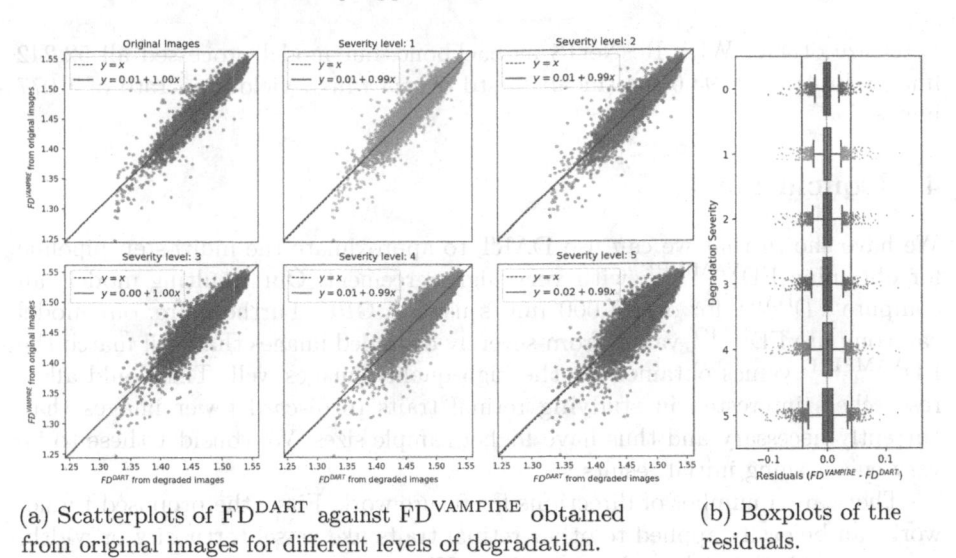

(a) Scatterplots of FD^{DART} against FD^{VAMPIRE} obtained from original images for different levels of degradation.

(b) Boxplots of the residuals.

Fig. 3. Agreement results for 14,907 held-out test set images. Best viewed zoomed in. **a)** Red line: best linear fit; dashed black line: $y = x$. **b)** Faint red line: $x = 0$; vertical black lines: $\pm$ one interquartile range (IQR) of FD^{VAMPIRE} for reference. (Color figure online)

veins, respectively). Another study comparing vessel caliber-related retinal traits obtained with VAMPIRE, SIVA, and IVAN found that they agreed with Pearson rs of 0.29 to 0.86. Thus, the observed agreement between FD^{VAMPIRE} and FD^{DART} with a Pearson $r = 0.9572$ and $R^2 = 0.9160$ is very high, and even when DART is applied the most degraded images the agreement (Pearson $r = 0.8817$ and $R^2 = 0.7773$) is higher than what could be expected when using two different tools on the same high quality images.

Finally, our method shows very low bias even as degradation severity is increased (Fig. 3). The best OLS fit is very close to the identity line for all levels of severity, or equivalently, the optimal linear translation function from FD^{DART} to FD^{VAMPIRE} is almost simply the identity function. This also implies that no post-hoc adjustment for image quality is needed and FD^{DART} values obtained for images of varying quality are on the same scale out-of-the-box. As degradation severity increases, the variance of the residuals also increases but most residuals are still less than one interquartile range (IQR), a robust equivalent of the standard deviation, even when applying the strongest degradation.

Speed. Images were loaded into RAM so that hard disk speed is not a factor. We then measured the time it took to process all 52,242 training images, including normalisation, moving them from RAM to GPU VRAM, as well as the time to move the results back to RAM. We used a modern workstation (Intel i9-9920X 24 core CPU, single Nvidia RTX A6000 24GB GPU, 126GB of RAM) and a batchsize of 440. With ResNet18 as backbone, our model processed all 52,242 images in 48.5s $\pm$ 93.6 ms (mean $\pm$ std over 5 runs), yielding a rate of 1,077 img/s.

4   Conclusion

We have shown that we can use DART to approximate the multi-step pipeline for obtaining $FD^{VAMPIRE}$ with very high agreement. Our resulting model can compute FD^{DART} for over 1,000 img/s using a GPU. Furthermore, our model can compute FD^{DART} values from severely degraded images that still match the $FD^{VAMPIRE}$ values obtained on the high quality images well. This could allow researchers interested in studying retinal traits to discard fewer images than currently necessary and thus have higher sample sizes. We consider these to be very encouraging initial results.

There are a number of directions for future work. First, the proposed framework can be easily applied to other retinal traits like vessel tortuosity or width, or FD as calculated by other pipelines. We would expect that this would be similarly successful. Second, the robustness of the resulting DART model should be evaluated in more depth and the cases with extreme residuals should be manually examined. We expect that robustness can be further improved, especially if we identify common failure cases and use those as data augmentations. Third, many straight-forward, incremental technical improvements should be possible such as improved training procedures to further increase performance, trying different architectures and resolutions, and speeding up inference speed further through common tricks like fusing batch norm layers into the convolutional layers. Finally, we hope that our approach will eventually enable other researchers to conduct better analyses, e.g. by not having to discard as many images and thus having a larger sample size available.

Acknowledgements. We thank our friends and colleagues for their help and support. This research has been conducted using the UK Biobank Resource (project number 72144). This work was supported by the United Kingdom Research and Innovation (grant EP/S02431X/1), UKRI Centre for Doctoral Training in Biomedical AI at the University of Edinburgh, School of Informatics. For the purpose of open access, the author has applied a creative commons attribution (CC BY) licence to any author accepted manuscript version arising. Support from Diabetes UK (grant 20/0006221) and Fight for Sight (grant 5137/5138) is gratefully acknowledged.

References

1. Ba, J.L., Kiros, J.R., Hinton, G.E.: Layer normalization. arXiv preprint arXiv:1607.06450 (2016)
2. Bello, I., et al.: Revisiting ResNets: improved training and scaling strategies. arXiv preprint arXiv:2103.07579 (2021)
3. Buslaev, A., Iglovikov, V.I., Khvedchenya, E., Parinov, A., Druzhinin, M., Kalinin, A.A.: Albumentations: fast and flexible image augmentations. Information **11**(2), 125 (2020). https://doi.org/10.3390/info11020125

4. He, K., Zhang, X., Ren, S., Sun, J.: Deep residual learning for image recognition. In: Proceedings of the IEEE Conference on Computer Vision and Pattern Recognition, pp. 770–778 (2016)
5. Hendrycks, D., Gimpel, K.: Gaussian error linear units (GELUs). arXiv preprint arXiv:1606.08415 (2016)
6. Lemmens, S., Devulder, A., Van Keer, K., Bierkens, J., De Boever, P., Stalmans, I.: Systematic review on fractal dimension of the retinal vasculature in neurodegeneration and stroke: assessment of a potential biomarker. Front. Neurosci. **14**, 16 (2020)
7. Loshchilov, I., Hutter, F.: SGDR: stochastic gradient descent with warm restarts. arXiv preprint arXiv:1608.03983 (2016)
8. Loshchilov, I., Hutter, F.: Decoupled weight decay regularization. arXiv preprint arXiv:1711.05101 (2017)
9. MacGillivray, T.J., et al.: Suitability of UK Biobank retinal images for automatic analysis of morphometric properties of the vasculature. PLoS ONE **10**(5), e0127914 (2015)
10. MacGillivray, T., Trucco, E., Cameron, J., Dhillon, B., Houston, J., Van Beek, E.: Retinal imaging as a source of biomarkers for diagnosis, characterization and prognosis of chronic illness or long-term conditions. Br. J. Radiol. **87**(1040), 20130832 (2014)
11. McGrory, S., et al.: Towards standardization of quantitative retinal vascular parameters: comparison of SIVA and VAMPIRE measurements in the Lothian Birth Cohort 1936. Transl. Vis. Sci. Technol. **7**(2), 12 (2018)
12. Mookiah, M.R.K., et al.: A review of machine learning methods for retinal blood vessel segmentation and artery/vein classification. Med. Image Anal. **68**, 101905 (2021)
13. Staal, J., Abràmoff, M.D., Niemeijer, M., Viergever, M.A., Van Ginneken, B.: Ridge-based vessel segmentation in color images of the retina. IEEE Trans. Med. Imaging **23**(4), 501–509 (2004)
14. Stosic, T., Stosic, B.D.: Multifractal analysis of human retinal vessels. IEEE Trans. Med. Imaging **25**(8), 1101–1107 (2006)
15. Trucco, E., et al.: Novel VAMPIRE algorithms for quantitative analysis of the retinal vasculature. In: 2013 ISSNIP Biosignals and Biorobotics Conference: Biosignals and Robotics for Better and Safer Living (BRC), pp. 1–4. IEEE (2013)
16. Velasco, A.V., et al.: Decreased retinal vascular complexity is an early biomarker of MI supported by a shared genetic control. medRxiv (2021)
17. Wang, X., Xie, L., Dong, C., Shan, Y.: Real-ESRGAN: training real-world blind super-resolution with pure synthetic data. In: Proceedings of the IEEE/CVF International Conference on Computer Vision, pp. 1905–1914 (2021)
18. Wightman, R.: PyTorch image models (2019). https://doi.org/10.5281/zenodo.4414861
19. Wightman, R., Touvron, H., Jégou, H.: ResNet strikes back: an improved training procedure in timm. arXiv preprint arXiv:2110.00476 (2021)
20. Yalniz, I.Z., Jégou, H., Chen, K., Paluri, M., Mahajan, D.: Billion-scale semi-supervised learning for image classification. arXiv preprint arXiv:1905.00546 (2019)
21. Zekavat, S.M., et al.: Deep learning of the retina enables phenome-and genome-wide analyses of the microvasculature. Circulation **145**(2), 134–150 (2022)

Localizing Anatomical Landmarks in Ocular Images Using Zoom-In Attentive Networks

Xiaofeng Lei[1], Shaohua Li[1(✉)], Xinxing Xu[1(✉)], Huazhu Fu[1], Yong Liu[1],
Yih-Chung Tham[2,3], Yangqin Feng[1], Mingrui Tan[1], Yanyu Xu[1],
Jocelyn Hui Lin Goh[2], Rick Siow Mong Goh[1], and Ching-Yu Cheng[2,3]

[1] Institute of High Performance Computing, A*STAR,
Singapore, Singapore
{lei_xiaofeng,li_shaohua,xuxinx}@ihpc.a-star.edu.sg
[2] Singapore Eye Research Institute, Singapore National Eye Centre,
Singapore, Singapore
[3] Department of Ophthalmology, Yong Loo Lin School of Medicine, NUS,
Singapore, Singapore

Abstract. Localizing anatomical landmarks are important tasks in medical image analysis. However, the landmarks to be localized often lack prominent visual features. Their locations are elusive and easily confused with the background, and thus precise localization highly depends on the context formed by their surrounding areas. In addition, the required precision is usually higher than segmentation and object detection tasks. Therefore, localization has its unique challenges different from segmentation or detection. In this paper, we propose a zoom-in attentive network (ZIAN) for anatomical landmark localization in ocular images. First, a coarse-to-fine, or "zoom-in" strategy is utilized to learn the contextualized features in different scales. Then, an attentive fusion module is adopted to aggregate multi-scale features, which consists of 1) a co-attention network with a multiple regions-of-interest (ROIs) scheme that learns complementary features from the multiple ROIs, 2) an attention-based fusion module which integrates the multi-ROIs features and non-ROI features. We evaluated ZIAN on two open challenge tasks, i.e., the fovea localization in fundus images and scleral spur localization in AS-OCT images. Experiments show that ZIAN achieves promising performances and outperforms state-of-the-art localization methods. The source code and trained models of ZIAN are available at https://github.com/leixiaofeng-astar/OMIA9-ZIAN.

Keywords: Fovea localization · Scleral spur localization · Self-attention

1 Introduction

Localization of anatomical landmarks in medical images is one common task of medical image analysis. Precise localization plays an important role for some

B. Antony et al. (Eds.): OMIA 2022, LNCS 13576, pp. 94–104, 2022.
https://doi.org/10.1007/978-3-031-16525-2_10

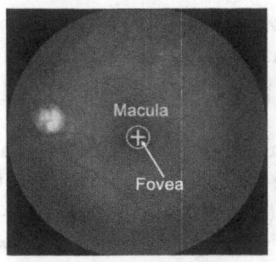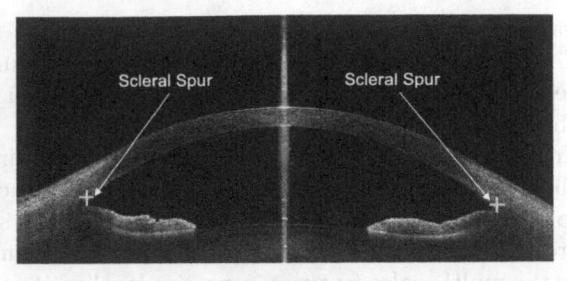

Fig. 1. Two typical localization tasks in ocular images. Left: fovea location in fundus image. Right: scleral spur location in AS-OCT image.

medical diagnosis. For example, the fovea is an important anatomical landmark on the posterior pole of the retina which is located in the center of a darker area of the eye [1]. Fovea location is important in diagnosing eye diseases such as glaucoma, diabetic retinopathy and macular edema. Similarly, the Scleral Spur (SS) location is an important anatomical landmark in imaging the anterior chamber angle, as it is a reference point to identify open and narrow/closed angles based on Optical Coherence Tomography (OCT) images (Fig. 1).

Manually labeling these landmarks by medical experts is expensive and tedious. Developing automated approaches for landmark localization is desirable and has been studied for decades. The conventional computer vision methods mainly utilize template matching or mathematical morphology techniques to localize the anatomical landmark [2–5]. However, these methods are sensitive to the low contrast of the image and the results vary if the images come from a different source. With more robust performance, machine learning based approaches are predominantly used for automatic localization of anatomical landmarks [6–8].

In general, there are three types of machine learning approaches for localization [9]. 1) Localization is viewed as a value regression problem [10,11], and the coordinates of the target location are directly predicted; 2) Localization is viewed as a binary segmentation problem that extends the single pixel label to a small region where the segmented mask center is used as the target position [12]; 3) Localization is viewed as heat-map regression task. First we generate a heatmap around the target position, and then employ regression, morphological or mathematical methods to estimate the target point [13–17]. Recently, the third heatmap-regression approach has outperformed the other 2 methods, and our method is also based on it.

Despite the huge progress in recent years, there are still challenges limiting the precision of these methods. A common challenge is that input images may have highly varying scales. A second challenge is that anatomical landmarks often lack prominent visual features, and the localization highly depends on the context formed by their surrounding areas.

In this paper, we propose "Zoom-In Attentive Network" (ZIAN) to address the two challenges above, with ocular images as a case study. First, to be adaptive to various scales of input images, ZIAN adopts a zoom-in and a multi-scale ROI schemes; Second, to better incorporate surrounding areas as context for more precise localization, ZIAN adopts co-attention [18] and self-attention [19] mechanisms.

In particular, different from the common "zoom-in" strategy in [16,20] which predicts the final value more accurately based on the first approximation of the region in coarse stage, ZIAN utilizes a "zoom-in" strategy, and a Regions-of-Interest (ROI) co-attention along with a self-attention mechanism that effectively fuses the multi-scales features in precise localization. Specifically, in the zoom-in step, our model performs preliminary positioning of the target through a coarse network. As a result, multiple ROIs in different scales are cropped according to the preliminary position, which are used as the input to the fine network. In the attention step, a ROI co-attention [21,22] module and a self-attention [23–26] module work together to fuse the multi-ROI features. The ROI co-attention module fuses and complements the features of multi-ROIs. In addition, the self-attention module fuses the multi-ROI features with the output features from the coarse network for more accurate localization. The main contributions of this paper are summarized as follows:

1. Different from most existing localization frameworks, we present a "Zoom-In Attentive Network" (ZIAN) that uses a coarse-to-fine zoom-in strategy, and a ROI co-attention/self-attention scheme in landmark localization.
2. A novel attentive fusion module is proposed to adaptively fuse features from different ROIs, and then fuse the multi-scale ROI features with the coarse features, so that the model learns to combine features of multiple scales and multiple ROIs for better prediction.
3. We evaluated ZIAN on two common ocular image tasks, i.e., fovea localization in fundus images, and Scleral Spur (SS) localization in Anterior Segment Optical Coherence Tomography (AS-OCT) images. The effectiveness of the method is validated by comparing it with various state-of-the-art methods.

2   Method

In this section, we provide details for our proposed Zoom-In Attentive Networks (ZIAN), which consists of two main components: the *Zoom-in Module* and the *Attentive Fusion Module* which includes the details of ROI co-attention and self-attention fusion module.

2.1   Zoom-In Module

As shown in Fig. 2, ZIAN has a coarse network and a fine network. The input image I_{input} is down-sampled by 4× and fed into a pre-trained base network HRNet [27] to get per-pixel heat-maps in the coarse network. The peak pixel is then located as the preliminary positioning of the target. Then, multiple scale ROIs centered at the preliminary location are cropped as the input of the fine

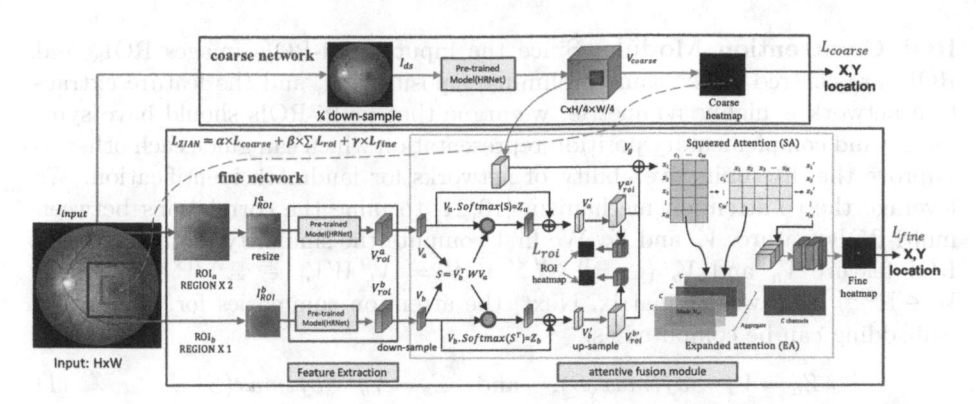

Fig. 2. The architecture of the proposed ZIAN, which comprises two main components: the *Zoom-in Module* and the *Attentive Fusion Module*. The input image is downsampled and fed into the coarse network to get the per-pixel coarse heat-map. The Multi-ROIs centered at the peak pixel on the coarse heat-map are cropped from the original input image, and fed into the fine network to generate features. Next, the multi-ROI features are refined by a co-attention module. Finally, the multi-ROI features are concatenated with the coarse-level features and transformed by self-attention module, and yield the fine heat-map.

network. The resized ROI images I^a_{roi} and I^b_{roi} are fed in parallel into the pre-trained model to build their feature representations individually. Next, multi-ROIs features V^a_{roi} and V^a_{roi} are processed through an attentive fusion module to get a fine-scale heat-map. The peak pixel in the fine-scale heat-map is located as the final coordinate of the target. We utilize HRNet [27] as the pre-trained backbone in the figure. It can be replaced with any state-of-the-art backbone (U-Net [28], EfficientNet [29], YOLO [30], RCNN [31], etc.).

2.2 Attentive Fusion Module

As shown at the bottom part in Fig. 2, the fine network takes a pair of ROI images I^a_{roi} and I^b_{roi}, and sequentially performs feature extraction and attentive fusion module which includes ROI co-attention and self-attention fusion. Two images ROI$_a$ and ROI$_b$ with different scales ($\times 1$ and $\times 2$, i.e. 256×256 and 512×512) are cropped on the input image I_{input} and centered at the predicted peak pixel in coarse heat-map. The multi-ROIs features V^a_{roi} and V^a_{roi} extracted from pre-trained model are down-sampled and refined by the ROI co-attention module. Next, the refined multi-ROIs features V'_a and V'_b are up-sampled and concatenated with coarse-level features V_g which we implement with "crop and resize" and "grid sample", then processed through a self-attention fusion module to get a fine-scale heat-map. Our two-level attention mechanism in fine network guarantees the full integration of the features from different receptive fields, it maintains the independence and integrity of the individual CNN network for single ROI, which enables any CNN backbone to be implemented inside simultaneously.

ROI Co-attention Module: Since the input multi-ROIs images ROI_a and ROI_b are centred in the same preliminary positioning, and the feature extraction network is highly symmetric, we argue that multi-ROIs should have symmetric and complementary position representation which can guide each other to improve the discriminative ability of networks for landmark identification. We leverage the co-attention mechanism [18,21] to mine the correlations between multi-ROIs features V_a and V_b. We first compute the similarity matrix between ROI feature V_a and V_b ($\in \mathbb{R}^{W \times H \times C}$): $S = V_b^T W V_a \in \mathbb{R}^{WH \times WH}$, where $W \in \mathbb{R}^{C \times C}$ is a weight matrix. Next, the attention summaries for the feature embedding can be computed as:

$$Z_a = V_a \cdot Softmax(S), \quad \text{and} \quad Z_b = V_b \cdot Softmax(S^T). \tag{1}$$

We concatenate the co-attention representation Z and the original ROI feature V_a and V_b: $X_a = [Z_a, V_a], X_b = [Z_b, V_b]$ ($X_a, X_b \in \mathbb{R}^{W \times H \times 2C}$). Finally, X_a and X_b pass through a 3×3 convolution and batch norm followed by ReLU activation to get V_a' and V_b' ($\in \mathbb{R}^{W \times H \times C}$) which keep the same 3D-tensor as V_a and V_b. We apply downsampling and upsampling ($\times \frac{1}{4}$, ×4) before and after the ROI co-attention module to reduce memory footprint. Co-attention ROI feature $V_{roi}^{a'}$ and $V_{roi}^{b'}$ pass through a 1×1 convolution to output a landmark heat-map.

Self-Attention Fusion Module: The co-attention ROI feature $V_{roi}^{a'}$ and $V_{roi}^{b'}$ concatenated with "crop and resize" coarse-level features V_g, are fed to a self-attention fusion module. Self-attention module uses Squeezed Attention Block (SAB) and Expanded Attention Block (EAB) from Segmentation Transformers network [19] so that our model can see the big picture in the features from the coarse network and fine details in the features from the fine network at the same time. SAB and EAB replace full self-attention and multi-head attention (MHA) in typical transformer to reduce noises and over-fitting in image tasks. SAB and EAB join forces to offer more capacity to model diverse data from coarse and fine networks.

The features X_{out} after the Self-Attention Fusion module are followed by two 3×3 convolution and one convolution for the final heat-map. The peak value in the heat-map is located as the landmark position. Given the coordinates (u_0, v_0) of landmark (Fovea or SS) point, the heat-map $G(u, v)$ as ground truth can be calculated as $G(u, v) = \exp\left(-\frac{(u-u_0)^2 + (v-v_0)^2}{2 \times \delta^2}\right)$, where δ is variance to control the heat-map radius, we use $\delta=2$ here.

The model is trained by minimizing the Mean Squared-Error (MSE) distance of the learned heat-map to a ground truth heat-map. Our ZIAN retains all loss functions of L_{coarse} in the coarse network, L_{roi} and L_{fine} in the fine network to improve their accuracy and combines them as

$$L_{ZIAN} = \alpha \times L_{coarse} + \beta \times \sum L_{roi}, + \gamma \times L_{fine}, \tag{2}$$

where L_{coarse}, L_{roi} and L_{fine} are the MSE loss coming from coarse heat-map, ROI heat-map and fine heat-map in Fig. 2 (ROI and fine ground truth heat-map are the same which are centered at the input ROI images). α, β and γ is the weight which is greater than or equal to 0 float, $\alpha=1$, $\beta=0.25$ and $\gamma=1$ here.

3 Experiments and Results

3.1 Datasets and Settings

To validate the effectiveness of our model, we use the REFUGE dataset [32] and AGE dataset [9]. The model is evaluated on two metrics: 1) Average Euclidean Distance (AVG L2) between the estimations and ground truth (unit is pixels, the lower the better) which is also the only evaluation criteria in two public challenges (REFUGE and AGE); 2) Successful detection rates (SDR, the higher the better)) with different thresholds (5 pixels, 10 pixels and 20 pixels).

REFUGE dataset[1] consists of 1200 retinal fundus images (1634 × 1634) for fovea localization (400 train, 400 val, 400 test). We split 800 images (80%:20%) into training and evaluation. AGE dataset[2] consists of 4800 AS-OCT images for Scleral Spur (SS) localization (1600 train, 1600 val, 1600 test). We use those 1600 train images (2130 × 998) with publicly available ground truth (GT) in training and evaluation (80%:20%), 1600 val images out of other 3200 images(no GT released) for test. The images are resized to 1064 × 1064, and center cropped to 1024×1024, then random cropped to a resolution of 896×896, next downsampled to 1/4 of cropped image size, i.e. 224 × 224 before being fed to pre-trained model in coarse network. In SS localization, we split each AS-OCT image into the left and right parts according to the centerline and locate the SS localization individually.

In SS localization task, GT of test dataset is not made public, all the results are obtained from online AGE Challenge Leaderboard for AVG L2 Distance.

3.2 Experimental Setup

ZIAN is implemented using PyTorch. All networks are trained using the Adam optimizer. We trained 140 epochs on the model with a learning rate of 0.0002, and weight decay of 0.1 after 90 epochs. For data augmentation, we apply random horizontal flipping, drifting, scaling and rotation. The initial weights of the base networks are loaded from pre-trained models based on ImageNet, and the parameters of the other modules are randomly initialized. We evaluate our ZIAN utilizing 2 state-of-the-art base networks: HRNet [27] and U-Net [28]. For each base network, we perform ablation studies to quantify the roles of different components namely base network, coarse-to-fine network with/without multi-ROIs scheme, self-attention or co-attention multi-ROIs scheme.

3.3 Results and Discussion

In this part, we report the results of fovea and SS localization in the REFUGE and AGE test dataset using AVG L2 and SDR. The performances of different methods are reported in Table 1 and 2 with some results in the REFUGE and AGE challenge leaderboard. Some output examples from the coarse and fine network are as Fig. 3.

---

[1] https://refuge.grand-challenge.org.

[2] https://age.grand-challenge.org.

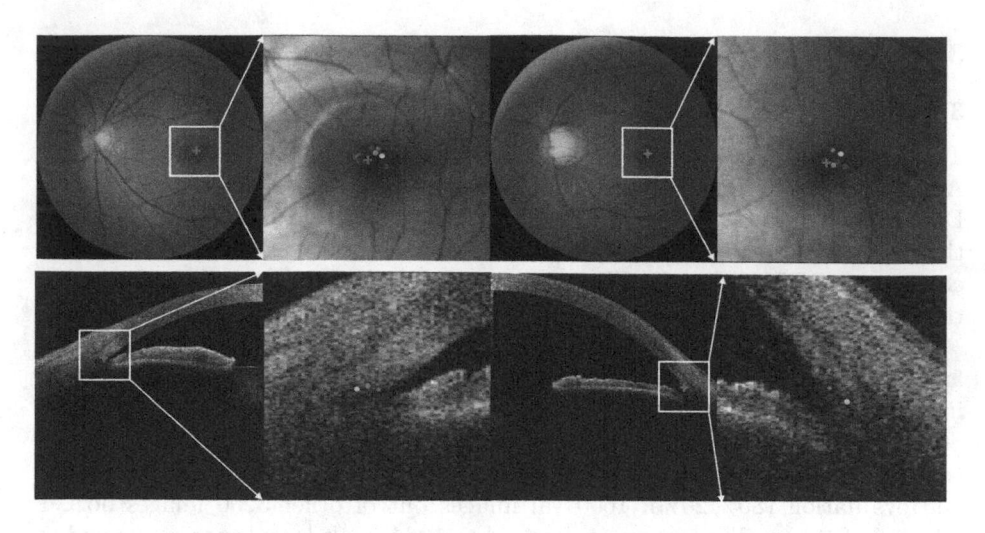

Fig. 3. The input and landmark locations in ZIAN coarse and fine network, Zoom-in localization results of ground truth and different methods. The red cross points + are the ground truth labels, while the circle points are the learned landmarks, •, •, •, • and • are for "HRNet", "HRNet+1ROI", "HRNet+1ROI+SA", "HRNet+MR+SA" and "ZIAN with HRNet" respectively. (Color figure online)

In the tables, HRNet, U-Net, EffcientUNet and GU2Net refer to the method and the CNN backbone we utilize. "1ROI" or "MR" means that we adopt a Coarse-to-Fine strategy with 1 ROI or multi-ROIs in fine network, "SA" means only the self-attention part is employed in the attentive fusion module. "ZIAN with HRNet/U-Net" is our proposed architecture using a coarse-to-fine strategy, a ROI co-attention along with a self-attention fusion mechanism. "SDSA and VRT team" and "Dream Sun and MIPAV team" are the top 2 in the REFUGE final rankings and AGE semifinal rankings, respectively, their results are presented for fair comparison. The corresponding methods of these teams are described in the REFUGE and AGE overview papers [9,32] and website.

From the results, we could have several observations:

Role of Coarse-to-Fine Strategy (C2F): We concur that the C2F strategy has been commonly used in localization and segmentation tasks to narrow down the ROI areas [9,26]. However, as indicated by our experiments, the C2F design is just a minor contributor for improvements compared with the other components (which are our main contribution) as described below.

Role of Multi-ROIs (MR): The localization accuracy is sensitive to the choices of the cropped ROI sizes which confine the context. MR avoids manually tuning the choice of ROI sizes which is more robust with better coverage and applicable to a wide range of tasks, relieving people from ad-hoc tuning. With a MR scheme, the model can choose from multiple contexts and learn to construct more predictive features. Multi-ROIs can achieve superior performance as compared to that of 1 ROI as demonstrated in Tables 1 and 2.

Table 1. Performances of different methods on REFUGE dataset. The best results are in **bold** and the second best results are underlined, - represents that no experimental results can be found in REFUGE challenge.

Method	AVG L2	SDR 5px(%)	SDR 10px(%)	SDR 20px(%)
REFUGE SDSA team[+]	*34.7*	–	–	–
REFUGE VRT team[+]	*37.1*	–	–	–
U-Net [28]	18.99	23.5	52.25	69.50
HRNet [27]	14.45	30.0	70.50	88.75
EffcientUNet-B0 [29][*]	18.62	24.5	59.00	72.50
EffcientUNet-B5 [29][*]	26.29	15.5	40.75	55.75
GU2Net [17]	24.91	24.0	47.5	60.75
U-Net+1ROI	16.56	29.75	61.0	78.75
U-Net+1ROI+SA	15.05	30.25	62.5	78.0
U-Net+ MR +SA	14.00	25.25	61.25	80.5
ZIAN W/U-Net (ours)	13.24	32.0	67.75	82.0
HRNet+1ROI	13.93	28.75	67.25	84.25
HRNet+1ROI+SA	9.51	<u>41.25</u>	**79.25**	90.0
HRNet+ MR +SA	<u>9.42</u>	38.0	76.25	<u>91.75</u>
ZIAN W/HRNet (ours)	**9.07**	**44.25**	<u>78.5</u>	**92.5**

[+] Top 2 teams in the REFUGE 1 final leaderboard. The model is trained on 400 train images instead of 800 train+val images like other methods.
[*] https://github.com/zhoudaxia233/EfficientUnet-PyTorch.

Role of Self-Attention Fusion Module (SA): SA is to learn to fuse the multi-scales features, so that the model learns to combine features for better prediction. With SA as shown in Tables 1 and 2 with HRNet, it significantly reduces the L2 distance further from 13.93 to 9.51, and from 14.786 to 14.264, in Fovea and SS tasks, respectively. In order to further investigate the advantages of multi-ROIs with SA, we evaluate the impact of SA without MR scheme, i.e. HRNet+1ROI+SA vs HRNet+MR+SA. This model achieved L2 distances of 9.42 and 13.891, compared to 9.52 and 14.264 in Fovea and SS tasks respectively. It indicates that self-attention works well under a single ROI and multi-ROIs.

Role of ROI Co-Attention (RCA): RCA mines the underlying correlations between Multi-ROIs features and selectively focuses on landmark regions. With RCA as shown in Tables 1 and 2, it slightly reduces the L2 distance from 9.42 to 9.07, and from 13.891 to 13.638, in Fovea and SS tasks, respectively.

Computational Efficiency: After incorporating the MR+SA+RCA in fovea localization, the GPU RAM usage increased from 2 GB to 11.9 GB with HRNet backbone, the training speed decreased from 12 images/s to 4 images/s, and the test speed decreased from 50 images/s to 7.4 images/s on one workstation with NVIDIA RTX3090 graphics card. Table 2 presents the number of parameters of

Table 2. Performances of different methods on AGE dataset

Method	AVG L2	Method	AVG L2	Params (M)[+]
AGE Dream Sun team*	*12.897*			
AGE MIPAV team*	13.761	HRNet [27]	15.032	28.544
EffcientUNet-B0 [29]**	17.657	HRNet+1ROI	14.783	57.102
EffcientUNet-B5 [29]**	15.594	HRNet+1ROI+SA	14.264	57.125
U-Net [28]	21.257	HRNet+ MR +SA	13.891	85.705
GU2Net [17]	23.024	ZIAN W/HRNet (ours)	**13.638**	85.710

* Top 2 teams in the AGE semi-final leaderboard, Dream Sun team utilizes Ensemble models with EffcientNet B2, B3, B5, and B6 [9].
** https://github.com/zhoudaxia233/EfficientUnet-PyTorch.
[+] Number of parameters in ablation study of ZIAN on a 224×224 input image.

our ZIAN method. As the top priority of medical applications is accuracy, we think the computational overhead of the ZIAN is still feasible and manageable.

4   Conclusions

In this paper, we propose a Zoom-In Attentive Network (ZIAN) for landmark localization tasks. ZIAN consists of a coarse-to-fine "zoom-in" module and an attentive fusion module. In the attentive fusion module, a ROI co-attention along with a self-attention fusion combine and fuse the multi-scale multi-ROI features. We performed extensive experiments and ablation studies on two public ocular image datasets. The results demonstrate that ZIAN has advantages over commonly used baselines. In the future work, we would like to extend ZIAN to make it robust against domain distribution shifts of the input images.

Acknowledgements. This work was supported by the Agency for Science, Technology and Research (A*STAR) under its AME Programmatic Funds (Grant Number: A20H4b0141), and its RIE2020 Health and Biomedical Sciences (HBMS) Industry Alignment Fund Pre-Positioning (IAF-PP, Grant Number: H20c6a0031). Xinxing Xu is the corresponding author.

References

1. Early Treatment Diabetic Retinopathy Study Research Group: Early photocoagulation for diabetic retinopathy. Ophthalmology **98**, 766–785 (1991)
2. Estudillo-Ayala, M.D.J., Aguirre-Ramos, H., Avina-Cervantes, J.G., Cruz-Duarte, J.M., Cruz-Aceves, I., Ruiz-Pinales, J.: Algorithmic analysis of vesselness and blobness for detecting retinopathies based on fractional Gaussian filters. Mathematics **8**(5), 744 (2020)
3. Meindert, N., Michael, D.A., Bram, V.G.: Fast detection of the optic disc and fovea in color fundus photographs. Med. Image Anal. **13**(6), 859–870 (2009)

4. Asim, K.M., Basit, A., Jalil, A.: Detection and localization of fovea in human retinal fundus images. In: 2012 International Conference on Emerging Technologies (ICET) (2012)
5. Li, T., et al.: Applications of deep learning in fundus images: a review. Med. Image Anal. **69**, 101971 (2021)
6. Sidey, G., Jenni, A.M.: Machine learning in medicine: a practical introduction. BMC Med. Res. Methodol. **19**, 64 (2019)
7. Zhao, Z.-Q., Zheng, P., Xu, S.-T., Wu, X.: Object detection with deep learning: a review. IEEE Trans. Neural Netw. Learn. Syst. **30**(11), 3212–3232 (2019)
8. Chen, C., Wang, B., Lu, C.X., Trigoni, N., Markham, A.: A survey on deep learning for localization and mapping: towards the age of spatial machine intelligence. arXiv preprint arXiv:2006.12567 (2020)
9. Fu, H., et al.: Age challenge: angle closure glaucoma evaluation in anterior segment optical coherence tomography. Med. Image Anal. **66**, 101798 (2020)
10. Noothout, J.M.H., et al.: Deep learning-based regression and classification for automatic landmark localization in medical images. IEEE Trans. Med. Imaging **39**, 4011–4022 (2020)
11. Huang, W., Yang, C., Hou, T.: Spine landmark localization with combining of heatmap regression and direct coordinate regression. arXiv preprint arXiv:2007.05355 (2020)
12. Tao, R., Zheng, G.: Spine-transformers: vertebra detection and localization in arbitrary field-of-view spine CT with transformers. In: de Bruijne, M., et al. (eds.) MICCAI 2021. LNCS, vol. 12903, pp. 93–103. Springer, Cham (2021). https://doi.org/10.1007/978-3-030-87199-4_9
13. Payer, C., Stern, D., Bischof, H., Urschler, M.: Integrating spatial configuration into heatmap regression based CNNs for landmark localization. Med. Image Anal. **54**, 03 (2019)
14. Bhalodia, R., et al.: Improving pneumonia localization via cross-attention on medical images and reports. In: de Bruijne, M., et al. (eds.) MICCAI 2021. LNCS, vol. 12902, pp. 571–581. Springer, Cham (2021). https://doi.org/10.1007/978-3-030-87196-3_53
15. Kang, J., Oh, K., Oh, I.S.: Accurate landmark localization for medical images using perturbations. Appl. Sci. **11**(21), 10277 (2021)
16. Liu, P., et al.: Reproducibility of deep learning based scleral spur localisation and anterior chamber angle measurements from anterior segment optical coherence tomography images. Br. J. Ophthalmol. (2022)
17. Zhu, H., Yao, Q., Xiao, L., Zhou, S.K.: You only learn once: universal anatomical landmark detection. In: de Bruijne, M., et al. (eds.) MICCAI 2021. LNCS, vol. 12905, pp. 85–95. Springer, Cham (2021). https://doi.org/10.1007/978-3-030-87240-3_9
18. Lu, X., Wang, W., Ma, C., Shen, J., Shao, L., Porikli, F.: See more, know more: unsupervised video object segmentation with co-attention Siamese networks. In: The IEEE Conference on Computer Vision and Pattern Recognition (CVPR) (2019)
19. Li, S., Sui, X., Luo, X., Xu, X., Yong, L., Goh, R.S.M.: Medical image segmentation using squeeze-and-expansion transformers. In: The 30th International Joint Conference on Artificial Intelligence (IJCAI) (2021)
20. Cina, A., et al.: 2-step deep learning model for landmarks localization in spine radiographs. Sci. Rep. **11**(1), 1–12 (2021)
21. Lu, J., Yang, J., Batra, D., Parikh, D.: Hierarchical question-image co-attention for visual question answering. CoRR, vol. abs/1606.00061 (2016)

22. Nguyen, D.K., Okatani, T.: Improved fusion of visual and language representations by dense symmetric co-attention for visual question answering. In: Proceedings of the IEEE Conference on Computer Vision and Pattern Recognition, pp. 6087–6096 (2018)

23. Vaswani, A., et al.: Attention is all you need. In: Proceedings of the 31st International Conference on Neural Information Processing Systems, NIPS 2017, pp. 6000–6010 (2017)

24. Voita, E., Talbot, D., Moiseev, F., Sennrich, R., Titov, I.: Analyzing multi-head self-attention: specialized heads do the heavy lifting, the rest can be pruned. In: Proceedings of the 57th Annual Meeting of the Association for Computational Linguistics (2019)

25. Cordonnier, J.B., Loukas, A., Jaggi, M.: Multi-head attention: collaborate instead of concatenate. arXiv preprint arXiv:2006.16362 (2020)

26. Xie, R., et al.: End-to-end fovea localisation in colour fundus images with a hierarchical deep regression network. IEEE Trans. Med. Imaging **40**(1), 116–128 (2021)

27. Ke, S., Bin, X., Dong, L., Jingdong, W.: Deep high-resolution representation learning for human pose estimation. In: Proceedings of the IEEE/CVF Conference on Computer Vision and Pattern Recognition (CVPR), pp. 5693–5703 (2019)

28. Ronneberger, O., Fischer, P., Brox, T.: U-net: convolutional networks for biomedical image segmentation. In: Navab, N., Hornegger, J., Wells, W.M., Frangi, A.F. (eds.) MICCAI 2015. LNCS, vol. 9351, pp. 234–241. Springer, Cham (2015). https://doi.org/10.1007/978-3-319-24574-4_28

29. Tan, M., Le, Q.V.: EfficientNet: rethinking model scaling for convolutional neural networks. In: Chaudhuri, K., Salakhutdinov, R. (eds.) Proceedings of the 36th International Conference on Machine Learning, ICML 2019, 9–15 June 2019, Long Beach, California, vol. 97, pp. 6105–6114. Proceedings of Machine Learning Research, PMLR 2019 (2019)

30. Redmon, J., Divvala, S., Girshick, R., Farhadi, A.: You only look once: unified, real-time object detection. In: 2016 IEEE Conference on Computer Vision and Pattern Recognition (CVPR), pp. 779–788 (2016)

31. Ren, S., He, K., Girshick, R., Sun, J.: Faster R-CNN: towards real-time object detection with region proposal networks. IEEE Trans. Pattern Anal. Mach. Intell. **39**(6), 1137–1149 (2017)

32. Orlando, J.I., et al.: Refuge challenge: a unified framework for evaluating automated methods for glaucoma assessment from fundus photographs. Med. Image Anal. **59**, 101570 (2020)

Intra-operative OCT (iOCT) Super Resolution: A Two-Stage Methodology Leveraging High Quality Pre-operative OCT Scans

Charalampos Komninos[1]([✉]), Theodoros Pissas[1], Blanca Flores[2],
Edward Bloch[2], Tom Vercauteren[1], Sébastien Ourselin[1], Lyndon Da Cruz[2,3],
and Christos Bergeles[1]

[1] School of Biomedical Engineering and Imaging Sciences, King's College London,
London SE1 7EU, UK
charalampos.komninos@kcl.ac.uk
[2] Moorfields Eye Hospital, London EC1V 2PD, UK
[3] Institute of Ophthalmology, University College London, London EC1V 9EL, UK

Abstract. Regenerative therapies have recently shown potential in restoring sight lost due to degenerative diseases. Their efficacy requires precise intra-retinal delivery, which can be achieved by robotic systems accompanied by high quality visualization of retinal layers. Intra-operative Optical Coherence Tomography (iOCT) captures cross-sectional retinal images in real-time but with image quality that is inadequate for intra-retinal therapy delivery. This paper proposes a two-stage super-resolution methodology that enhances the image quality of the low resolution (LR) iOCT images leveraging information from pre-operatively acquired high-resolution (HR) OCT (preOCT) images. First, we learn the degradation process from HR to LR domain through Cycle-GAN and use it to generate pseudo iOCT (LR) images from the HR preOCT ones. Then, we train a Pix2Pix model on the pairs of pseudo iOCT and preOCT to learn the super-resolution mapping. Quantitative analysis using both full-reference and no-reference image quality metrics demonstrates that our approach clearly outperforms the learning-based state-of-the art techniques with statistical significance. Achieving iOCT image quality comparable to preOCT quality can help this medical imaging modality be established in vitreoretinal surgery, without requiring expensive hardware-related system updates.

Supported by King's Centre for Doctoral Studies - Centre for Doctoral Training in Surgical & Interventional Engineering and funded in whole, or in part, by the Wellcome Trust [WT203148/Z/16/Z]. For the purpose of open access, the author has applied a CC BY public copyright licence to any Author Accepted Manuscript version arising from this submission.

Supplementary Information The online version contains supplementary material available at https://doi.org/10.1007/978-3-031-16525-2_11.

Keywords: Image quality · Super-resolution · iOCT

1   Introduction

Regenerative therapies (e.g. [6,20]) have emerged as novel treatment methods for degenerative eye diseases such as Age-Related Macular Degeneration [15], which gradually leads to sight loss. Their success, however, depends on precise delivery to the intra-retinal or sub-retinal space. To this end, alongside novel robotic tools that enable the required implantation precision [5], excellent visualization capabilities are crucial for intra-operative guidance. Intra-operative Optical Coherence Tomography (iOCT) can support such vitreoretinal interventions by providing cross-sectional visualization of the retina and the targeted layers.

In the pre-operative setting, the gold standard for imaging this targeted anatomy, is Optical coherence tomography (OCT), which is a non-invasive imaging modality using infrared light interferometry to visualise retinal layer information. Modern OCT systems use spatiotemporal signal averaging to capture OCT images of excellent quality, enabling clinicians to easily differentiate retinal tissues and layers. However, the long acquisition time during pre-operative OCT scanning makes it unsuitable for the real-time visualization of an intervention. Real-time acquisition is achieved by iOCT albeit at the expense of image quality. More specifically, iOCT images have increased levels of speckle noise [24] and low signal strength [21], which limit their interventional utility. Therefore, we focus on computationally enhancing the quality of iOCT images provided by current commercial clinical systems with the goal of augmenting the capabilities of iOCT technology in the surgical setting without requiring expensive hardware updates.

Image quality enhancement of OCT images has been addressed by various works. Wiener filters [21], segmentation-based [8], registration-based [23] and diffusion-based [2] methods, as well as methods that consider empirical speckle statistics [18], successfully enhanced the OCT quality by reducing speckle noise (denoising) and preserving image structures. However, similar methods can not efficiently be applied on iOCT images and real-time scenarios due to their high computational cost as well as the need of perfect image alignment and prolonged scanning time.

Learning-based techniques using Generative Adversarial Networks (GANs) [9] have been proposed for image quality enhancement or domain translation of natural images [13,14,27]. Similar approaches have been adopted for medical imaging modalities such as CT [26], PET [25] and OCT [1,7,10]. However, few works have focused on intra-operative OCT image quality enhancement. In [16] iOCT quality was improved using iOCT 3D cubes as the high resolution domain, while in [17] super-resolution achieved through surgical biomicroscopy guidance.

This work concerns self-supervised super-resolution[1] of iOCT images transferring the quality from high-resolution (HR) pre-operative OCT images to low-

---

[1] We interchange "super resolution" and "quality enhancement" as usual in the literature.

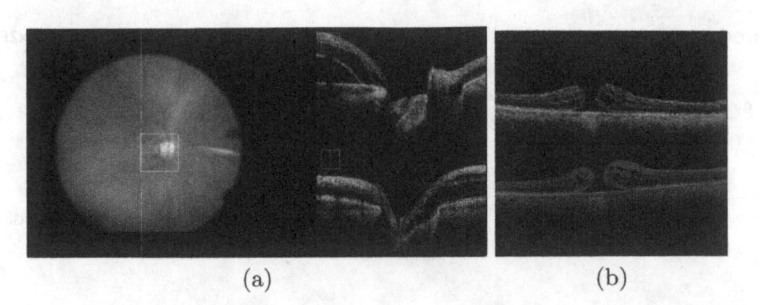

(a)   (b)

Fig. 1. (a): Surgery video frame. Left: Surgical biomicroscope view. Right: iOCT frames. (b): From top to bottom: iOCT and preOCT with macular hole.

resolution (LR) iOCT images. As access to aligned LR-HR pairs is not available, previous approach [17] focused on estimating the HR image of each LR by fusing multiple aligned iOCT video frames and then performing paired super-resolution. Given the fact that their estimated HR images are still of inferior quality compared to preOCT, we propose here a two-stage methodology for the task of unpaired image quality enhancement of iOCT using available preOCT images as HR domain. First, we train a CycleGAN [27] model using iOCT as input and pre-operative, high quality, OCT as the target domain and learn the image degradation process by training the backwards mapping network (HR to LR). Subsequently, the latter is leveraged to generate pseudo iOCT images, which contrary to the starting unpaired dataset, are now aligned with their pre-OCT counterparts. Then, we apply super-resolution with pixel-level supervision through Pix2Pix [13] using the generated pseudo iOCT images. To establish the effectiveness of this approach we provide extensive quantitative analysis showing we outperform existing, state-of-the-art learning based iOCT super-resolution approaches.

2   Methods

In this section, we present the data used in our study, the two-stage super-resolution approach and the quantitative metrics used for evaluation.

2.1   Datasets

The data used in this work are derived from an internal database of intra-operative and pre-operative OCT scans accompanied with vitreoretinal surgery videos acquired at Moorfields Eye Hospital, London, UK (see Fig. 1). The data was acquired in accordance with the Declaration of Helsinki (1983 Revision) and its ethical principles. We use HR pre-operative OCT data (resolution of $512 \times 1024 \times 128$ voxels) of 61 subjects which were acquired prior to the surgery using Cirrus 5000 as well as LR intra-operative OCT data (resolution

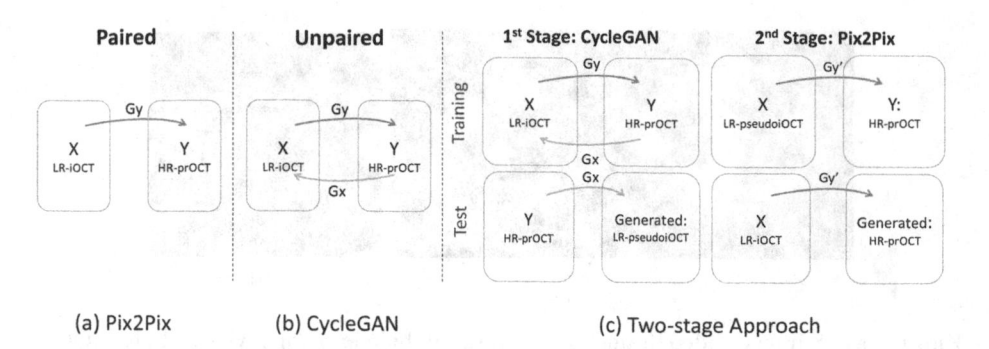

Fig. 2. Different approaches for learning the mapping (G) between X and Y domains.

of 440×300 pixels) acquired during the intervention using RESCAN 700 integrated into the Zeiss OPMI LUMERA 700. Pre-operative OCT 2D frames were extracted from the recorded 3D OCT scans.

2.2   Two-Stage Super-Resolution Approach

The task addressed in this work is super-resolution (SR) and quality enhancement of iOCT images. Specifically, this task is formulated as domain translation from the iOCT domain to the preOCT domain. In our first attempt, we used CycleGAN's architecture (Fig. 2.b) as one-stage approach to learn the bidirectional domain translation between HR preOCT and LR iOCT images. However, given that our iOCT and preOCT images are unpaired, and despite the fact that CycleGAN has shown superior performance in unpaired tasks where no pixel-level loss can be employed, as shown in our quantitative analysis it failed to generate consistent results.

We therefore propose a two-stage approach (Fig. 2.c). In the first stage, we use a CycleGAN model to learn the mappings between iOCT and preOCT domains. We leverage the capability of the model to learn with consistency the backwards mapping (from preoCT to iOCT), thus providing a generator that approximates the degradation and domain translation from HR to LR. We then use the trained backwards generator G_x to generate a pseudo (fake) iOCT that is pixel-wise aligned with each real preOCT image. In the second stage, we train a model that learns to map pseudo iOCT images (LR) to the preOCT domain (HR) leveraging pixel-level supervision through the Pix2Pix model. Crucially, as we show in the experimental section, the generator in the second stage sees **only** pseudo iOCT inputs but is able to effectively generalize to real iOCT images.

2.3   Implementation Details

The dataset, 7808 pairs of preOCT and pseudo iOCT images, was split into: training set (70%, 43 patients), validation set (15%, 9 patients) and test set

(15%, 9 patients). Each patient's image data were used only in one set. Pseudo iOCT images were generated through the inference of the first stage network achieving similarity of 87.49 Fréchet Inception Distance (see next section) with respect to the real iOCT images.

We based the implementation of the building blocks (Pix2Pix, CycleGAN) of our two-stage approach on the code available online[2]. Both networks use ResNet-based generator [14] of nine residual blocks and are trained on input resolution of 440×300. All models are trained using Adam optimizer with initial learning rate of 10^{-4} and a batch size of 4 for a total of 200 epochs. We used NVIDIA Quadro P6000 GPU with 24 GB memory for our experiments.

2.4   Evaluation Metrics

To evaluate the performance of the proposed approach compared to the state-of-the art learning based methods, given that the ground truth HR images do not exist, we use five no-reference Image Quality Assessment (IQA) metrics, i.e. Fréchet Inception Distance (FID) [11], Kernel Inception Distance (KID) [3], perceptual loss function ℓ_{feat} [16], Global Contrast Factor (GCF) [19] and Fast Noise Estimation (FNE) [12]. FID calculates the distance between distributions of features of two image sets extracted from the ImageNet-pretrained Inception-v3. KID is the squared Maximum Mean Discrepancy between Inception representations extracted from Inception-v3. Perceptual loss ℓ_{feat} demonstrates how perceptually similar are two image sets by calculating the distance of their representations extracted by Deep Convolutional Network pretrained on Imagenet [22]. GCF calculates the contrast at different resolution levels to calculate the global contrast of the image while FNE measures the noise level of each image of the dataset. We use $|\Delta GCF|$, which quantifies the absolute difference of the GCF that SR image yields compared to preOCT, and $|\Delta FNE|$, which is the absolute difference of the FNE that SR image yields with respect to preOCT.

Furthermore, we use full-reference metrics following the SR approaches in natural images which apply image degradation techniques to the HR ground truth images to create the LR counterparts. Peak signal-to-noise ratio (PSNR) and Structural Similarity Index (SSIM) are used in our case to evaluate the performance of each model using as input the pseudo iOCT images and comparing its output with real preOCT images.

3   Results

In this section, we present the results obtained from the quantitative analysis conducted to evaluate our approach.

---

[2] https://github.com/junyanz/pytorch-CycleGAN-and-pix2pix.

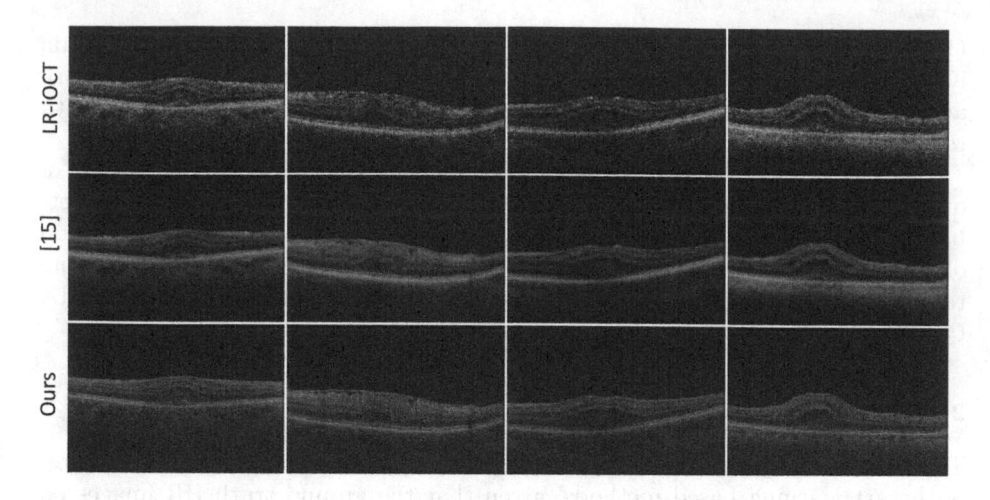

Fig. 3. From top to bottom: LR iOCT images, SR using [17], SR using our proposed method.

3.1   Evaluation on Real iOCT Images

We compare the improvements in image quality of the iOCT images generated by our model with respect to images from the preOCT domain. A total number of 2352 iOCT frames, extracted from iOCT surgery videos of 9 patients, not present in the train set, was used as test set. As ground truth HR images do not exist, we use five different no-reference IQA metrics, described in Sect. 2.4: FID, KID, ℓ_{feat}, $|\Delta GCF|$ and $|\Delta FNE|$.

Table 1 summarises the results of our analysis. Super-resolution using our method ranks first in terms of three out of five no-reference metrics, which demonstrates that the iOCT image quality has been improved (see also Fig. 3) and is closer to preOCT images. Our method is compared to the real iOCT images, the state-of-the-art iOCT SR techniques [16,17] and the SR using Cycle-GAN with unpaired LR and HR datasets (UnCycGAN). Regarding perceptual metrics, our method exhibit the best FID value and close to the best KID and ℓ_{feat} values, which demonstrates that our methods can generate SR images that are perceptually more similar to the HR domain. In addition, $|\Delta GCF|$ and $|\Delta FNE|$ metrics demonstrate that contrast and noise values of SR images through our method are closer to the values of HR preOCT images, which are the images with the best quality in our dataset. We assessed the statistical significance of the reported values for $|\Delta GCF|$ and $|\Delta FNE|$ using a paired t-test and all p-values were p < 0.001. Statistical significance can not be examined for perceptual metrics (FID, KID, ℓ_{feat}) which return one value for all the test set. Furthermore, our approach performs at 18.05 frames per second (FPS) with iOCT images of size 440×300 as input, which is appropriate for the real-time requirement of our application.

3.2   Evaluation on Pseudo iOCT Images

Prior works [4,14] used this standard evaluation technique but they applied heuristic degradation processes to generate LR images from their HR counterparts. However, iOCT quality can be affected by speckle noise, low signal strength, different pathologies which are not trivial to simulate. Therefore, we opt for learning the degradation processes. As described in Sect 2.2, during the first training stage we learn the mapping from preOCT to pseudo iOCT and we use it to create pseudo iOCT images that are aligned with our real preOCT for testing, allowing full-reference metrics to be computed.

Table 1. Quantitative analysis on iOCT images. Arrows show whether higher/lower is better.

	No-reference				
	FID($\downarrow$)	KID($\downarrow$)	$\ell_{feat}(\downarrow)$	$|\Delta\text{GCF}|(\downarrow)$	$|\Delta\text{FNE}|(\downarrow)$
iOCT	166.06	0.183	527.00	2.33±0.6	7.95±0.6
[16]	171.40	0.191	445.91	2.42±0.5	2.83±0.1
[17]	125.67	**0.115**	435.48	0.85±0.4	3.99±0.1
UnCycGAN	133.33	0.132	**356.48**	0.87±0.3	2.26±0.1
Ours	**123.09**	0.120	379.37	**0.41±0.3**	**2.09±0.1**

Table 2. Quantitative analysis. Arrows show whether higher/lower is better.

	Full-reference		No-reference				
	PSNR ($\uparrow$)	SSIM ($\uparrow$)	FID ($\downarrow$)	KID ($\downarrow$)	$\ell_{feat}(\downarrow)$	$|\Delta\text{GCF}|$ ($\downarrow$)	$|\Delta\text{FNE}|$ ($\downarrow$)
pseudo iOCT	23.05±2.1	0.65±0.1	121.30	0.114	336.04	1.43±0.5	**2.49±0.5**
[16]	16.81±1.8	0.58±0.1	123.18	0.127	362.40	2.48±0.5	3.17±0.1
[17]	24.09±2.2	0.64±0.1	75.43	0.058	277.89	0.41±0.3	4.11±0.1
UnCycGAN	28.93±1.6	**0.82±0.0**	58.87	0.041	237.66	0.34±0.2	2.81±0.1
Ours	**31.45±0.9**	**0.82±0.0**	**16.62**	**0.007**	**76.02**	**0.27±0.1**	2.61±0.4

Thus, quantitative analysis using both full-reference, i.e. PSNR, SSIM, and no-reference metrics was performed on 1152 pairs of pseudo iOCT and preOCT images. The results are reported in Table 2. Our method outperforms all other approaches both numerically and visually as shown in Fig. 4. According to six out of seven metrics, our approach can generate SR images that have high perceptual and structural similarity as well as similar levels of contrast and noise to preOCT images. Paired t-test was used to assess the statistical significance of the pairwise comparisons of the PSNR, SSIM, $|\Delta\text{GCF}|$ and $|\Delta\text{FNE}|$ reported values and all p-values were p < 0.001.

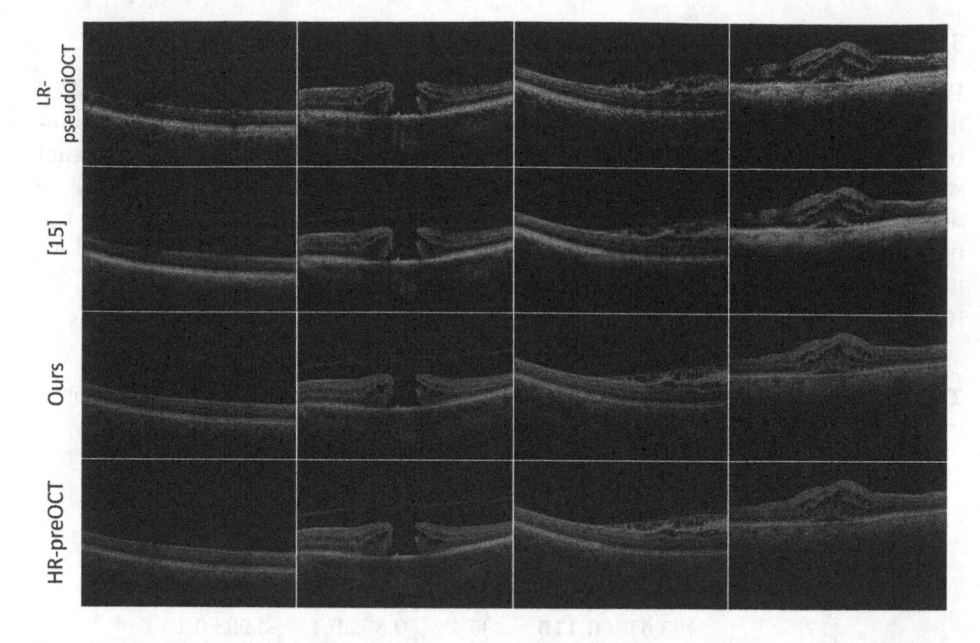

Fig. 4. From top to bottom: LR pseudo iOCT images, SR using [17], SR using our proposed method, HR preOCT images.

4   Discussion and Conclusions

In our study, we propose a Super-resolution pipeline for iOCT images acquired during vitreoretinal surgeries using pre-operatively acquired OCT images as HR domain. Our methodology clearly outperforms both numerically and visually previous proposed image quality enhancement methods.

First, we learn the degradation from preOCT (HR) domain to iOCT (LR) domain through a CycleGAN model trained on unpaired images of the two domains. Then, we apply the learned degradation process to generate pseudo iOCT images from preOCT ones which allows us to create pairs of LR-HR images. Finally, we train a Pix2Pix model on the LR-HR pairs to perform super-resolution.

We quantitatively evaluate our pipeline using as input both iOCT images extracted from real surgery videos and pseudo iOCT images generated through the learned degradation process. The results demonstrate the superior improvement that our method can achieve compared to already proposed techniques.

Future work will include qualitative analysis from expert clinicians and will consider temporal information for the iOCT video super-resolution.

References

1. Apostolopoulos, S., et al.: Automatically enhanced oct scans of the retina: a proof of concept study. Sci. Rep. **10**(1), 1–8 (2020)
2. Bernardes, R., Maduro, C., Serranho, P., Araújo, A., Barbeiro, S., Cunha-Vaz, J.: Improved adaptive complex diffusion despeckling filter. Opt. Express **18**(23), 24048–24059 (2010)
3. Bińkowski, M., Sutherland, D.J., Arbel, M., Gretton, A.: Demystifying MMD GANs. arXiv preprint arXiv:1801.01401 (2018)
4. Bulat, A., Yang, J., Tzimiropoulos, G.: To learn image super-resolution, use a GAN to learn how to do image degradation first. In: Proceedings of the European Conference on Computer Vision (ECCV), pp. 185–200 (2018)
5. Cornelissen, P., Ourak, M., Borghesan, G., Reynaerts, D., Vander Poorten, E.: Towards real-time estimation of a spherical eye model based on a single fiber OCT. In: 2019 19th International Conference on Advanced Robotics (ICAR), pp. 666–672. IEEE (2019)
6. da Cruz, L., et al.: Phase 1 clinical study of an embryonic stem cell-derived retinal pigment epithelium patch in age-related macular degeneration. Nat. Biotechnol. **36**(4), 328 (2018)
7. Devalla, S.K., et al.: A deep learning approach to denoise optical coherence tomography images of the optic nerve head. Sci. Rep. **9**(1), 1–13 (2019)
8. Fang, L., Li, S., Cunefare, D., Farsiu, S.: Segmentation based sparse reconstruction of optical coherence tomography images. IEEE Trans. Med. Imaging **36**(2), 407–421 (2016)
9. Goodfellow, I., et al.: Generative adversarial nets. Adv. Neural Inf. Process. Syst. **27** (2014)
10. Halupka, K.J., et al.: Retinal optical coherence tomography image enhancement via deep learning. Biomed. Opt. Express **9**(12), 6205–6221 (2018)
11. Heusel, M., Ramsauer, H., Unterthiner, T., Nessler, B., Hochreiter, S.: GANs trained by a two time-scale update rule converge to a local Nash equilibrium. Adv. Neural Inf. Process. Syst. **30** (2017)
12. Immerkaer, J.: Fast noise variance estimation. Comput. Vis. Image Underst. **64**(2), 300–302 (1996)
13. Isola, P., Zhu, J.Y., Zhou, T., Efros, A.A.: Image-to-image translation with conditional adversarial networks. In: Proceedings of the IEEE Conference on Computer Vision and Pattern Recognition, pp. 1125–1134 (2017)
14. Johnson, J., Alahi, A., Fei-Fei, L.: Perceptual losses for real-time style transfer and super-resolution. In: Leibe, B., Matas, J., Sebe, N., Welling, M. (eds.) ECCV 2016. LNCS, vol. 9906, pp. 694–711. Springer, Cham (2016). https://doi.org/10.1007/978-3-319-46475-6_43
15. de Jong, E.K., Geerlings, M.J., den Hollander, A.I.: Age-related macular degeneration. In: Genetics and Genomics of Eye Disease, pp. 155–180 (2020)
16. Komninos, C., et al.: Intra-operative OCT (iOCT) image quality enhancement: a super-resolution approach using high quality iOCT 3D scans. In: Fu, H., Garvin, M.K., MacGillivray, T., Xu, Y., Zheng, Y. (eds.) OMIA 2021. LNCS, vol. 12970, pp. 21–31. Springer, Cham (2021). https://doi.org/10.1007/978-3-030-87000-3_3
17. Komninos, C., et al.: Surgical biomicroscopy-guided intra-operative optical coherence tomography (iOCT) image super-resolution. Int. J. Comput. Assist. Radiol. Surg. **17**(5), 877–883 (2022). https://doi.org/10.1007/s11548-022-02603-5

18. Li, M., Idoughi, R., Choudhury, B., Heidrich, W.: Statistical model for OCT image denoising. Biomed. Opt. Express **8**(9), 3903–3917 (2017)
19. Matkovic, K., Neumann, L., Neumann, A., Psik, T., Purgathofer, W.: Global contrast factor-a new approach to image contrast. Comput. Aesthetics **2005**(159–168), 1 (2005)
20. Nazari, H., et al.: Stem cell based therapies for age-related macular degeneration: the promises and the challenges. Prog. Retin. Eye Res. **48**, 1–39 (2015)
21. Ozcan, A., Bilenca, A., Desjardins, A.E., Bouma, B.E., Tearney, G.J.: Speckle reduction in optical coherence tomography images using digital filtering. JOSA A **24**(7), 1901–1910 (2007)
22. Russakovsky, O., et al.: ImageNet large scale visual recognition challenge. Int. J. Comput. Vision **115**(3), 211–252 (2015). https://doi.org/10.1007/s11263-015-0816-y
23. Sander, B., Larsen, M., Thrane, L., Hougaard, J.L., Jørgensen, T.M.: Enhanced optical coherence tomography imaging by multiple scan averaging. Br. J. Ophthalmol. **89**(2), 207–212 (2005)
24. Viehland, C., et al.: Enhanced volumetric visualization for real time 4D intraoperative ophthalmic swept-source OCT. Biomed. Opt. Express **7**(5), 1815 (2016)
25. Xu, J., Gong, E., Pauly, J., Zaharchuk, G.: 200x low-dose PET reconstruction using deep learning. arXiv preprint arXiv:1712.04119 (2017)
26. Yang, Q., et al.: Low-dose CT image denoising using a generative adversarial network with Wasserstein distance and perceptual loss. IEEE Trans. Med. Imaging **37**(6), 1348–1357 (2018)
27. Zhu, J.Y., Park, T., Isola, P., Efros, A.A.: Unpaired image-to-image translation using cycle-consistent adversarial networks. In: Proceedings of the IEEE International Conference on Computer Vision, pp. 2223–2232 (2017)

Domain Adaptive Retinal Vessel Segmentation Guided by High-frequency Component

Haojin Li[1,2,3], Heng Li[2,3(✉)], Zhongxi Qiu[1,3], Yan Hu[2,3(✉)], and Jiang Liu[1,2,3,4]

[1] Guangdong Provincial Key Laboratory of Brain-inspired Intelligent Computation,
Southern University of Science and Technology, Shenzhen, China
[2] Department of Computer Science and Engineering, Southern University of Science
and Technology, Shenzhen, China
{lih3,huy3}@sustech.edu.cn
[3] The School of Computer and Communication Engineering, University of Science
and Technology, Beijing, China
[4] Singapore Eye Research Institute, Singapore National Eye Centre, Singapore,
Singapore

Abstract. The morphological structure of retinal fundus blood vessels is of great significance for medical diagnosis, thus the automatic retinal vessel segmentation algorithm has become one of the research hotspots in the field of medical image processing. However, there are still several unsolved difficulties in this task: the existed methods are too sensitive to the low-frequency noise in the fundus images, and there are few annotated data sets available, and meanwhile, the retinal images of different datasets vary greatly. To solve the above problems, we propose a domain adaptive vessel segmentation algorithm with multiple image entrances called MIUnet, which is robust to the etiological noises and domain shift between diverse datasets. We apply Fourier domain adaptation and the high-frequency component filtering modules to transform the raw images into two styles, and simultaneously reduce the discrepancy between the source domain and target domain retinal images. After that, images produced by the two modules are fed into a multi-input deep segmentation model, and the full utilization of features from different modalities is ensured by the deep supervision mechanism. Experiments prove that, compared with other segmentation methods, the MIUnet has better performances in cross-domain experiments, where the IoU reaches 63% when trained on ARIA dataset and tested on the DRIVE dataset and 53% in the opposite direction.

Keywords: Retinal fundus image · Retinal vessel segmentation · Domain adaptation

1 Introduction

Many ophthalmic diseases can show corresponding symptoms in the morphology of retinal vessels, such as diabetic retinopathy, glaucoma, age-related macular degeneration, hypertension, and atherosclerosis [12]. Consequently, fundus photography has been used as a routine clinical examination [10,22], and vascular structure extraction is one of the most important procedures. In the early age of digital technology, vessels were extracted by hand; however, manual segmentation is not precise and requires lots of labor and material costs [24]. The above demands inspire the invention and development of automatic retinal vessel segmentation algorithms.

In the computer vision field, image segmentation is a prerequisite for many advanced image processing tasks, thus segmentation algorithms are always a hot research field. Conventional segmentation algorithms can be roughly sorted into two categories [15]: region-based approach [1], and edge-based approach [1,20]; these approaches usually focus on the characteristics of pixels and relationship between pixels. In the recent decade, deep learning (DL) has become a universal paradigm for plenty of machine learning algorithms, and the recent competitive segmentation results are commonly achieved by DL-based methods. DL-based methods offer end-to-end models which are more efficient in capturing the contextual relationship between pixels compared with traditional methods. There are some representative models, such as Fully Convolutional Network [14], Deep Parsing Network [13], SegNet [2], U-net [17], UNet++ [25], DeepLab family [3–6] and so on; and in particular, many valuable methods have been proposed for the sub-task of vascular segmentation, for instance, CE-Net [8] and CS-Net [16].

However, previous segmentation algorithms based on supervised learning could not solve the following problems in retinal fundus vascular segmentation well: 1) fundus images always suffer from imaging noise, and the vessels are of limited contrast with the background; 2) domain shift between the training (source) and test (target) data is unavoidable in practice [11,23], which severely impacts the performance of segmentation models.

To deal with the above problem, we propose a domain adaptive segmentation model named MIUnet. This model leverages the Fourier domain adaptation (FDA) [21] module and the high-frequency filtering (HFC) module to impose the model's generality and robustness. Within the model, the deep convolutional modules with two input images are designed with a deep supervision mechanism, which is adopted in the two entrance branches to supervise the feature extraction from the outputs of FDA and HFC modules. Our main contributions are listed as follows:

- Our proposed segmentation method, MIUnet, uses FDA, HFC, and specifically built multi-input convolutional modules to address the problem of noise and domain shift in the retinal vessel segmentation task.
- FDA and HFC modules are introduced to reduce the domain shift between data domains and compress the imaging noise. The deep convolutional modules with a deep supervision mechanism are designed to fuse the feature information of the outputs of FDA and HFC modules.
- Comparison experiments and ablation study are conducted, and the experimental results show that MIUnet has better segmentation effect and generalization ability compared to other state-of-the-art methods.

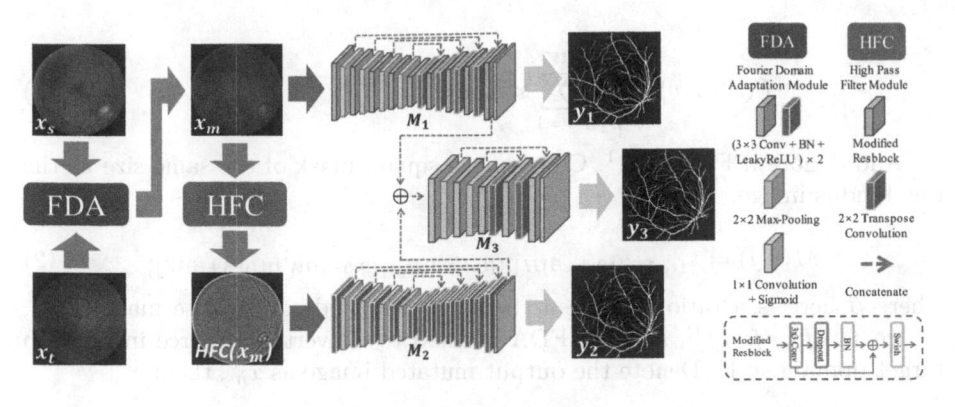

Fig. 1. Illustration of our proposed method. In this figure, the source domain fundus image is sampled from the DRIVE dataset, and the target domain image is from the ARIA dataset. The FDA mutated image and the high-frequency component are input into modules M_1 and M_2 respectively. The convolutional blocks in these two modules have the same structure, and are distinguished by different colors; meanwhile, the convolutional blocks in M_3 are changed to residual blocks.

2 Methodology

Figure 1 shows the workflow of our proposed method MIUnet. Source domain fundus image and the target domain image sampled from different datasets are synthesized into the mutated image by Fourier Domain Adaptation (FDA) module [21], and then input the mutated image into the HFC module to extract the high-frequency component. The FDA mutated image and the high-frequency component image are fed into two entrances of the multi-input segmentation model. Finally, three vessel segmentation results are generated; the output of M_3 which combined two feature vectors is considered the final result, while the other two outputs are used for deep supervision.

2.1 Fourier Domain Adaptation

FDA [21] is a kind of unsupervised domain adaptation method. The main idea of FDA is that: convert fundus images into the frequency domain by fast Fourier transformation (FFT), and then the low-frequency part of the amplitude of the source domain image is replaced by the corresponding part of the target domain image, in the end, the fused amplitude image and the phase image from the source domain image are combined, and restored to a mutated fundus image by inverse fast Fourier transformation (iFFT).

Given source domain dataset $D^s = \{(x_s^i, y_s^i) \sim P(x_s, y_s)\}_{i=1}^{N_s}$ and target domain dataset $D^t = \{x_t^i \sim P(x_t)\}_{i=1}^{N_t}$, while $x_s, x_t \in \mathbb{R}^{H \times W \times 3}$ are color picture with height of H and width of W, and $y_s \in \mathbb{R}^{H \times W}$ is the vessel segmentation ground truth of the source domain fundus image. Denote FFT as $\mathcal{F}$ (only consider gray-scale image here, in color image each channel should be calculated respectively):

$$\mathcal{F}(x)(u,v) = \sum_{h=1}^{H} \sum_{w=1}^{W} x(h,w)e^{-j2\pi(\frac{uh}{H} + \frac{vw}{W})}, j^2 = -1 \qquad (1)$$

And denote iFFT as $\mathcal{F}^{-1}$. Construct a square mask of the same size as the raw fundus image:

$$M(i,j) = \mathbb{1}_{(i,j)\in[\lfloor(0.5-\beta)H\rfloor:\lfloor(0.5+\beta)H\rfloor, \lfloor(0.5-\beta)W\rfloor:\lfloor(0.5+\beta)W\rfloor]} \qquad (2)$$

where β here is a ratio coefficient. Say the amplitude and phase maps of x_s, x_t are f_s^A/f_s^P, f_t^A/f_t^P, and use FDA method to convert the source image into target domain style. Denote the output mutated image as x_m, then:

$$x_m = \mathcal{F}^{-1}((M \circ f_s^P + (1-M) \circ f_t^P)e^{jf_A^s}) \qquad (3)$$

As shown in Fig. 2, the mutated image retain not only the high-frequency features from the source domain fundus image such as vascular thickness, branch, etc., and also the low-frequency style information from target domain.

2.2 High-frequency Component Extraction Based on Gaussian Filtering

Gaussian filtering is a common linear filtering method, it's commonly used in fundus image processing to deal with the noises caused by abnormal lighting conditions, interference of electronic components, or ophthalmic diseases. There are two important factors in this algorithm: σ refers to the standard variance, and the size of the Gaussian kernel is $2k+1$. Conduct a two-dimensional convolution between the kernel matrix and the fundus image with a step size of 1, and this is the so-called Gaussian filtering. Say the raw image is I, and all pixel values are between $[0,1]$. The Gaussian filtered image is G. Then, subtract the Gaussian blurring map from the raw image, so it can be considered that the remaining part is the high-frequency component of the fundus image:

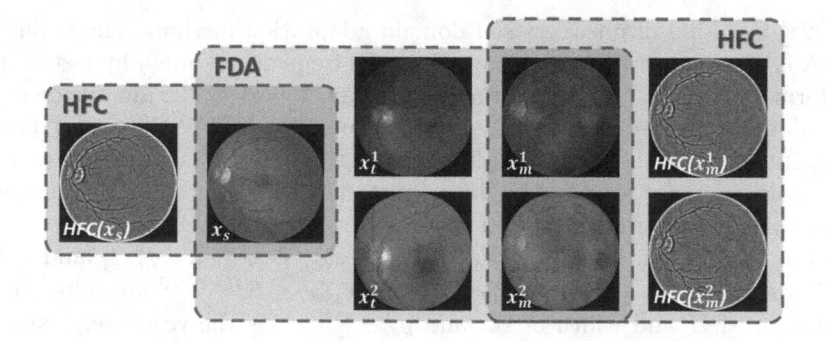

Fig. 2. Samples of outputs of FDA and HFC modules.

$$HFC(i,j) = I(i,j) - G(i,j) \tag{4}$$

As shown in Fig. 2, the vascular structure in the high-frequency component retinal image is much more pronounced in contrast to the background, compared to the raw fundus image.

2.3 Multi-input Deep Vessel Segmentation Model

In the image segmentation task, pre-processing the raw images is one of the most important procedures. In most cases, the selection of pre-processing methods is usually based on empirical cognition, and in fact, it is hard to compare the feature accessibility of outputs of fundus images by different pre-processing techniques. The main idea of our proposed multi-input U-net is to take advantage of features of fundus images pre-processed in different ways, and the aim is to make the segmentation results outperform the results with inputs produced by two pre-processing methods respectively.

As shown in Fig. 1, there are three modules M_1, M_2 and M_3 and their architecture are all based on U-net [17]. M_1 and M_2 are the entrances for fundus images from two modules: FDA mutated image and the high-frequency component image. We suppose the two inputted images are equivalent in feature accessibility, so the M_1 and M_2 share the same architecture, which is almost the same as U-net. The difference between the two modules and U-net is that the activation function is replaced with Leaky-ReLU, and the padding value in the convolution blocks of M_1 and M_2 is set to 1 to preserve the size during convolution. Regularize the final by Sigmoid function, and then the final outputs y_1 and y_2 are:

$$y_1 = (M_1(FDA(x_s, x_t))) \tag{5}$$

$$y_2 = M_2(HFC(FDA(x_s, x_t))) \tag{6}$$

M_3 is also a unet-like module. Different from M_1 and M_2, M_3 has only 3 layers, and inspired by [9,19] we replace the double-convolution block by a kind of modified residual convolution blocks, which contains a 3×3 convolution module, a batch normalization module, a dropout module (with a dropout ratio of 0.5) and Swish activation function. The outputs of the last double-convolution blocks in M_1 and M_2 are denoted as y_1^{latent} and y_2^{latent}. Concatenate y_1^{latent} and y_2^{latent}, and input the result into M_3 such that the input of M_3 fuses the features of images in two different modalities. The above procedure is formulated as:

$$y_3 = M_3([y_1^{latent}, y_2^{latent}]) \tag{7}$$

The output of M_3, y_3, is the final segmentation result of MIUnet. y_1, y_2 and y_3 are all aligned with label y_s, and y_1 and y_2 are used for deep supervision; the alignment of y_1 and y_2 to y_s could make sure that M_1 and M_2 can be consider to be independent segmentation models, such that the information in fundus images in different modality can be fully utilized. We use binary cross entropy as loss function to measure the distance between the prediction result and ground truth, so the total loss function is:

$$L_{total} = \lambda_1 BCE(y_1, y_s) + \lambda_2 BCE(y_2, y_s) + BCE(y_3, y_s) \qquad (8)$$

where λ_1 and λ_2 are empirically set to 0.2 and 0.2.

3   Experiments

In order to prove the segmentation effect of MIUnet, comparison experiment and ablation study are conducted. To test the cross-domain generality of the models, the training set and testing set are from different datasets.

3.1   Experiment Settings

Datasets   In our experiments, there are two datasets used:

1) **ARIA** [7] contains 147 labeled fundus images with a resolution of 768×576, with over 2/3 of them collected from people suffering from ophthalmic diseases. The ARIA dataset is split randomly into the training set and validation/testing set in a ratio of 3:1. To make the fundus images from different datasets similar in general styles such as field of view (FoV) and aspect ratio, we crop the raw images into the shape of a square, and use a circle mask to make the FoV a circle tangent to the edge of the squares.
2) **DRIVE** [18] contains 40 labeled images with a resolution of 565×584, and vascular structure in most of the images in the DRIVE dataset is relatively clear. All images were manually cropped such that the FoV area could be tangent to all the edges of the images. DRIVE dataset had been already split in half into training and testing set by its author.

All images are resized to a size of 512×512, and images in training set of both datasets were all rotational augmented in four angles of $90/135/180/225°$. **Evaluation metrics** 1) **F1 score**, which is the harmonic average of precision and recall; 2) **Accuracy**, referring to the proportion of all correctly classified pixels among all pixels; 3) **AUC**, which means the area between the Receiver Operating Characteristic Curve and x-axis; 4) **IoU**, the interaction area of the prediction and ground truth over the union area.

Implementation details: The experiments of comparison and ablation study were all based on the Pytorch framework and used NVIDIA GeForce RTX 3060 (12GB) graphics card. The numbers of channels in each convolution block of M_1 and M_2 are set to [64, 128, 256, 612, 1024] from top to bottom, and in M_3 the numbers are [64, 128, 256]. The initial learning rate of the models was 0.001 and dropped to 0.1 times per 3 rounds when the ARIA dataset was used as a training set and per 20 rounds when the training set was from the DRIVE dataset (ARIA and DRIVE differ from each other in size). The Adam optimizer

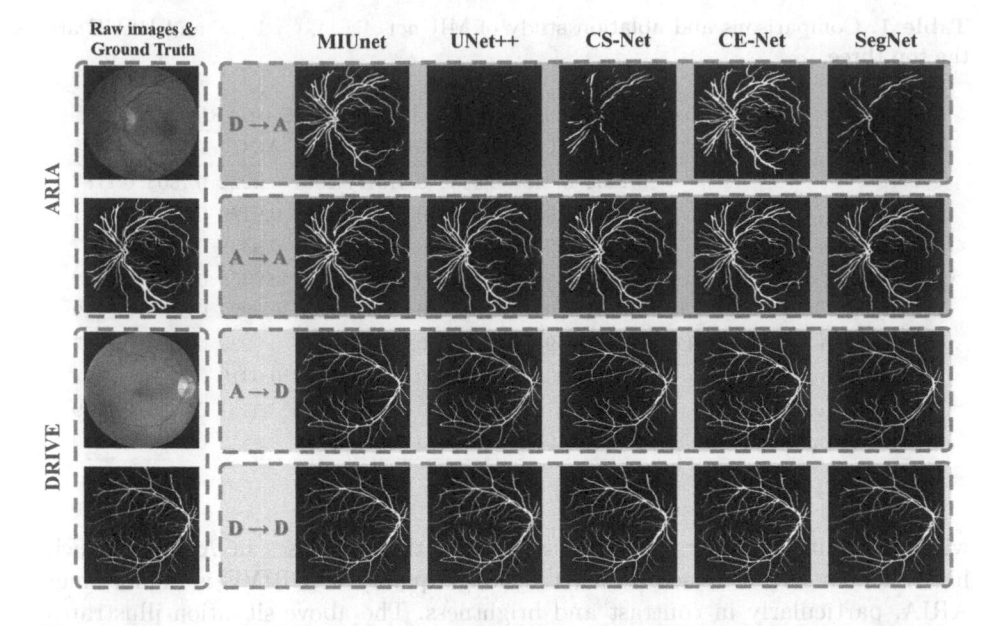

Fig. 3. Comparison on the segmentation result between MIUnet and baseline methods. The colors of the dotted boxes and the background represent the source of training set and testing set respectively.

was used, with $\beta = (0.9, 0.999)$. The batch size was set to 2 due to the limitation of computational resources. In the training process, epochs for all experiments were 50 and an early stop strategy was applied.

3.2 Comparison and Ablation Study

To prove the cross-domain generalization ability of our proposed method, we conducted a comparison experiment with several baseline methods and an ablation experiment. Five baselines were introduced, including U-net [17], UNet++ [25], SegNet [2], CE-Net [8] and CS-Net [16]. In the ablation study, modules were removed one by one, firstly the FDA module was removed, and then we removed the "multi-input" mechanism (only use U-net with HFC module), and finally removed the HFC module.

(1) Comparison Table 1 presents the comparison result of all the methods on the cross-domain experiment. From the table, it can be seen that our method shows the optimal effect in almost all metrics among all the involved methods. In the cross-domain experiment from ARIA to DRIVE (training set and validation set is from ARIA and testing set is from DRIVE, hereinafter referred to as A-to-D), all algorithms could produce meaningful results, which is manifested in their high performance among baselines. However, some of the models perform badly in the D-to-A experiment. A possible reason is that the fundus images in ARIA are noisier than those in DRIVE because the proportion of images from patients

Table 1. Comparisons and ablation study of MIUnet. RED, GREEN and BLUE are the top three.

Method	ARIA → DRIVE				DRIVE → ARIA			
	F1	ACC	AUC	IoU	F1	ACC	AUC	IoU
U-net	0.7252	0.9489	0.9630	0.5161	0.2907	0.9222	0.7503	0.1787
UNet++	0.7468	0.9519	0.9665	0.5286	0.3082	0.9199	0.7790	0.1701
SegNet	0.7129	0.9499	0.9070	0.5539	0.5141	0.9338	0.8177	0.3577
CE-Net	0.7256	0.9466	0.9630	0.5367	0.6862	0.9356	0.9593	0.5348
CSNet	0.7394	0.9509	0.9653	0.5038	0.3864	0.9222	0.8390	0.2049
MIUnet w/o HFC, MI, FDA	0.7252	0.9489	0.9630	0.5161	0.2907	0.9222	0.7503	0.1787
MIUnet w/o MI, FDA	0.7304	0.9482	0.9614	0.5276	0.6822	0.9319	0.9617	0.5409
MIUnet w/o FDA	0.7677	0.9542	0.9715	0.6246	0.5655	0.9387	0.9405	0.4129
MIUnet (proposed)	0.7723	0.9559	0.9744	0.6307	0.7038	0.9442	0.9639	0.5359

with ophthalmic diseases and the severity of these diseases in ARIA is much high than in DRIVE, meanwhile, the image quality of DRIVE is higher than ARIA, particularly in contrast and brightness. The above situation illustrates the domain shift between the two datasets, and apparently, it is better for A-to-D experiments, and bad for D-to-A ones. Although UNet++ and CS-Net show terrible results in the D-to-A experiment, they are the best two baselines in A-to-D datasets, and also CE-Net achieves good performance in the D-to-A experiment; but the proposed MIUnet still outperforms the above method greatly.

Figure 3 shows the actual segmentation effect of several sample data, and at the same time, we also show the corresponding segmentation result testing on the validation set of the same dataset as the training set (called the same-domain experiment). There are two samples shown, the first from the ARIA dataset, and the second from DRIVE. As mentioned above, the segmentation results in the D-to-A experiment of UNet++ and CS-Net are largely meaningless. In contrast, the results of the same-domain experiment and the A-to-D experiment are relatively good. It is found that the segmentation ability of CE-Net is more stable, as it gives acceptable results in all cross-domain experiments. However, in the outputs of CE-Net in the D-to-A experiment and CS-NET/UNet++ in the A-to-D experiment, many small vessels are mislabeled in the segmentation result, which means the segmentation capability of these baseline models are not as good as the output MIUnet in detail. The experimental result proves the cross-domain generalization ability of MIUnet.

(2) Ablation Study The ablation study is also contained in Table 1, which is conducted to prove the necessity of the three main modules of MIUnet. Firstly we tested the performance of MIUnet w/o HFC, MI, FDA modules, which is exactly the naive U-net. After that, MIUnet w/o MI and FDA is also included, which means the outputs of M_2 were taken as final outputs. In the last experiment, only the FDA module was removed.

The experimental results show that, the FDA module significantly reduces the domain discrepancy between source and target domain, especially in the D-to-A experiment. The HFC module removes the low-frequency noises and style-related information and thus enhances the robustness of the model. And the multi-input convolutional model combines the outputs of the two modules and turns the single parts into a whole. As a result, the segmentation model MIUnet could have great robustness and generalization ability.

4   Conclusion

The retinal vessel segmentation algorithm is important for ophthalmic disease diagnosis, but due to the noisy fundus images and little labeled data, the researchers call for a robust model with generalization capability. This paper proposes a domain adaptive method called MIUnet to address the above problem, which could take advantage of both the feature information from the outputs of FDA and HFC modules, and use a deep supervision mechanism to support the training process. In the experiments, the comparison and ablation study proves the cross-domain generalization ability of MIUnet.

References

1. Al-Amri, S.S., Kalyankar, N.V., et al.: Image segmentation by using threshold techniques. arXiv preprint arXiv:1005.4020 (2010)
2. Badrinarayanan, V., Kendall, A., Cipolla, R.: SegNet: a deep convolutional encoder-decoder architecture for image segmentation. IEEE Trans. Pattern Anal. Mach. Intell. **39**(12), 2481–2495 (2017)
3. Chen, L.C., Papandreou, G., Kokkinos, I., Murphy, K., Yuille, A.L.: Semantic image segmentation with deep convolutional nets and fully connected CRFs. arXiv preprint arXiv:1412.7062 (2014)
4. Chen, L.C., Papandreou, G., Kokkinos, I., Murphy, K., Yuille, A.L.: DeepLab: semantic image segmentation with deep convolutional Nets, Atrous convolution, and fully connected CRFs. IEEE Trans. Pattern Anal. Mach. Intell. **40**(4), 834–848 (2017)
5. Chen, L.C., Papandreou, G., Schroff, F., Adam, H.: Rethinking atrous convolution for semantic image segmentation. arXiv preprint arXiv:1706.05587 (2017)
6. Chen, L.C., Zhu, Y., Papandreou, G., Schroff, F., Adam, H.: Encoder-decoder with atrous separable convolution for semantic image segmentation. In: Proceedings of the European Conference on Computer Vision (ECCV), pp. 801–818 (2018)
7. Farnell, D.J., et al.: Enhancement of blood vessels in digital fundus photographs via the application of multiscale line operators. J. Franklin Inst. **345**(7), 748–765 (2008)
8. Gu, Z., et al.: CE-Net: context encoder network for 2D medical image segmentation. IEEE Trans. Med. Imaging **38**(10), 2281–2292 (2019)
9. He, K., Zhang, X., Ren, S., Sun, J.: Deep residual learning for image recognition. In: Proceedings of the IEEE Conference on Computer Vision and Pattern Recognition, pp. 770–778 (2016)

10. Li, H., et al.: An annotation-free restoration network for cataractous fundus images. IEEE Trans. Med. Imaging (2022)
11. Li, H., et al.: Restoration of cataract fundus images via unsupervised domain adaptation. In: 2021 IEEE 18th International Symposium on Biomedical Imaging (ISBI), pp. 516–520. IEEE (2021)
12. Li, T., et al.: Applications of deep learning in fundus images: a review. Med. Image Anal. **69**, 101971 (2021)
13. Liu, Z., Li, X., Luo, P., Loy, C.C., Tang, X.: Semantic image segmentation via deep parsing network. In: Proceedings of the IEEE International Conference on Computer Vision, pp. 1377–1385 (2015)
14. Long, J., Shelhamer, E., Darrell, T.: Fully convolutional networks for semantic segmentation. In: Proceedings of the IEEE Conference on Computer Vision and Pattern Recognition, pp. 3431–3440 (2015)
15. Lucchese, L., Mitra, S.K.: Colour image segmentation: a state-of-the-art survey. Proc. Indian National Sci. Acad. **67**(2), 207–222 (2001)
16. Mou, L., et al.: CS-Net: channel and spatial attention network for curvilinear structure segmentation. In: Shen, D., et al. (eds.) MICCAI 2019. LNCS, vol. 11764, pp. 721–730. Springer, Cham (2019). https://doi.org/10.1007/978-3-030-32239-7_80
17. Ronneberger, O., Fischer, P., Brox, T.: U-Net: convolutional networks for biomedical image segmentation. In: Navab, N., Hornegger, J., Wells, W.M., Frangi, A.F. (eds.) MICCAI 2015. LNCS, vol. 9351, pp. 234–241. Springer, Cham (2015). https://doi.org/10.1007/978-3-319-24574-4_28
18. Staal, J., Abràmoff, M.D., Niemeijer, M., Viergever, M.A., Van Ginneken, B.: Ridge-based vessel segmentation in color images of the retina. IEEE Trans. Med. Imaging **23**(4), 501–509 (2004)
19. Tan, Y., Yang, K.F., Zhao, S.X., Li, Y.J.: Retinal vessel segmentation with skeletal prior and contrastive loss. IEEE Trans. Med. Imaging (2022)
20. Wang, A., Liu, X.: Vehicle license plate location based on improved roberts operator and mathematical morphology. In: 2012 Second International Conference on Instrumentation, Measurement, Computer, Communication and Control, pp. 995–998. IEEE (2012)
21. Yang, Y., Soatto, S.: FDA: Fourier domain adaptation for semantic segmentation. In: Proceedings of the IEEE/CVF Conference on Computer Vision and Pattern Recognition, pp. 4085–4095 (2020)
22. Zhang, X.Q., Hu, Y., Xiao, Z.J., Fang, J.S., Higashita, R., Liu, J.: Machine learning for cataract classification/grading on ophthalmic imaging modalities: a survey. Mach. Intell. Res. **19**(3), 184–208 (2022)
23. Zhang, X., et al.: Adaptive feature squeeze network for nuclear cataract classification in AS-OCT image. J. Biomed. Inform. **128**, 104037 (2022)
24. Zhang, Y., et al.: A multi-branch hybrid transformer network for corneal endothelial cell segmentation. In: de Bruijne, M., et al. (eds.) MICCAI 2021. LNCS, vol. 12901, pp. 99–108. Springer, Cham (2021). https://doi.org/10.1007/978-3-030-87193-2_10
25. Zhou, Z., Rahman Siddiquee, M.M., Tajbakhsh, N., Liang, J.: UNet++: a nested U-Net architecture for medical image segmentation. In: Stoyanov, D., et al. (eds.) DLMIA/ML-CDS -2018. LNCS, vol. 11045, pp. 3–11. Springer, Cham (2018). https://doi.org/10.1007/978-3-030-00889-5_1

Tiny-Lesion Segmentation in OCT via Multi-scale Wavelet Enhanced Transformer

Meng Wang[1], Kai Yu[2], Xinxing Xu[1], Yi Zhou[3], Yuanyuan Peng[3], Yanyu Xu[1], Rick Siow Mong Goh[1], Yong Liu[1], and Huazhu Fu[1(✉)]

[1] Institute of High Performance Computing, A*STAR, Singapore 138632, Singapore
hzfu@ieee.org
[2] The Children's Hospital, Zhejiang University School of Medicine, National Clinical Research Center for Child Health, Hangzhou, Zhejiang 310057, China
[3] School of Electronics and Information Engineering, Soochow University, Suzhou, Jiangsu 215006, China

Abstract. The accurate segmentation of retinal lesions from OCT images can greatly aid ophthalmologists in evaluating retinal diseases. However, it remains a challenge to accurately segment retinal lesions in OCT images. This is due to the complicated pathological features of retinal diseases, resulting in severe regional scale imbalance between different lesions, and leading to the problem of target tendency of the network during training, subsequently resulting in the segmentation performance reduction for tiny-lesion. Aiming to solve these challenges, we propose a novel multi-scale wavelet enhanced transformer network for tiny-lesion segmentation in retinal OCT images. In the proposed model, we first design a novel adaptive wavelet down-sampling module combined with the pre-trained ResNet blocks as the feature extractor network, which can generate a wavelet representation to improve the model's interpretability while avoiding feature loss, and further enhancing the ability of the network to represent local detailed features. Meanwhile, we also develop a novel multi-scale transformer module to further improve the model's capacity of extracting the multi-scale long-dependent global features of the retinal lesions in OCT images. Finally, the proposed method is evaluated on the public database of AI-Challenge 2018 for retinal edema lesions joint segmentation, and the results indicate that the proposed method achieves better segmentation performance than other state-of-the-art networks, especially for tiny PED lesions with very small regional proportions.

Keywords: OCT images · Lesion segmentation · Wavelet · Transformer

---

M. Wang, K. Yu and H. Fu—Contributed equally.

1 Introduction

Retinal optical coherence tomography(OCT) is a non-invasive imaging technology that enables the visualization of the cross-sectional structure of the retina, and it has been widely used in the diagnosis of retinal diseases [11]. The accurate segmentation of retinal lesions from OCT images can greatly assist ophthalmologists in the evaluation of retinal diseases. Recently, many convolutional neural networks(CNNs) [5,8,13,16,20] have been proposed for medical image segmentation. Although these CNN-based methods have achieved excellent performance, there are limitations in modeling explicit long-range dependent global features due to the inherent locality of convolutional operations. To tackle these limitations, existing studies improved the ability of the model to learn long-distance dependency information by introducing transformer [4,18]. Several transformer-based methods have been proposed for medical image segmentation and achieved comparable performance with CNN-based approaches [2,7,12]. Retinal diseases often co-occur in multiple morphologies, and as the disease progresses, there is a severe imbalance in the ratio between different lesion regions. The problem of target tendency during network training will lead to the performance drop for the tiny-lesion. Despite the promising results of these CNN-and transformer-based methods in image segmentation tasks, there are still considerable challenges when applying these methods to the segmentation of retinal lesions in OCT images. These challenges include: 1) How to avoid feature loss when down-sampling the feature map while improving the interpretability of the model and further enhancing the network's ability to represent local detailed features. 2) How to improve the ability of the model to learn complex multi-scale global contextual information in retinal OCT images.

Aiming to solve these challenges, we propose a novel multi-scale wavelet enhanced transformer network for tiny-lesion segmentation in retinal OCT images. Our main contributions are summarized as follows: (1) We propose a novel adaptive wavelet down-sampling(AWDS) module combined with the pre-trained ResNet blocks as the feature extractor network, which can generate a wavelet representation to improve the model's interpretability while avoiding feature loss, and enhancing the ability of the network to represent local detailed features in retinal OCT images. (2) A novel adaptive multi-scale transformer(AMsTrans) module is developed based on the transformer concept, which can guide the model to explore complex multi-scale long-dependent global features for different retinal lesions in OCT images. (3) We conduct extensive experiments to evaluate the performance of the proposed method on the public database: AI-Challenge 2018 for retinal edema lesions joint segmentation. The experimental results show that, compared with other state-of-the-art segmentation methods, the proposed method can significantly improve the segmentation performance of tiny-lesion while maintaining the segmentation performance for large lesions.

2   Method

2.1   Overall Architecture

As shown in Fig. 1(a), the proposed multi-scale wavelet enhanced transformer network is designed based on the U-shaped architecture, which mainly consists of three components: the encoder path which integrates the pre-trained ResNet blocks with AWDS module, and is adopted to extract the feature information of different scale receptive fields in the input image, the AMsTrans module is appended on the top layer of encoder path to guide the model to explore complex multi-scale long-dependent global features of retinal lesions, and the decoder path to restore the spatial information with strong multi-scale global features generated by AMsTrans module, and gradually fuse the multi-semantic contextual information from different stages of encoder path.

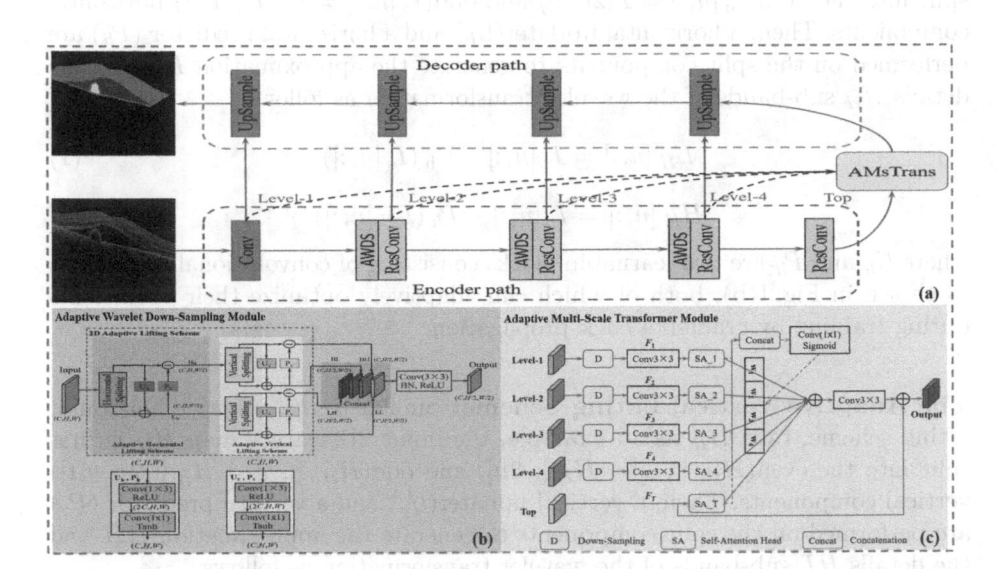

Fig. 1. The overview of the proposed method. (a) The architecture of multi-scale wavelet enhanced transformer network, (b) The details of adaptive wavelet down-sampling module, (c) The structure of adaptive multi-scale transformer module.

2.2   The Encoder Path

Although CNNs have achieved significant performance in many challenging computer vision tasks [5,8,10], they are essentially spatial approaches that lack interpretability, and usually ignore the spectral information which is equally important for representing image features. Wavelet transformation has a good local detailed feature representation capacity in the time-frequency domain and can present any local details in the image, so it is widely used to deal with various image problems [1,3,17]. Several prior works are dedicated to further improving the feature representation capacity by incorporating wavelet transformation into CNNs [6,14,15]. Therefore, inspired by [15], to supplement those missing spectral information in CNNs while improving the model's interpretability, we develop a novel feature extractor network by combining our newly proposed AWDS module with pre-trained ResNet blocks [10], as shown in Fig. 1(a). The details for the proposed AWDS module is shown in Fig. 1(b). In AWDS module, we adopt 2D adaptive lifting scheme [15] to perform multi-resolution wavelet transformation on the input feature maps **Input** $\in R^{(C,H,W)}$ to generate four wavelet sub-bands feature maps of **LL** $\in R^{(C,H/2,W/2)}$, **LH** $\in R^{(C,H/2,W/2)}$, **HL** $\in R^{(C,H/2,W/2)}$, and **HH** $\in R^{(C,H/2,W/2)}$.

The Adaptive Horizontal Lifting Scheme: The input 2D feature map is first split into the even($I_e [n,:] = I [2n,:]$) and odd($I_o [n,:] = I [2n+1,:]$) horizontal components. Then, a horizontal updater(U_h) and a horizontal predictor (P_h) are performed on the split components to generate the approximation L_H and the details H_H sub-bands of the wavelet transformation as follows,

$$L_H [n,:] = I_e [n,:] + U_h (I_o [n,:]) \tag{1}$$

$$H_H [n,:] = I_o [n,:] - P_h (L_H [n,:]) \tag{2}$$

where U_h and P_h are two learnable blocks consisting of convolutional operations as shown in Fig. 1(b), both of which can adaptively optimize their coefficients during training by gradients back-propagation.

The Adaptive Vertical Lifting Scheme: Similar to the adaptive horizontal lifting scheme, take H_H as an example, the input 2D feature map H_H is first split into the even($H_{He} [:,n] = H_H [:,2n]$) and odd($H_{Ho} [:,n] = H_H [:,2n+1]$) vertical components. Then, a vertical updater(U_v) and a vertical predictor (P_v) are performed on the split components to generate the approximation HH and the details HL sub-bands of the wavelet transformation as follows,

$$HL [:,n] = H_{He} [n,:] + U_v (H_{Ho} [n,:]) \tag{3}$$

$$HH [n,:] = H_{Ho} [n,:] - P_v (HL [n,:]) \tag{4}$$

like U_h and P_h, both U_v and P_v are also learnable blocks consisting of convolutional operations as shown in Fig. 1(b), both of which can adaptively optimize their coefficients during training by gradients back-propagation.

It can be seen from Fig. 1 and Eq. (1, 2, 3 and 4) that the input feature map can be down-sampled without lossing any feature information by 2D adaptive lifiting scheme. Finally, **LL** $\in R^{(C,H/2,W/2)}$, **LH** $\in R^{(C,H/2,W/2)}$, **HL** $\in R^{(C,H/2,W/2)}$, and **HH** $\in R^{(C,H/2,W/2)}$ are concatenated fed into a Conv3 × 3 convolutional layer to adaptively fuse the features of different wavelet sub-bands.

2.3 The Adaptive Multi-scale Transformer Module

The large variation in shape and sizes between different retinal lesions result in seriously imbalanced regional ratios, which often causes the problem of target tendency in the training process of the network, and then leads to the reduction of the segmentation performance for the lesions with a small regional proportion. Therefore, it is crucial to improve the model's ability to learn multi-scale global features for accurate segmenting retinal lesions in OCT images. Transformer, with excellent ability to model long-range dependencies for sequence signal, is initially proposed for natural language processing(NLP) tasks [18]. With the remarkable achievements of Transformer in NLP, many researchers have explored the application of transformer in medical image segmentation [2,7]. However, these transformer-based methods mainly focused on exploring single-scale long-dependent global features, ignoring the equally important modeling of multi-scale long-dependent global features in medical images. Therefore, as shown in Fig. 1(c), dedicated to exploring multi-scale global long-dependent feature modeling in retinal OCT images, we propose a novel AMsTrans module appended to the top layer of the encoder path. It can be seen from Fig. 1 that, different from commonly transformer which focusing on single scale features, the proposed AMsTrans module takes feature maps with different scale receptive fields at different stages of encoder path as input. First, the feature maps from level-1(F_1), level-2(F_2), level-3(F_3), and level-4(F_4) are fed into a bilinear interpolation down-sampling module followed by a Conv3 × 3 layer to normalize the resolution and channels to the top layer feature map(F_T). Then, the normalized feature maps(F_1, F_2, F_3, and F_4) and the top layer feature map (F_T) are respectively fed into a self-attention(SA) module, so as to explore the multi-scale long-dependent global features in different receptive fields, which can be analogized to the multi-head SA operation in the common transformer structure, where the SA operation of each scale feature map branch represents a SA head of common transformer. In addition, inspired by artificial neuron(AN) [9], the feature maps with multi-scale long-dependent global features are obtained by weighted sum operation of different SA branch features followed by a Conv3 × 3 feature fusion layer,

$$F_{Ms} = Conv3 \times 3 \left(1 * F_T + \sum_{i=1}^{4} w_i F_i \right) \tag{5}$$

where 1 is analogized to the bias in AN, while w_i is the learnable weights obtained by Conv1 × 1 followed by Sigmoid normalization layer, as shown in Fig. 1(c),

$$W = \text{Sigmoid}\left(Conv1 \times 1 \left(\text{Concat}\left(F_T, F_1, F_2, F_3, F_4\right)\right)\right) \in R^{B,4,H,W} \tag{6}$$

where B, H, and W are the batch size, height and width of the feature maps, respectively. Finally, the residual architecture is constructed by summing F_T with F_{Ms} to further enhance the model's ability to model strong semantic abstract features contained in the top layer, while avoiding the gradient vanishing.

3   Experiments and Results

3.1   Dataset

We systematically evaluate the proposed method on the public database of AI-Challenge 2018 for retinal edema lesions joint segmentation, including the segmentation of retina edema(RE), sub-retinal fluid(SRF), and PED with severely imbalanced regional proportions. The regional ratio of RE, SRF, and PED in this database is counted as 0.8441:0.1493:0.0066, where the proportion of PED is much smaller than RE and SRF, which poses a great challenge to accurate segment PED lesion. The dataset contains 85 retinal OCT cubes (1024 × 512 × 128) with ground truth. We randomly divide the dataset into three exclusive subsets for training, validation, and testing based on 3D cubes with a ratio of 6:2:2. Therefore, the training dataset contains 6528 B-Scan OCT images, while validation and testing contain 2176 B-Scan OCT images, respectively.

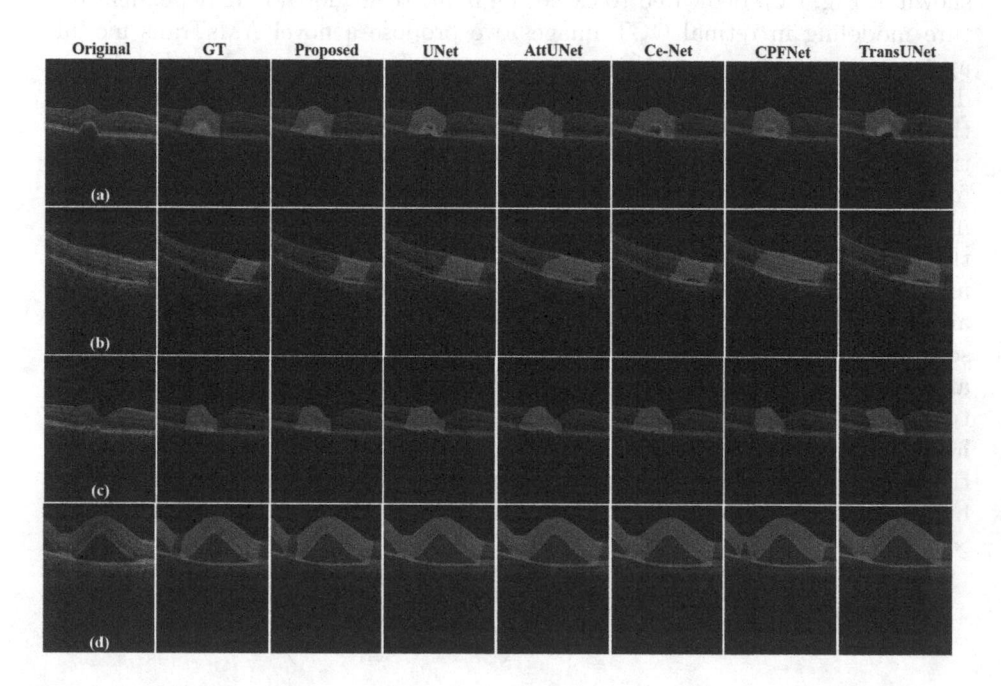

Fig. 2. Segmentation results of different models, where red represents RE, blue is SRF, and green indicates PED. (Color figure online)

3.2   Implementation Detail

For data preprocessing, we resize the retinal OCT B-Scan to 512 × 256 to improve the computational efficiency, while avoiding excessive detail loss and maintaining the average aspect ratio. All experiments involved in this paper were performed on the public platform Pytorch and RTX3090 GPU (24G). All networks are optimized by Adam with the batch size 8 and maximum training epochs of 100. The initial learning rate and weight decay were set to 0.0005 and 0.0001, respectively.

3.3 Comparison Study

As shown in Table 1, the proposed method achieves the highest average jaccard coefficient and dice similarity score of 0.802 and 0.878, respectively. Although the segmentation result of SRF lesion is slightly lower than UNet, the segmentation performance of PED and RE are significantly improved, especially for PED, the jaccard and dice of the proposed method are 20.23% and 17.53% higher than UNet. Meanwhile, compared with AttUnet, which achieves the highest PED lesion segmentation index among all comparison methods, the jaccard and dice indices of PED lesion segmented by the proposed method are improved by 9.68% and 5.96%, respectively. Worth noting that, the segmentation performance of most transformer-based methods degrades in this task. It may be caused by the weak ability of the transformer-based method to model complex local detailed features in OCT images. We also compare with MsTGANet which was designed for the Drusen small object segmentation task in retinal OCT images, and the proposed method also achieves better segmentation performance. Furthermore, Fig. 2 shows the segmentation results of different methods. As shown in Fig. 2, the proposed method obtains better segmentation results than other models, the mis-segmentation and missing-segmentation problems are significantly alleviated, especially for the PED lesion(Fig. 2(a) and Fig. 2(c)). These quantitative and qualitative analysis results show that our proposed method can significantly improve the segmentation performance of tiny-lesion while maintaining the segmentation performance for large regional lesions in retinal OCT images.

Table 1. Quantitative results of different segmentation methods.

Methods	Jaccard			Average	Dice			Average
	PED	SRF	RE		PED	SRF	RE	
UNet [16]	0.603	**0.893**	0.783	0.759	0.696	**0.940**	0.872	0.836
AttUNet [13]	0.661	0.839	0.766	0.755	0.772	0.896	0.863	0.844
Ce-Net [8]	0.474	0.885	0.778	0.712	0.585	0.936	0.870	0.797
CPFNet [5]	0.571	0.888	0.787	0.749	0.681	0.936	0.875	0.831
UNet++ [20]	0.583	0.888	0.787	0.753	0.695	0.937	0.874	0.835
TransUNet [2]	0.611	0.887	0.776	0.758	0.718	0.938	0.870	0.842
UTNet [7]	0.450	0.864	0.710	0.675	0.571	0.923	0.820	0.771
MsTGANet [19]	0.629	0.889	0.782	0.767	0.742	0.937	0.871	0.850
Proposed	**0.725**	0.888	**0.793**	**0.802**	**0.818**	0.937	**0.879**	**0.878**

3.4   Wavelet Feature Representation Visualization

Figure 3 shows the feature reconstruction results of different sub-bands generated by the lifting scheme in different levels. The feature reconstruction results of different sub-bands are very similar to traditional wavelet transformation. It can be seen from Fig. 3 that the PED lesion features and retinal structure information at different levels of the encoder path are preserved and enhanced. The reconstruction results show that the proposed AWDS module can generate a wavelet representation to improve the model's interpretability while avoiding feature loss, and further enhancing the ability of the network to represent local detailed features.

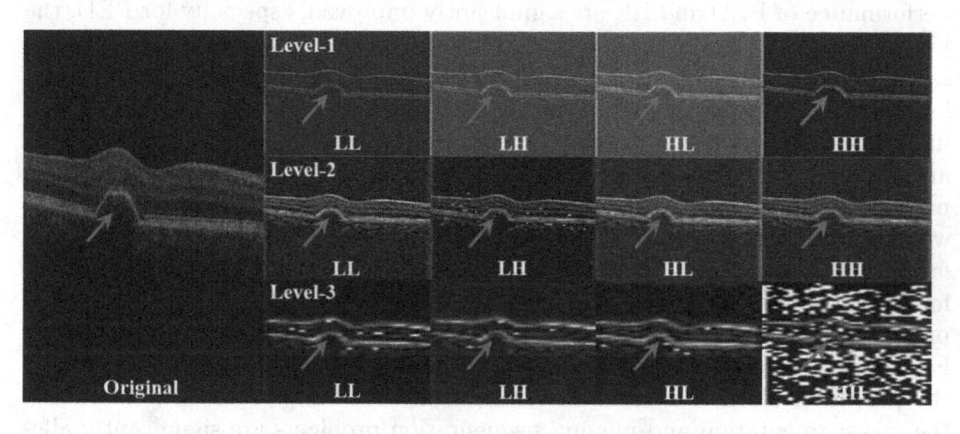

Fig. 3. Wavelet feature representation visualization. Red arrows indicate PED lesions. (Color figure online)

3.5   Ablation Study

We also conducted a variety of ablation studies to validate the effectiveness of the mainly components in the proposed framework, where the modified U-shaped network with pre-trained ResNet blocks and decoder is employed as the 'Backbone' model. Compared with Backbone model, the average jaccard and dice of Backbone+AWDS are improved from 0.755 and 0.844 to 0.781 and 0.860 with 3.44% and 1.90% improvements, respectively. Meanwhile, the average jaccard and dice of the Backbone+AMsTrans achieves 4.24% and 2.49% improvement over Backboned, reaching 0.787 and 0.865, respectively. Finally, the proposed method (Backbone+AWDS+MsA-Trans) achieves the highest average jaccard and dice of 0.802 and 0.878, respectively, which are 6.23% and 4.03% higher than Backbone model. These ablation experiment results demonstrate the effectiveness of the mainly components in the proposed framework.

4 Conclusion

In this paper, focusing on the challenges of the segmentation for retinal lesions in OCT images, we propose a novel multi-scale wavelet enhanced transformer network by integrating CNN, wavelet transformation, and transformer concept for tiny-lesion segmentation in retinal OCT images. Specifically, the pre-trained ResNet blocks combined with the newly proposed AWDS module is designed as the extractor network to capture complicated pathological features in retinal OCT images. Meanwhile, a novel AMsTrans module is developed to further improve the model's capacity to learn multi-scale long-dependent global features. Finally, we evaluate the model's performance by applying the proposed method to a public database: AI-Challenge 2018 for retinal edema lesions joint segmentation, where the proportion between different retinal lesions is severely imbalanced. The experimental results show that, compared with other state-of-the-art segmentation methods, the proposed method can significantly improve the segmentation performance of tiny-lesion while maintaining the segmentation performance for large lesions in retinal OCT images.

In the future, we will collect more retinal OCT data to build a larger and more comprehensive database to further validate the performance of the proposed method. Furthermore, working on improving the efficiency of the proposed model is also an important task in our future research works.

Acknowledgements. This work was supported by A*STAR Advanced Manufacturing and Engineering (AME) Programmatic Fund (A20H4b0141); Exploration Project of Natural Science Foundation of Zhejiang Province(LQ22F010003).

References

1. Abdulrahman, A.A., Rasheed, M., Shihab, S.: The analytic of image processing smoothing spaces using wavelet. In: Journal of Physics: Conference Series, vol. 1879, p. 022118. IOP Publishing (2021)
2. Chen, J., et al.: Transunet: transformers make strong encoders for medical image segmentation. CoRR **abs/2102.04306** (2021). https://arxiv.org/abs/2102.04306
3. Chervyakov, N., Lyakhov, P., Kaplun, D., Butusov, D., Nagornov, N.: Analysis of the quantization noise in discrete wavelet transform filters for image processing. Electronics **7**(8), 135 (2018)
4. Dosovitskiy, A., et al.: An image is worth 16x16 words: transformers for image recognition at scale. arXiv preprint arXiv:2010.11929 (2020)
5. Feng, S., Zhao, H., Shi, F., Cheng, X., Wang, M., Ma, Y., Xiang, D., Zhu, W., Chen, X.: Cpfnet: context pyramid fusion network for medical image segmentation. IEEE Trans. Med. imaging **39**(10), 3008–3018 (2020)
6. Fujieda, S., Takayama, K., Hachisuka, T.: Wavelet convolutional neural networks. arXiv preprint arXiv:1805.08620 (2018)
7. Gao, Y., Zhou, M., Metaxas, D.N.: UTNet: a hybrid transformer architecture for medical image segmentation. In: de Bruijne, M., et al. (eds.) MICCAI 2021. LNCS, vol. 12903, pp. 61–71. Springer, Cham (2021). https://doi.org/10.1007/978-3-030-87199-4_6

8. Gu, Z., et al.: Ce-net: context encoder network for 2d medical image segmentation. IEEE Trans. Med. Imaging **38**(10), 2281–2292 (2019)
9. Harmon, L.D.: Artificial neuron. Science **129**(3354), 962–963 (1959)
10. He, K., Zhang, X., Ren, S., Sun, J.: Deep residual learning for image recognition. In: Proceedings of the IEEE Conference on Computer Vision and Pattern Recognition, pp. 770–778 (2016)
11. Huang, D., et al.: Optical coherence tomography. Sci. (Am. Assoc. Adv. Sci) **254**(5035), 1178–1181 (1991)
12. Liu, Z., et al.: Swin transformer: hierarchical vision transformer using shifted windows. CoRR **abs/2103.14030** (2021), https://arxiv.org/abs/2103.14030
13. Oktay, O., et al.: Attention u-net: learning where to look for the pancreas (2018)
14. Oyallon, E., Belilovsky, E., Zagoruyko, S.: Scaling the scattering transform: deep hybrid networks. In: Proceedings of the IEEE International Conference on Computer Vision, pp. 5618–5627 (2017)
15. Rodriguez, M.X.B., et al.: Deep adaptive wavelet network. In: Proceedings of the IEEE/CVF Winter Conference on Applications of Computer Vision, pp. 3111–3119 (2020)
16. Ronneberger, O., Fischer, P., Brox, T.: U-net: convolutional networks for biomedical image segmentation. In: Navab, N., Hornegger, J., Wells, W.M., Frangi, A.F. (eds.) MICCAI 2015. LNCS, vol. 9351, pp. 234–241. Springer, Cham (2015). https://doi.org/10.1007/978-3-319-24574-4_28
17. Sathiyanathan, N.: Medical image compression using view compensated wavelet transform. J. Glob. Res. Comput. Sci. **9**(9), 01–04 (2018)
18. Vaswani, A., et al.: Attention is all you need. In: Advances in Neural Information Processing Systems, pp. 5998–6008 (2017)
19. Wang, M., et al.: Mstganet: automatic drusen segmentation from retinal oct images. IEEE Trans. Med. Imaging **41**(2), 394–406 (2021)
20. Zhou, Z., Rahman Siddiquee, M.M., Tajbakhsh, N., Liang, J.: UNet++: a nested u-net architecture for medical image segmentation. In: Stoyanov, D., et al. (eds.) DLMIA/ML-CDS -2018. LNCS, vol. 11045, pp. 3–11. Springer, Cham (2018). https://doi.org/10.1007/978-3-030-00889-5_1

Dataset and Evaluation Algorithm Design for GOALS Challenge

Huihui Fang[1], Fei Li[2], Huazhu Fu[3], Junde Wu[1], Xiulan Zhang[2(✉)], and Yanwu Xu[1(✉)]

[1] Intelligent Healthcare Unit, Baidu Inc., Beijing, China
ywxu@ieee.org
[2] State Key Laboratory of Ophthalmology, Zhongshan Ophthalmic Center, Guangdong Provincial Key Laboratory of Ophthalmology and Visual Science, Sun Yat-sen University, Guangzhou, China
zhangxl2@mail.sysu.edu.cn
[3] Institute of High Performance Computing, Agency for Science, Technology and Research, Singapore, Singapore

Abstract. Glaucoma causes irreversible vision loss due to damage to the optic nerve, and there is no cure for glaucoma. OCT imaging modality is an essential technique for assessing glaucomatous damage since it aids in quantifying fundus structures. To promote the research of AI technology in the field of OCT-assisted diagnosis of glaucoma, we held a Glaucoma OCT Analysis and Layer Segmentation (GOALS) Challenge in conjunction with the International Conference on Medical Image Computing and Computer Assisted Intervention (MICCAI) 2022 to provide data and corresponding annotations for researchers studying layer segmentation from OCT images and the classification of glaucoma. This paper describes the released 300 circumpapillary OCT images, the baselines of the two sub-tasks, and the evaluation methodology. The GOALS Challenge is accessible at https://aistudio.baidu.com/aistudio/competition/detail/230.

Keywords: GOALS Challenge · Glaucoma classification · OCT layer segmentation · Circumpapillary OCT

1 Introduction

Glaucoma is a chronic neurodegenerative condition that is one of the leading causes of irreversible blindness in the world. It is a multifactorial optic neuropathy characterized by progressive neurodegeneration of retinal ganglion cells (RGCs) and their axons, resulting in retinal nerve fiber layer (RNFL) attenuation, a specific pattern of damage to the optic nerve head, and visual field loss [1]. In 2020, about 80 million people have glaucoma worldwide [2], and this number is projected to be 111.8 million in 2040 [3]. Optical coherence tomography (OCT) is a powerful tool for diagnosing ocular diseases because of its no radiation, non-invasive, high resolution, high detection sensitivity and other characteristics [4,5]. In contrast to color fundus images, which can only provide information about the surface of the retina, OCT images can provide cross-sectional information about fundus structures. The retinal structures contain RNFL, ganglion cell-inner plexiform layer (GCIPL), inner nuclear layer (INL), outer plexiform layer (OPL), outer nuclear layer (ONL), external limiting membrane (ELM), inner photoreceptor segment, inner/outer photoreceptor segment junction, outer photoreceptor segment, retinal pigment epithelium (RPE) interdigitation, RPE/Bruch's membrane complex, as well as choroid layer [6,7]. In the diagnosis of glaucoma, the disease can be judged by observing changes in the thickness of the optic nerve fiber layer, etc., which is easier to detect early glaucoma than by observing fundus color images. The circumpapillary OCT image corresponds to a circular scan located around the optic nerve head, where a wealth of information about the different retinal layers can be found [8].

Currently, there are only a limited number of OCT datasets [9,10] available in public, to facilitate researchers to conduct research on OCT images, we hold a GOALS Challenge in conjunction with MICCAI 2022, aiming to provide circumpapillary OCT images for studying layer segmentation and glaucoma classification. This paper mainly introduces the 300 circumpapillary OCT images released in the GOALS challenge, and provides baselines for the two sub-tasks (Layer segmentation, and Glaucoma classification). Meanwhile, the evaluation methods are described in detail.

2   Dataset

The 300 circumpapillary OCT images are randomly selected from previous glaucoma study cohorts collected over the past five years in Zhongshan Ophthalmic Center, Sun Yat-sen University, Guangzhou, China. The images are all acquired by using a TOPCON DRI Swept Source OCT [11]. The acquired images are saved in BMP format with a resolution of 1024×247 or in JPG format with 1270×763. In the GOALS Challenge, we store the images in PNG format with a resolution of 1100×800. The summary of the GOALS dataset and its population demographic are shown in Table 1.

Table 1. Summary of the GOALS dataset and the demographic of the population.

		Person	Eyes	Age	Gender (Female)
Total dataset	Total	66	99	45.91±15.04	36.40%
	Glaucoma	13	22	44.59±12.77	30.80%
Training set	Total	16	24	39.08±14.08	31.30%
	Glaucoma	4	7	40.86±9.23	25%
Preliminary set	Total	19	30	44.8±16.32	42.11%
	Glaucoma	4	7	42.92±17.09	75%
Final set	Total	31	45	50.05±14.48	35.50%
	Glaucoma	5	8	50±8.48	0%

The GOALS dataset provides the glaucoma labels and the segmentation masks of RNFL, GCIPL and choriod layers in the circumpapillary OCT images. The glaucoma labels are determined by the clinical records, which can reflect the findings from a series of eye examinations. The annotations of the layer segmentation are manually marked by the ophthalmologists of the iChallenge-GOALS study group. The iChallenge-GOALS study group contains ten ophthalmologists from different hospitals who have been working in the ocular field for 5 years or more. The 300 images are randomly divided into 2 subsets, and repeating this operation 5 times, we obtain 10 subsets of the data, where each image appears in 5 different subsets. The 10 subsets are randomly assigned to the 10 ophthalmologists, that is, each image is labeled by 5 different ophthalmologists. The results of the 5 initial labeling results are then aggregated by a more senior ophthalmologist for fusion. Specifically, The ophthalmologist need to delineate the upper and lower margin of the RNFL, GCIPL and choroid regions, as shown in Fig. 1(A). After that, the senior ophthalmologist analyze the 5 initial annotations of each image, remove the annotations with large deviations, and average the remaining initial annotations as the final annotation result for each image. We then assign different pixel values to pixels within the boundaries of RNFL, GCIPL and choroid layer to obtain the final ground truths of the layer segmentation (RNFL: 0, GCIPL:80, choroid:160, elsewhere:255, as shown in Fig. 1(B)).

In GOALS Challenge, 300 images are divided into three partitions according to the patient dimension, i.e. the images acquired from the same patient's eyes are guaranteed to be divided into the same partition. These three data partitions correspond to the training set, the preliminary set, and the final set. The data in the training set contains the original OCT images and their glaucoma labels and layer segmentation masks, which are used for training models. While the preliminary and final sets only contain the original OCT images, which are used for testing models in preliminary and final rounds.

3 Baseline

We design a baseline model for each of the two challenge sub-tasks. As shown in Figs. 2 and 3, we utilize a U-shape network with residual concept to achieve the layer segmentation, and utilize a ResNet50 to perform the glaucoma classification. The baseline codes are available at https://aistudio.baidu.com/aistudio/competition/detail/230/0/related-material.

We implement the baselines via PaddlePaddle. During training, we use an Adam optimizer with learning rate $= 10^{-3}$ in the layer segmentation task, as well as with learning rate $= 10^{-6}$ in the glaucoma classification task. The training procedure consist of 3000 iterations and 1000 iterations for layer segmentation and glaucoma classification with a Nvidia Tesla V100-SXM2 GPU, respectively. The batch sizes are 8 for both tasks.

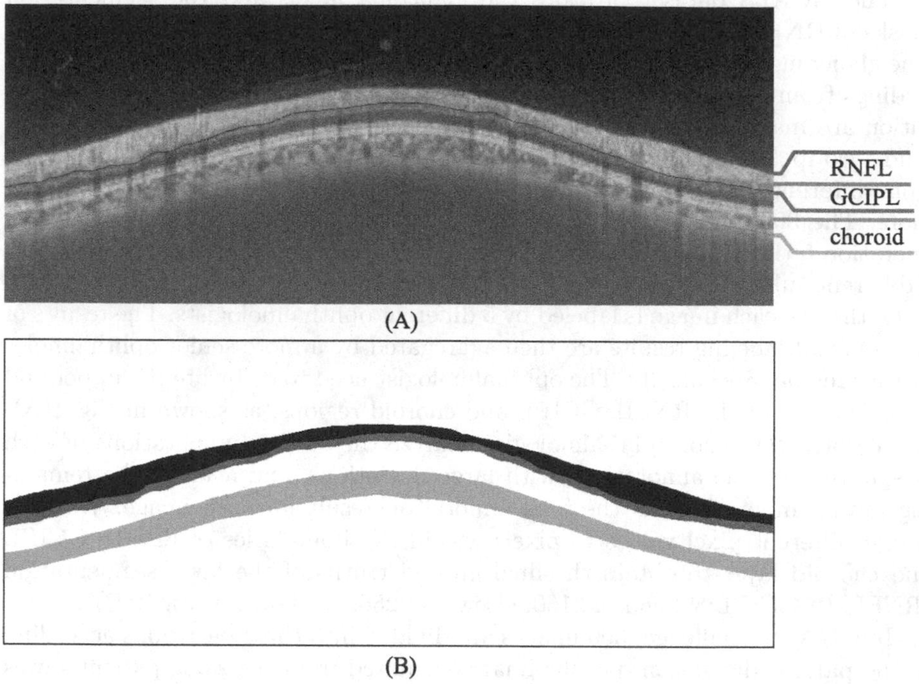

RNFL
GCIPL
choroid

(A)

(B)

Fig. 1. Schematic diagram of the annotations for RNFL, GCIPL, and choroid layer segmentation. (A) Annotations for the boundaries of the targets; (B) Segmentation masks.

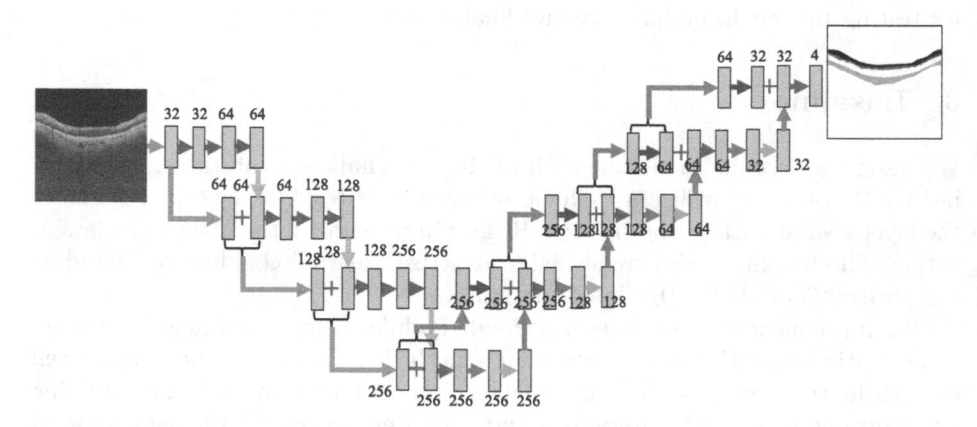

➤ Conv <3×3, stride=2> with Batch Normalization and ReLU   ➤ Conv2DTranspose with Batch Normalization   ➤ ReLU
➤ Conv <3×3> with Batch Normalization and ReLU   ➤ Max Pooling   ➤ Conv <3×3> with Batch Normalization
+ Element-wise add   ➤ Conv2DTranspose with Batch Normalization and ReLU   ➤ Upsample   ➤ Conv <1×1>

Fig. 2. A baseline framework for OCT layer segmentation.

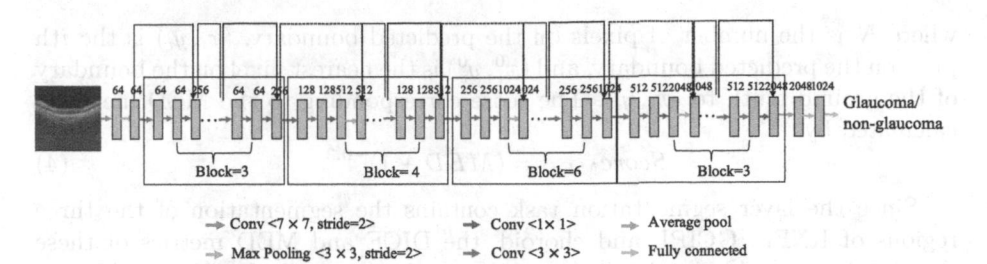

Fig. 3. A baseline framework for glaucoma classification.

4 Evaluation

In this section, we introduce the evaluation metrics for the two challenge sub-tasks. For the layer segmentation task, a DICE coefficient and a mean Euclidean distance (MED) are used to evaluate the predicted region and boundary, respectively. For the glaucoma classification, the weighted combination of sensitivity (Sen), specificity (Spe), accuracy (Acc), F_1 score, and area under the receiver operating characteristic curve (AUC) are utilized to evaluate the predicted results.

4.1 Task 1: Layer Segmentation

To measure the accuracy of the predicted region, we use the frequently-used DICE coefficient in the segmentation task:

$$Dice = \frac{2|X \cap Y|}{|X| + |Y|} \qquad (1)$$

where, X represents the segmented target pixel point set in the ground truth; Y represents the segmented pixel point set in the prediction result; $|X \cap Y|$ represents the intersection between X and Y; $|X|$ and $|Y|$ represent the number of the elements of X and Y. The formula for calculating the score corresponding to the DICE metric is

$$Score_{Dice} = DICE \times 10 \qquad (2)$$

In addition to evaluating the accuracy of the region segmentation, we also evaluate the accuracy of the boundary of the segmentation results by using Euclidean distance, due to the importance of the boundaries between the structural layers in the OCT images. Specifically, we first traverse each pixel on the predicted boundary, and calculate the Euclidean distance from each pixel to the nearest pixel on the gold standard boundary. Then the sum of the above Euclidean distances is averaged based on the number of pixels on the predicted boundary:

$$MED = \frac{1}{N} \sum_{i=1}^{N} \sqrt{(x_i - x_i^0)^2 + (y_i - y_i^0)^2} \qquad (3)$$

where N is the number of pixels on the predicted boundary, (x_i, y_i) is the ith pixel on the predicted boundary, and (x_i^0, y_i^0) is the nearest pixel on the boundary of the ground truth to (x_i, y_i). The score corresponding to the MED metric is calculated by

$$Score_{MED} = (MED + 1)^{-0.3} \tag{4}$$

Since the layer segmentation task contains the segmentation of the three regions of RNFL, GCIPL and choroid, the DICE and MED metrics of these three regions should be taken into account in the score calculation. In addition, because the RNFL layer is more important for the diagnosis of glaucoma, we assign higher weights to the scores obtained from RNFL segmentation:

$$Score_{task1} = 0.4 \times Score_{RNFL} + 0.3 \times Score_{GCIPL} + 0.3 \times Score_{choroid} \tag{5}$$

$$Score_{region} = 0.5 \times Score_{DICE_{region}} + 0.5 \times Score_{MED_{region}}, \\ region \in \{RNFL, GCIPL, choroid\} \tag{6}$$

4.2   Task 2: Glaucoma Classification

For glaucoma classification, we adopt five common metrics including Sen, Spe, Acc, F_1, and AUC:

$$Sen = \frac{TP}{TP + FN} \tag{7}$$

$$Spe = \frac{TN}{TP + FP} \tag{8}$$

$$Acc = \frac{TP + TN}{TP + FN + TN + FP} \tag{9}$$

$$F_1 = \frac{2 \times TP}{2 \times TP + FP + FN} \tag{10}$$

where TP, TN, FP and FN represent the numbers of true positive, true negative, false positive, and false negative detection of the glaucoma. Sen, Spe and Acc can reflect the proportions of positive samples, negative samples and all samples predicted correctly, respectively. F_1 provides a overall metric of the model's ability to detect comprehensively and accurately. And AUC reflects the classification ability of the model when the positive and negative samples are unbalanced. In our evaluation framework, these metrics are implemented via scikit-learn package [12], which is an open source machine learning toolkit base on Python. Since the GOALS dataset has a balanced distribution of positive and negative samples, we assign the lowest weight to the AUC metric in the score calculation.

$$Score_{task2} = (0.1 \times AUC + 0.25 \times Sen + 0.25 \times Spe + 0.2 \times ACC + 0.2 \times F_1) \times 10 \tag{11}$$

Based on the results of the baseline model, we find that positive and negative samples in the GOALS dataset have obvious distinguishable image features, and therefore score high in Task 2. Hence, for preliminary and final rounds, a lower weight is assigned to Task 2 in the score calculation:

$$Score_{round} = 0.8 \times Score_{task1} + 0.2 \times Score_{task2},$$
$$round \in \{preliminary, final\} \tag{12}$$

Since the preliminary leaderboard is visible to the players, one can adjust the model parameters or strategies to get the best prediction on the preliminary set. To avoid players' results from getting overfitting results on the preliminary set and getting high scores, we assign lower weights to the preliminary score when counting the total challenge scores. Hence, the total score is:

$$Score = 0.3 \times Score_{preliminary} + 0.7 \times Score_{final} \tag{13}$$

Based on the evaluation criteria, our baselines receive 7.2802 score on the preliminary set and 7.2398 score on the final set. The results of each specific evaluation index are shown in Table. 2.

Table 2. The evaluation results of the baseline model on different datasets.

Dataset		Preliminary set	Final set
Score		7.2802	7.2398
Layer Segmentation	RNFL_DICE	0.8161	0.8433
	RNFL_ED	4.0597	4.151
	GCIPL_DICE	0.6295	0.6234
	GCIPL_ED	3.318	3.6011
	choroid_DICE	0.8193	0.8746
	choroid_ED	8.9155	9.8953
Glaucoma Classification	AUC	0.9984	0.9927
	F1	0.9346	0.8829
	ACC	0.93	0.8687
	SEN	1	1
	SPE	0.86	0.74

5 Conclusion

In this paper, we introduce the GOALS Challenge at MICCAI 2022. In the challenge, we focus on OCT which is a powerful imaging technology for glaucoma diagnostics. We design two challenge sub-tasks, including OCT layer segmentation of RNFL, GCIPL and choroid, and glaucoma classification. The dataset collection and labeling process, as well as the result evaluation design are described in detail in the paper. GOALS Challenge dataset and evaluation framework are publicly accessible through the AI Studio website at https://aistudio.baidu.com/aistudio/competition/detail/230. Participants are welcome to join the GOALS Challenge and submit their predicted results on the website.

References

1. Sehi, M., et al.: Retinal nerve fiber layer atrophy is associated with visual field loss over time in glaucoma suspect and glaucomatous eyes. Am. J. Ophthalmol. **155**(1), 73–82 (2013)
2. Glaucoma: Facts and figures. https://www.brightfocus.org/glaucoma/article/glaucoma-facts-figures
3. Tham, Y.C., Li, X., Wong, T.Y., Quigley, H.A., Aung, T., Cheng, C.Y.: Global prevalence of glaucoma and projections of glaucoma burden through 2040: a systematic review and meta-analysis. Ophthalmology **121**(11), 2081–2090 (2014)
4. Puzyeyeva, O., et al.: High-resolution optical coherence tomography retinal imaging: a case series illustrating potential and limitations. J. Ophthalmol. **2011** (2011)
5. Yaqoob, Z., Jigang, W., Yang, C.: Spectral domain optical coherence tomography: a better oct imaging strategy. Biotechniques **39**(6), S6–S13 (2005)
6. Mohandass, G., Natarajan, R.A., Sendilvelan, S.: Retinal layer segmentation in pathological SD-OCT images using boisterous obscure ratio approach and its limitation. Biomed. Pharmacol. J. **10**(3), 1585–1591 (2017)
7. Medeiros, F.A., et al.: Detection of glaucoma progression with stratus oct retinal nerve fiber layer, optic nerve head, and macular thickness measurements. Invest. Ophthalmol. Vis. Sci. **50**(12), 5741–5748 (2009)
8. García, G., del Amor, R., Colomer, A., Naranjo, V.: Glaucoma detection from raw circumpapillary oct images using fully convolutional neural networks. In 2020 IEEE International Conference on Image Processing (ICIP), pp. 2526–2530. IEEE (2020)
9. Rasti, R., Rabbani, H., Mehridehnavi, A., Hajizadeh, F.: Macular oct classification using a multi-scale convolutional neural network ensemble. IEEE Trans. Med. Imaging **37**(4), 1024–1034 (2017)
10. Gholami, P., Roy, P., Parthasarathy, M.K., Lakshminarayanan, V.: OCTID: optical coherence tomography image database. Comput. Electr. Eng. **81**, 106532 (2020)
11. Dri oct triton series. https://topconhealthcare.eu/uploads/media/60cb7b98ea585/topcon-triton-brochure-rev5-27-05-21-e325-lores.pdf
12. Pedregosa, F., et al.: Scikit-learn: machine learning in python. J. Mach. Learn. Res. **12**, 2825–2830 (2011)

Self-supervised Learning for Anomaly Detection in Fundus Image

Sangil Ahn and Jitae Shin[✉]

Department of Electrical and Computer Engineering, SungKyunKwan University,
Suwon 16419, Republic of Korea
{il2s,jtshin}@skku.edu

Abstract. Since medical data with different characteristics can be observed even with the same disease in a clinical environment, an anomaly detection algorithm should be well applied to medical data that are not seen. Focusing on a fact that an object photograph consists of reflectance and illumination information, we propose a new data augmentation method that can change illumination information for creating a new fundus image by preserving the reflectance information including the disease lesion information. Then our framework which is trained with only normal data during training employs a reconstruction manner with a self-supervised learning technique capable of identifying anomalous images. Based on the reconstruction manner, our model is trained to reconstruct the reflectance image, not the original image to leverage the useful information which is the main component of the fundus image. Furthermore, in order to boost the anomaly detection capability of our proposal, we propose a pretext task for a self-supervised learning manner to reduce intra-class variance by considering the distance of each feature representation. An anomaly score, as a measure to classify the anomalous data, is constructed based on the reconstruction error between the original image and the reconstructed image. In addition, We extensively evaluate our framework on the diabetic retinopathy fundus dataset. The results demonstrate our framework's superiority over the latest state-of-the-art methods.

Keywords: Self-supervised learning · Anomaly detection · Fundus image

1 Introduction

Clinically, anomaly detection of image-based biomarker [6–8] correlated with disease information to determine patient status is an important task. In order to diagnose the status of the retina, a fundus image is one of the standard methods widely used to observe diseases that cause blindness, such as Diabetic Retinopathy [5].

Although deep learning-based studies that are helpful for the identification of image-based biomarker in a clinical environment have shown high-accuracy

© The Author(s), under exclusive license to Springer Nature Switzerland AG 2022
B. Antony et al. (Eds.): OMIA 2022, LNCS 13576, pp. 143–151, 2022.
https://doi.org/10.1007/978-3-031-16525-2_15

research results, many studies are based on annotation information. However two limitations can arise in research based on medical data with expert annotations that can derive high performance. First, the acquisition of abnormal data is more difficult than normal data that it is difficult to obtain sufficient characteristics of data required to distinguish between normal and abnormal. Second, it can have a much greater variety of features (e.g., size, shape, color) in unseen medical data that can be encountered in an actual clinical environment compared to observable features from the data used in learning. In other words, various features of anomalies which can be occurred make it difficult to accurately identify the biomarker by methods built on the basis of annotation.

The main focus of this paper is to propose an anomaly image-based biomarker method based on a reconstruction approach with a self-supervised learning manner to have a capability about distinction between normal and abnormal data by considering the possible problems. The main contribution of this work can be summarized into four-fold:

1. A novel reconstruction model is presented by exploiting a self-supervised method to aid image-based biomarker to detect anomalies that are not seen through the use of only normal data during training.
2. Based on the fact that objects can be divided into reflectance and illumination information, we propose an augmentation method to generate a new augmented fundus image by preserving the reflectance information.
3. Our model is to reconstruct the reflectance image from which illumination information has been removed so that we learn the representation of required features to reconstruct data regardless of less useful information.
4. Pretext task technique with a self-supervised learning manner based on the semi-hard negative mining strategy is combined in our framework to control the distance of intra-class variance, which further boosts the anomaly detection performance.

2   Methodology

2.1   Illumination Information Change Augmentation

Medical data such as fundus images with different illumination information can be obtained depending on the difference in the amount of light through the aperture between the person and the measuring equipment. Even the data obtained from the same person may have different illumination information. Since color information may vary depending on the observation method, the features constituting the image may be more important in medical data such as fundus images. In consideration of the fact and focusing the object photograph can be divided into two elements: reflectance and illumination information [11], we make a division algorithm to get the reflectance image and illumination image from the fundus image and construct a new fundus image that is changed the illumination information, with reflectance information fixed as shown the Fig. 1.

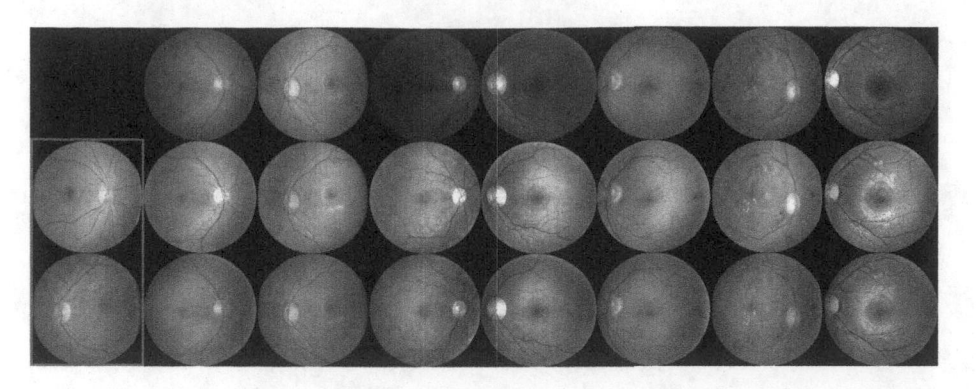

Fig. 1. Example of fundus images observed in an actual clinical environment. First row: fundus images with various illumination information. Second and Third row: new fundus images in which the illumination information of the image in the first line has been changed using the illumination information of the fundus image in the red box. (Color figure online)

2.2   Reconstruction for Reflectance Image

We first prepare two different fundus images x^1, x^2 to obtain a reflectance image and an illumination image from each image by applying the division algorithm (**yellow lines** on the Fig. 2). Then, as shown **blue lines** in Fig. 2, we make a new normal fundus image x^3 that has the reflectance information same with the image x^1 and the illumination information same with the image x^2. Eventually, we regard the new fundus image x^3 as an original fundus image as well as the fundus images x^1 and x^2. A little difference from the recent anomaly detection based on the reconstruction approach is to restore input to the original image. In order to encourage a model to fully exploit the feature representation exactly from the normal fundus image, we let our model M restore the reflectance image from the original image by giving less consideration to the information of illumination. In other words, since our model exploit the reflectance information, illumination information that can occur in a clinical environment is not significantly affected by various problems for our model. Particularly, even if the image x^3 has the illumination information of the fundus image x^2, our model is trained to restore the reflectance image $x^3_{r_1}{'}$ to have a characteristic similar to x_{r_1} based on embedded feature representation $z^3_{r_1}$ which indicate the encoded reflectance information through an encoder M_E. Then, x^1 and x^2 also are embedded into feature space to get the representations $z^1_{r_1}$ and $z^2_{r_2}$ through the encoder, and based on these, $x^{1}_{r_1}{'}$ and $x^{2}_{r_2}{'}$ are generated, respectively. Finally, as shown Fig. 2, the reconstructed reflectance images $x^{1}_{r_1}{'}$, $x^{3}_{r_1}{'}$, and $x^{2}_{r_2}{'}$ are converted into the reconstructed fundus images $x^{1}{'}$, $x^{3}{'}$, and $x^{2}{'}$ by combining the illumination information extracted from original fundus image x^1 or x^2 corresponding to the same reflectance information.

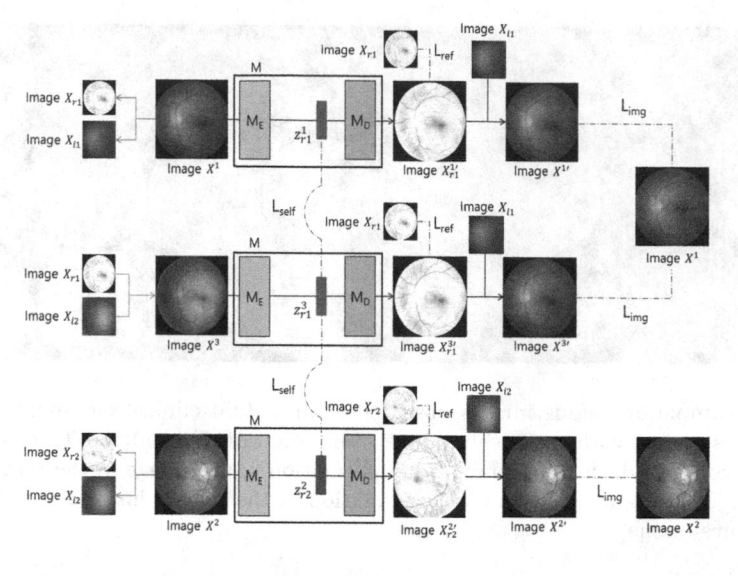

Fig. 2. Overview of the proposed methodology with self-supervised learning.

We employ the reconstruction process not only to compare the reconstructed fundus images x' and original fundus images x but also to compare the reconstructed reflectance images x'_r and original reflectance images x_r. To train our model based on the reconstruction process, the reconstruction loss function is defined as:

$$\mathcal{L}_{ref} = \left\| x_{r_1}^{1'} - x_{r_1} \right\| + \left\| x_{r_1}^{3'} - x_{r_1} \right\| + \left\| x_{r_2}^{2'} - x_{r_2} \right\| \tag{1}$$

$$\mathcal{L}_{img} = \| x'_1 - x_1 \| + \| x'_3 - x_1 \| + \| x'_2 - x_2 \| \tag{2}$$

$$\mathcal{L}_{rec} = \mathcal{L}_{ref} + \mathcal{L}_{img} \tag{3}$$

2.3 Semi-hard Negative Mining Strategy

In order for our model to estimate anomaly by reconstructing manner, the model needs to be trained to minimize the intra-class variance of feature representations. However, even though the intra-class variance is minimized, similar features should be embedded close to each other, and those with relatively different features should be embedded far away in the distribution of intra-class. In order to improve our model capability for detecting anomalies by considering both the intra-class variance and the distance of embedded feature representation, we leverage a pretext task based on a self-supervised learning technique with the semi-hard negative mining strategy [10] to assist the reconstruction process. We define the new fundus image x^3 as an anchor image, the fundus image x^1 which has the same reflectance information of the anchor image as a positive image, and the fundus image x^2 which has different reflectance information of the anchor image as a negative image. The three images are passed through the encoder M_E

to represent the feature of reflectance in the feature space, respectively. At this time, we embed a negative features representation $z_{r_2}^2$ through the encoder to closer to the anchor features representation $z_{r_1}^3$ in the feature space, but further than the positive features representation $z_{r_1}^1$, but closer than the positive feature representation $z_{r_1}^1$ with margin α: $\|z_{r_1}^3 - z_{r_1}^1\| < \|z_{r_1}^3 - z_{r_2}^2\| < \|z_{r_1}^3 - z_{r_1}^1\| + \alpha$. With this strategy, we train our modified mapping function by the encoder M_E with the following triplet loss:

$$\mathcal{L}_{self} = \mathbf{d}_1 + \begin{cases} 0, & \mathbf{d}_1 \leq \mathbf{d}_2 \leq \mathbf{d}_1 + \alpha \\ \mathbf{d}_2 - \mathbf{d}_1, & \mathbf{d}_1 + \alpha \leq \mathbf{d}_2 \\ \mathbf{d}_1 + \alpha - \mathbf{d}_2, & \mathbf{d}_2 \leq \mathbf{d}_1 \end{cases} \tag{4}$$

where $\mathbf{d}_1$ and $\mathbf{d}_2$ denote the Euclidean distances of the positive feature $z_{r_1}^1$ and negative feature $z_{r_2}^2$ to anchor feature $z_{r_1}^3$, respectively. Therefore we train our model to embed the feature representations with small intra-class variance by considering the relative distance between feature representations.

Finally, with the previously defined loss functions, the overall training loss is defined as:

$$\mathcal{L} = \mathcal{L}_{rec} + \mathcal{L}_{self} \tag{5}$$

3   Experiments and Result

3.1   Dataset

We perform experiments on the EyePACS dataset [2] which has the largest publicly-accessible dataset for classifying the grade information of fundus images. However, some fundus images have the problem of the variation in the quality that can be considered anomaly data. Thus we employ the EyeQ [3] dataset which is a subset of EyePACS and has fundus image quality grading information. By excluding the low-quality fundus images, we set a training dataset consisting of 11,892 fundus images with only normal class and a validation dataset consisting of 832 fundus images with mixed-status both normal and abnormal.

3.2   Anomaly Score

In the testing phase, a test image x^t is fed to our model, M, which yields a reconstructed reflectance image $x_r^{t'}$. Then, we generate the reconstructed fundus image $x^{t'}$. Compared with the original image and the reconstructed image in both the reflectance-based and the fundus-based, respectively, we calculate the reconstruction error namely anomaly score. The anomaly score will be low if the fundus image with no anomaly will be restored similar to the input, but on the contrary, the anomaly score will be high if the fundus image with anomalies will be restored differently from the input. Based on the anomaly score, we classify the input data whether the normal or the abnormal.

Table 1. Ablation study results for three major components of our proposal.

Methods	Ablation	Precision	Sensitivity	Specificity	AUC
Color distortion	1	0.5860	0.5563	0.5647	0.6244
Cutout	1	0.5318	0.5197	0.5214	0.5406
Sobel filtering	1	0.5723	0.5446	0.5726	0.6091
Local pixel shuffling	1	0.5632	0.5399	0.5732	0.6098
Fundus image reconstruction	2	0.5751	0.5586	0.5709	0.6343
Without strategy	3	0.5690	0.5517	0.5720	0.6272
Hard negative mining strategy	3	0.5612	0.5521	0.5542	0.6129
Ours		0.5889	0.5670	0.5949	0.6550

3.3 Ablation Study

This comparison aims at investigating whether our framework can be an evaluation model for the anomaly detection task or not. We first delineate the contribution of our proposal via ablation studies of the three major components of our model: illumination information change, reflectance image reconstruction, and semi-hard negative mining strategy.

Illumination Information Change. In order to demonstrate that illumination information change has the advantage for pretext tasks with self-supervised learning, we first keep our model learning scheme and compare the different augmentation methods for pretext tasks. The result is shown in the second to fifth rows in Table 1. For the pretext task for self-supervised learning, the illumination information change leads to signification better performance. Furthermore, from this comparison result, we can infer that from the pretext task set up to do self-supervised learning well, the best result can be derived when the physical properties of the object remain unchanged as much as possible.

Reflectance Image Reconstruction. The sixth row in the Table 1 is the performance if our model restores the fundus image directly. This suggests that generating the original image can impair the capability of the model to perform anomaly detection, given that the fundus image with various illumination can occur in the clinical environment.

Semi-hard Negative Mining Strategy. If the normal data is only used to perform anomaly detection, the intra-class variance of the extracted features must be small. As shown in the seventh and eighth rows in Table 1, the use of semi-hard negative mining which consider the distance between the feature representations resulted in the best results, even though the use of a simple hard negative mining strategy can lead to worse performance than not being used.

3.4 Comparison with the State-of-the-Arts(SOTA)

We compared our proposal with representative SOTA researches which worked in the field of ophthalmology for anomaly detection. The abnormality of the

Table 2. Performance of the comparison with SOTA for DR anomaly detection.

Methods	Precision	Sensitivity	Specificity	AUC
AutoEncoder [1]	0.4920	0.4870	0.4734	0.4777
F-AnoGAN [9]	0.5303	0.5188	0.5263	0.5384
SALAD [12]	0.5264	0.5274	0.5232	0.5572
Lesion2Void [4]	0.5680	0.5548	0.5664	0.6237
Ours	0.5889	0.5670	0.5949	0.6550

data was determined using the anomaly score derived from each model. Experimental results identify the effectiveness of the reconstruction approach based on reflectance information with the self-supervised technique in Table 2 and Fig. 3. Furthermore, as shown Fig. 4, our model can distinguish the distinction between the normal and the abnormal based on the anomaly score. Even though the F-AnoGAN and SALAD researches are exploited for retinal status evaluation with optical coherence tomography (OCT), compared with researches (Lesion2Void, Ours), it can be observed that it's not suitable for the anomaly detection task with fundus image.

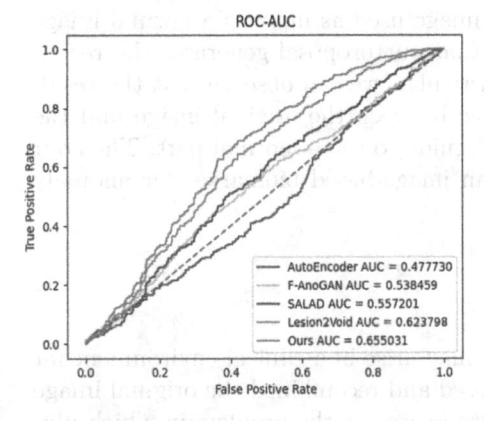

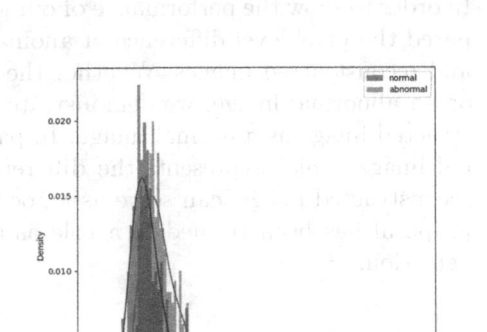

Fig. 3. Demonstration of ROC Curves. We demonstrate that our proposal's AUC value is the highest compared to other methods.

Fig. 4. The histogram of anomaly scores for DR. We can observe that the distribution of anomaly scores of both normal and abnormal is different.

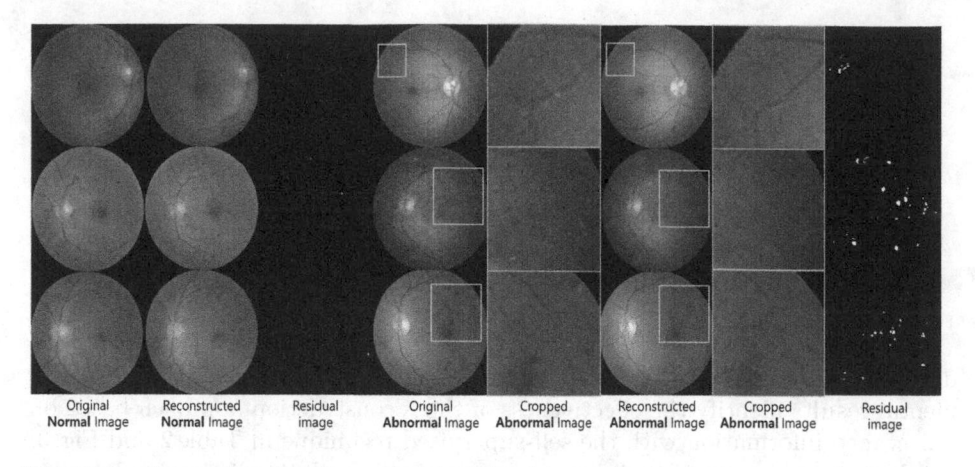

| Original
Normal Image | Reconstructed
Normal Image | Residual
image | Original
Abnormal Image | Cropped
Abnormal Image | Reconstructed
Abnormal Image | Cropped
Abnormal Image | Residual
image |

Fig. 5. Qualitative results of our model on the dataset for fundus images including two example images for normal and abnormal, respectively.

3.5   Qualitative Analysis

In order to show the performance of our proposal, we present a qualitatively compared the pixel-level difference of anomaly localization between original images and reconstructed images. Whether the image used as input is a normal image or an abnormal image, we demonstrate that our proposal generates the reconstructed image as a normal image. In particular, we can observe that the residual image, which represents the difference between the original image and the reconstructed image, can serve as a good guide to the abnormal part. Thus our proposal has been trained to a role as an image-based biomarker for anomaly detection.

4   Conclusion

This paper is to study the problems that may arise in a clinical environment for the anomaly detection task. We decomposed and recombined the original image into reflectance and illumination images to overcome the problem in which illumination information varies depending on the method of acquisition in a clinical environment. We propose a framework that is trained with only normal data based on the reconstruction manner for anomaly detection of fundus images. In order to pay attention to the feature representation of normal data, unlike other reconstruction-based models, we employ a technique of reproducing, not original images, but reflectance images with the exclusion of illumination information that can degrade the model's performance. Furthermore, we employ the self-supervised learning technique to fully exploit useful information from the feature representations by considering the distance within the distribution of intra-class. Furthermore, the experiments have proved that our framework can be used as a biomarker for fundus images.

Acknowledgements. This research was supported by the MSIT(Ministry of Science and ICT), Korea, under the ITRC(Information Technology Research Center) support program(IITP-2022-0-01798) supervised by the IITP(Institute for Information & Communications Technology Planning & Evaluation).

References

1. Chen, Z., Yeo, C.K., Lee, B.S., Lau, C.T.: Autoencoder-based network anomaly detection. In: 2018 Wireless Telecommunications Symposium (WTS), pp. 1–5 (2018). https://doi.org/10.1109/WTS.2018.8363930
2. Cuadros, J., Bresnick, G.: EyePACS: an adaptable telemedicine system for diabetic retinopathy screening. J. Diab. Sci. Technol. **3**(3), 509–516 (2009). https://doi.org/10.1177/193229680900300315. pMID: 20144289
3. Fu, H., et al.: Evaluation of retinal image quality assessment networks in different color-spaces. In: Shen, D., et al. (eds.) MICCAI 2019. LNCS, vol. 11764, pp. 48–56. Springer, Cham (2019). https://doi.org/10.1007/978-3-030-32239-7_6
4. Huang, Y., Huang, W., Luo, W., Tang, X.: Lesion2void: unsupervised anomaly detection in fundus images. In: 2022 IEEE 19th International Symposium on Biomedical Imaging (ISBI), pp. 1–5 (2022). https://doi.org/10.1109/ISBI52829.2022.9761593
5. Leasher, J.L., et al.: Global estimates on the number of people blind or visually impaired by diabetic retinopathy: a meta-analysis from 1990 to 2010. Diab. Care **39**(9), 1643–1649 (2016). https://doi.org/10.2337/dc15-2171
6. Lee, G., et al.: Radiomics and its emerging role in lung cancer research, imaging biomarkers and clinical management: State of the art. Eur. J. Radiol. **86**, 297–307 (2017). https://doi.org/10.1016/j.ejrad.2016.09.005, https://www.sciencedirect.com/science/article/pii/S0720048X16302741
7. Markan, A., Agarwal, A., Arora, A., Bazgain, K., Rana, V., Gupta, V.: Novel imaging biomarkers in diabetic retinopathy and diabetic macular edema. Ther. Adv. Ophthalmol. **12**, 2515841420950513 (2020). https://doi.org/10.1177/2515841420950513. pMID: 32954207
8. Martí Bonmatí, L.: Imaging biomarkers, quantitative imaging, and bioengineering. Radiología (Engl. Ed.) **54**(3), 269–278 (2012). https://doi.org/10.1016/j.rxeng.2012.05.001, https://www.sciencedirect.com/science/article/pii/S2173510712000675
9. Schlegl, T., Seeböck, P., Waldstein, S.M., Langs, G., Schmidt-Erfurth, U.: f-AnoGAN: fast unsupervised anomaly detection with generative adversarial networks. Med. Image Anal. **54**, 30–44 (2019). https://doi.org/10.1016/j.media.2019.01.010, https://www.sciencedirect.com/science/article/pii/S1361841518302640
10. Schroff, F., Kalenichenko, D., Philbin, J.: Facenet: A unified embedding for face recognition and clustering. In: Proceedings of the IEEE Conference on Computer Vision and Pattern Recognition (CVPR) (2015)
11. Tu, G.J., Karstoft, H., Pedersen, L.J., Jørgensen, E.: Illumination and reflectance estimation with its application in foreground detection. Sensors **15**(9), 21407–21426 (2015). https://doi.org/10.3390/s150921407, https://www.mdpi.com/1424-8220/15/9/21407
12. Zhao, H., Li, Y., He, N., Ma, K., Fang, L., Li, H., Zheng, Y.: Anomaly detection for medical images using self-supervised and translation-consistent features. IEEE Trans. Med. Imaging **40**(12), 3641–3651 (2021). https://doi.org/10.1109/TMI.2021.3093883

GARDNet: Robust Multi-view Network for Glaucoma Classification in Color Fundus Images

Ahmed Al-Mahrooqi$^{(\boxtimes)}$ ⓘ, Dmitrii Medvedev ⓘ, Rand Muhtaseb ⓘ,
and Mohammad Yaqub ⓘ

Mohamed bin Zayed University of Artificial Intelligence, Abu Dhabi, UAE
{ahmed.mahrooqi,mohammad.yaqub}@mbzuai.ac.ae

Abstract. Glaucoma is one of the most severe eye diseases, characterized by rapid progression and leading to irreversible blindness. It is often the case that diagnostics is carried out when one's sight has already significantly degraded due to the lack of noticeable symptoms at early stage of the disease. Regular glaucoma screenings of the population shall improve early-stage detection, however the desirable frequency of etymological checkups is often not feasible due to the excessive load imposed by manual diagnostics on limited number of specialists. Considering the basic methodology to detect glaucoma is to analyze fundus images for the *optic-disc-to-optic-cup ratio*, Machine Learning algorithms can offer sophisticated methods for image processing and classification. In our work, we propose an advanced image pre-processing technique combined with a multi-view network of deep classification models to categorize glaucoma. Our *Glaucoma Automated Retinal Detection Network (GARDNet)* has been successfully tested on Rotterdam EyePACS AIROGS dataset with an AUC of 0.92, and then additionally fine-tuned and tested on RIM-ONE DL dataset with an AUC of 0.9308 outperforming the state-of-the-art of 0.9272. Our code is available on https://github.com/ahmed1996said/gardnet

Keywords: Glaucoma classification · Color fundus images · Computer aided diagnosis · Deep learning

1 Introduction

Glaucoma is an eye disease which is considered the leading cause of blindness. It is caused by an increased pressure in the eyes as a result of fluid build up, clinically known as *intraocular pressure (IOP)*, which damages the optic nerve.

A. Al-Mahrooqi, D. Medvedev and R. Muhtaseb—Equal contribution.

Supplementary Information The online version contains supplementary material available at https://doi.org/10.1007/978-3-031-16525-2_16.

Patients with glaucoma do not usually experience symptoms, as such, it is referred to as the "silent thief of sight" [8]. A recent study [1] reported that by the year 2040, 111.8 million people will be affected by this disease. Among many types of glaucoma, there are two common types, specified by the structural nature of the disease: *angle closure glaucoma (ACG)* and *open angle glaucoma (OAG)*. The former type is more common, while the latter progresses much faster to complete blindness with no early intervention. While measuring the IOP may sometimes help clinicians in diagnosis, it is difficult to take accurate readings due to the unstable nature of the optical pressure. Clinicians have resorted to examining the structure and appearance of *optic disc (OD)*, such as the increase of the *cup-to-disc ratio (CDR)* [8]: the ratio of the optic cup diameter to the diameter of the OD. However, manual examination is time-consuming and is a subject to the availability of a specialist. In order to release optometrists and ophthalmologists from the burden of manual glaucoma screening, multiple deep learning approaches are explored.

In this paper, we propose *Glaucoma Automated Retinal Detection Network (GARDNet)*: a combined methodology of sophisticated image pre-processing and robust multi-view network architecture for glaucoma classification. Our model was trained and tested on AIROGS training dataset [17] with images of different quality and resolution. In order for our model to produce consistent and robust results regardless of the input's quality, we introduced a localization of the area of interest with the following pre-processing pipeline. GARDNet extracts bounding boxes around the OD, and then applies multiple random affine and non-linear transformations, as well as such image processing techniques as *Contrast Limited Adaptive Histogram Equalization (CLAHE)*. Overall, we have validated eight models with over 150 experiments, and combined three best performing models in a multi-view network manner. Our proposed methodology allowed us to achieve AUC of 0.9308 on an external testing dataset, outperforming the state-of-the-art model by Fumero et al. [5] which achieved 0.9272 on the same dataset. This work does not aim to propose a new algorithm nor expand on an existing one. We aim to propose and validate a robust solution for glaucoma classification.

2   Related Works

Glaucoma related research is mainly focused on automated screening methods and OD segmentation as well as its outer area, with the following classification of referable/no-referable glaucoma. For example, Dibia et al. in [2] proposed to extract from segmented OD such features of eye fundus images as OD area, cup diameter, rim area and other important features to calculate *then Cup-to-disc ratio (CDR)*, which is commonly used as glaucoma indicator. Although the proposed methodology has a strong logical foundation, it was tested on a rather small dataset. Furthermore, many papers introduce deep-learning methods to classify glaucoma. Lee et al. in [9] proposed fully automated CNN, called M-Net, based on a modified U-Net [12] to segment OD and *optic cup (OC)*. For the glaucoma classification task, the team used pretrained ResNet50 and affine transformations for image preprocessing, achieving AUC of 0.96 on the small dataset, REFUGE [4]. Similar approach of two-step glaucoma screening was presented by Sreng et al. [16], segmenting OD with DeepLabV3, and then classifying glaucoma with various deep CNNs such as AlexNet, GoogleNet, and InceptionV3. The authors worked with several datasets and achieved promising results, but faced some limitations when generalizing between datasets. Maadi et al. in [10] followed the same segment-and-classify approach. As a novelty, the authors modified classical U-Net model, introducing pre-trained SE-ResNet50 on the encoding layers, which achieved better results.

In a more recent work, Phasuk et al. in [11], proposed improvements of *disc-aware ensemble network (DENet)* which incorporate the information from general fundus image with the information from optic disc area. This allowed to achieve AUC of 0.94 on a combined testing set from RIM-ONE-R3 [7] and Drishti-GS [15].

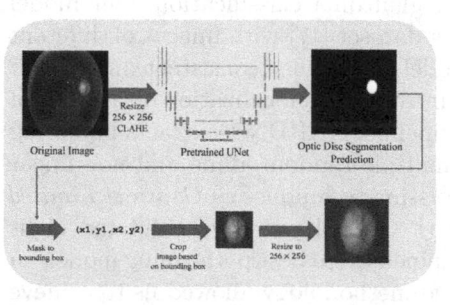

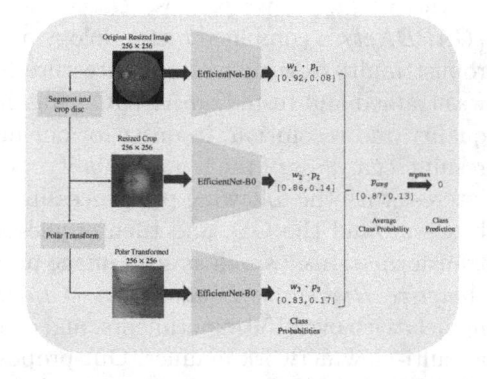

Fig. 1. Preprocessing pipeline used in our experiments on the AIROGS dataset to crop the regions of interest from the original images.

Fig. 2. Our multi-view network is composed of three different CNNs trained on different views of the color fundus images. w_n refers to the weight coefficient corresponding to model n, and p_n is the soft-max probability predictions in model n.

3   Method

3.1   Preprocessing

The AIROGS dataset [17] used in our experiments have non-uniform dimensions. We therefore begin by resizing all images to a fixed dimension of 256 × 256 pixels. In addition, we apply CLAHE transformation with a clipping limit value of 0.01, and then feed our resized images to a U-Net model [12] pretrained on optic disc segmentation [14] using the RIM-ONE v3 dataset [6]. The generated optic disc segmentation masks are then converted to bounding box coordinates, with padding determined by taking 30% of the segmented optic disc's diameter. We then proceed with cropping the original image based on the values of the bounding box coordinates, and finally resize the cropped image to a uniform dimension of 256 × 256 pixels. In the case where the pretrained network fails to segment the optic disc, we default by taking a center crop of size 85% of the image width, followed by a resize to 256 × 256 pixels. This accounts for approximately 20% of our dataset. Figure 1 illustrates our overall preprocessing pipeline.

3.2 Multi-view Classification Network

Our glaucoma classification model, GARDNet, is composed of a multi-view network of three different convolutional neural networks (CNNs) trained on different views of the color fundus images, as illustrated in Fig. 2. The first network is trained on the original resized images, whereas the second network is trained on the cropped disc area generated from the preprocessing strep, and finally, the third network is trained on the polar transformed cropped images. The training of each model is done independently. The model choice in the final multi-view network is based on ablation studies using different architectures, as reported in later sections. The intuition behind the multi-view network is that, experimentally, the model with uncropped images performed better than the cropped images. This is likely due to the error introduced by the pretrained disc segmentation model that is used to crop the images. At the same time, cropped images containing the optic disc area are most important for glaucoma diagnosis, as stated in the literature [9] and shown experimentally in our GradCAM [13] visualization Fig. A.1. We therefore retain both models in the final multi-view network. Lastly, in the final model, we apply polar transformation, which converts the image representation from Cartesian coordinates to polar coordinates system. For a point (u, v) in the Cartesian space, we obtain the radius r and angle θ as follows [3]:

$$\begin{cases} r = \sqrt{u^2 + v^2} \\ \theta = \tan^{-1}(\frac{v}{u}) \end{cases} \quad \leftrightarrow \quad \begin{cases} u = r\cos\theta \\ v = r\sin\theta \end{cases} \tag{1}$$

The transformation converts the radial relationship between the optic disc, cup, and background to a spatial hierarchical structure, which may provide an alternative view to the classification model and help capture more complex features. Phasuk et al. [11] claims that this transformation enhances the low level information in the optic disc region. The final classification prediction is obtained by taking a weighted average of the three soft-max predictions, followed by assigning the prediction label to the class that scored the highest probability. In the final multi-view network, we assign higher weight ($w = 2$) to the model trained on uncropped images, as it performed better on the validation set. The other two models generally performed similarly and therefore share the same weight.

4   Datasets

Rotterdam EyePACS AIROGS. The Rotterdam EyePACS AIROGS dataset [17] consists of 113,893 color fundus images. Only the training set is public and available to be downloaded, which has 101,442 gradable images (images of acceptable quality). The testing set consists of 11,000 gradable and ungradable images but it is not accessible to the public which limited our ability to use in this paper. Each image in the dataset is annotated by an expert as "referable glaucoma" or "no referable glaucoma". The images are high in resolution and do vary in size. The dataset has significant class imbalance, where the size of "no referable glaucoma" (normal) class is approximately 15 times greater than the "referable glaucoma" class.

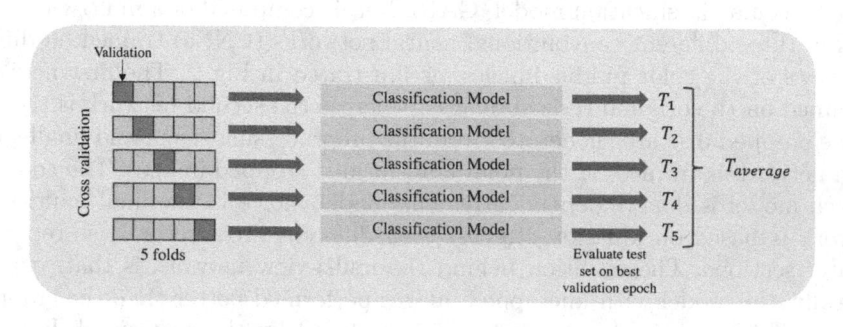

Fig. 3. 5-fold cross-validation applied on our dataset, where T_n is the test results evaluated using the model trained on fold n and $T_{average}$ is the average test results across all $k = 5$ folds.

RIM-ONE DL. Retinal IMage database for Optic Nerve Evaluation for Deep Learning (RIM-ONE DL) dataset [5] is used in this project as an external testing dataset, which consists of 313 normal and 172 glaucomatous fundus images. All images were segmented, then cropped around the cup-disc area. There are two training/testing split versions of this dataset; one was split randomly and the other was split by hospitals in Madrid and Zaragoza. We chose to report the results on the one split by the hospitals. The training set consists of 311 images, and the testing set contains 174 images.

5   Experimental Setup

For the following datasets, all the images were resized to 256 × 256. To address the problem of the imbalanced classes in both datasets, we utilize weighted cross entropy as a loss function, with the weights assigned for class j being $w_j = n_{samples}/(n_{classes} \cdot n_{samples_j})$. In other words, the class weights are inversely proportional to their respective class probabilities. The evaluation metrics used are receiver operating characteristic area under curve (ROC AUC) and F-score (F1).

Rotterdam EyePACS AIROGS. Our models were trained for 50 epochs on a single NVIDIA A100 GPU with a batch size of 64. An Adam optimizer was used with a learning rate ranging between $1 \times 10^{-4} - 1 \times 10^{-3}$. For some experiments, we apply data augmentations consisting of random vertical flip ($p = 0.5$), random horizontal flip ($p = 0.5$) and random rotation (degrees=$(-10°, +10°)$). In some experiments, we apply CLAHE transformation, as inspired by previous works. The advantage of using CLAHE is that it enhances the contrasts and dampens any noise amplification [11]. Given that the original testing set is not available, we split the training data into training and testing splits, using approximately 90/10 percents. To validate the robustness of our models, we performed 5-fold cross-validation by splitting the training data into training and validation, with approximately 80/20%, as illustrated in Fig. 3. As a result, the dataset sizes for training, validation, and testing are 73,154, 18,288 and 10,000, respectively.

RIM-ONE DL. For this dataset, our main goal is to validate our model trained on the Rotterdam EyePACS AIROGS generalizability on a completely new unseen dataset. We visually noticed that the optic disc occupied a larger area in the image. We therefore retrain our best model with scaling augmentation that mimics this behavior, and results in a model invariant to images with different scales. We fine-tuned our pretrained models using dropout rate of 0.2, learning rate of 5×10^{-3} and augmentations such as random horizontal and vertical flips as well as scaling. Since the RIM-ONE DL dataset is already cropped around the optic disc (OD) area, our multi-view network for this experiment consisted of only two models, while ignoring the model trained on original uncropped images. This makes our proposed solution applicable to different datasets with varying sizes and crops.

6   Experiments and Results

Rotterdam EyePACS AIROGS. Table 1 shows a summary of our experiments on the Rotterdam EyePACS AIROGS dataset. On the cropped data, we performed multiple experiments using different convolutional neural networks such as EfficinetNet-B0, EfficinetNet-B1, MobileNet-V3, ResNet18, ResNet34, ResNet50 and DenseNet in addition to Vision Transformer (ViT-Base) with patch size 16. We experimented with several experimental hyperparameters such as dropout, applying CLAHE and augmentations. Our best performance on the cropped images was obtained with EfficientNet-B0 model with dropout ($p = 0.5$), CLAHE and augmentations, gaining an AUC of 0.90 ± 0.01 and F1-score of 0.77 ± 0.01. To verify the performance of our cropped images vs. the original images, we trained the original images on the same model configurations as our best model, and obtained a higher AUC of 0.91 ± 0.01 and F1-score of 0.79 ± 0.01. Additionally, we further repeated the training of the best scoring model on the uncropped images using polar transformations, which obtained a slightly inferior performance of AUC 0.85 ± 0.02 and F1-score of 0.76 ± 0.01.

RIM-ONE DL. Table 2 summarizes our testing results on the RIM-ONE DL dataset after fine-tuning our pretrained models (Experiment #10 and #14) on the RIM-ONE DL training split. As shown in Table 2, our multi-view network achieves a better performance compared to [5], obtaining an AUC of 0.9308 and F1-Score 0f 0.9170. The individual CNNs corresponding to Experiments #10 and #14 obtained an inferior performance of AUC 0.87954 and 0.9088 respectively.

Table 1. Experimental results on the Rotterdam EyePACS AIROGS dataset. D=dropout, A=augmentations, C=CLAHE, S=scaling transformation, P=polar transformation. EfficientNet-B0$_{original}$ refers to EfficientNet-B0 model trained on the original (uncropped) data.

ID	Model	D	A	C	P	S	Test AUC	Test F-1
1	Resnet34						0.74 ± 0.02	0.74 ± 0.01
2	Resnet18						0.75 ± 0.02	0.74 ± 0.01
3	Resnet34			✓			0.78 ± 0.01	0.75 ± 0.01
4	ViT-B$_{224 \times 224}$						0.78 ± 0.01	0.75 ± 0.01
5	DenseNet-121						0.79 ± 0.04	0.71 ± 0.06
6	MobileNet-V3 Large						0.79 ± 0.02	0.78 ± 0.00
7	EfficientNet-B1						0.81 ± 0.02	0.80 ± 0.01
8	EfficientNet-B0						0.81 ± 0.02	0.79 ± 0.01
9	Resnet50						0.82 ± 0.02	0.80 ± 0.00
10	EfficientNet-B0	✓	✓	✓	✓		0.85 ± 0.02	0.76 ± 0.01
11	EfficientNet-B0		✓	✓			0.87 ± 0.01	0.80 ± 0.01
12	MobileNet-V3 Large	✓	✓	✓			0.89 ± 0.01	0.77 ± 0.01
13	EfficientNet-B0	✓	✓	✓		✓	0.89 ± 0.01	0.76 ± 0.01
14	EfficientNet-B0	✓	✓	✓			0.90 ± 0.01	0.77 ± 0.01
15	EfficientNet-B0$_{original}$	✓	✓	✓			0.91 ± 0.01	0.79 ± 0.01
16	Multi-view network (#14, #15)						**0.92**	0.80
17	Multi-view network (#10, #14, #15)						**0.92**	0.80

7 Discussion

Our results indicate that the models trained on the uncropped images performed much better than the cropped images. We hypothesize that this is due to errors introduced by the pretrained disc segmentation model that is used to crop the images. Furthermore, our experiments show that using dropout improves the performance, and therefore is a good strategy for overfitting. Additionally, using

Table 2. Experimental results on RIM-One DL dataset.

Model	Test AUC	Test F-1
Fumero et al. [5]	0.9272	–
Experiment #10 (Ours)	0.8795	0.8517
Experiment #14 (Ours)	0.9088	0.8974
Multi-view network (#10, #14) (Ours)	**0.9308**	**0.9170**

augmentations and CLAHE on top of dropout significantly improves the performance. By using augmentations and CLAHE, we increase the effective dataset size and also overcome model overfitting, making it robust to spatial and color transformations.

Furthermore, the ViT-B model did not perform as good as the EfficientNet-B0 model. The Vision Transformer model requires a large amount of data to perform as well as CNNs, therefore we hypothesize that its inferior performance is probably due to the relatively small number of training samples. In addition, ResNet18 and ResNet34 models performed worse, as smaller models are not able to capture the complex features in our dataset.

The multi-view network outperformed all previous experiments in the AIROGS dataset. By combining our three best performing CNNs, each trained on a different view of the same data, we achieve an AUC of 0.92. Furthermore, we give more classification decision weight to the best performing CNN, Experiment #15 (Table 1), which helped achieve this performance.

For the RIM-ONE DL experiments, we can conclude that our multi-view network, GARDNet, generalizes well on this dataset when fine-tuned on the training set. While experiment #10 and #14 did not exceed in performance compared to the previous state-of-the-art, the multi-view network composed of these two models scored a higher AUC score than Fumero et al. [5]. We hypothesize that our model performed better due to our image processing methods such as CLAHE and polar transformations, as well as the availability of a large dataset for pretraining. Furthermore, as our results indicate, multi-view networks outperform individual models.

Finally, we address the results obtained in Experiment #16 from Table 1. As we can see, on the AIROGS dataset, our multi-view model without the polar network performs as good as the Multi-view model with all three networks (Experiment #16). While this may indicate that the polar network has no positive contribution to the overall model, we argue that our results on the external dataset prove the opposite. As shown in Table 2, the polar model alone (Experiment #10) had achieved inferior performance in comparison to the cropped model (Experiment #14), but when combined in a multi-view network, the result achieved is significantly higher than the individual networks.

8   Conclusion

In this paper, we introduced a multi-view network GARDNet for glaucoma classification composed of three different CNNs trained on different views of color fundus images. Trained on the AIROGS dataset and tested on an external dataset, RIM-ONE DL, our results indicate that the multi-view network significantly improves the performance when compared to individual models. On the external test dataset, we get superior performance to the previous state-of-the-art model by Fumero et al. [5]. In future works, we would like to extend the weighted averaging of the multi-view network predictions, such that the weights are determined systematically as learnable parameters rather than being constant.

References

1. Allison, K., Patel, D., Alabi, O.: Epidemiology of glaucoma: the past, present, and predictions for the future. cureus, November 2020. https://doi.org/10.7759/cureus.11686, https://www.cureus.com/articles/42672-epidemiology-of-glaucoma-the-past-present-and-predictions-for-the-future
2. Dibia, A.C., Nwawudu, S.E.: Automated detection of glaucoma from retinal images using image processing techniques, vol. 7, pp. 2321–9009, September 2018
3. Fu, H., Cheng, J., Xu, Y., Wong, D.W.K., Liu, J., Cao, X.: Joint optic disc and cup segmentation based on multi-label deep network and polar transformation. IEEE Trans. Med. Imaging **37**(7), 1597–1605 (2018). https://doi.org/10.1109/tmi.2018.2791488
4. Fu, H., et al.: Refuge: retinal fundus glaucoma challenge (2019). https://doi.org/10.21227/tz6e-r977, https://dx.doi.org/10.21227/tz6e-r977
5. Fumero, F., Diaz-Aleman, T., Sigut, J., Alayón, S., Arnay, R., Angel-Pereira, D.: Rim-one dl: a unified retinal image database for assessing glaucoma using deep learning. Image Anal. Stereology **39** (2020). https://doi.org/10.5566/ias.2346
6. Fumero, F., Sigut, J., Alayón, S., González-Hernández, M., González de la Rosa, M.: Interactive tool and database for optic disc and cup segmentation of stereo and monocular retinal fundus images, July 2015
7. Fumero, F., Sigut, J., Alayón, S., González-Hernández, M., González de la Rosa, M.: Interactive tool and database for optic disc and cupsegmentation of stereo and monocular retinal fundus images, June 2015
8. Lee, D.A., Higginbotham, E.J.: Glaucoma and its treatment: a review. Am. J. Health-Syst. Pharm. **62**(7), 691–699 (2005). https://doi.org/10.1093/ajhp/62.7.691, https://academic.oup.com/ajhp/article/62/7/691/5134357
9. Lee, J., Lee, J., Song, H., Lee, C.: Development of an end-to-end deep learning system for glaucoma screening using color fundus images. JAMA Ophthalmol. **137**, 1353–1360 (2019)
10. Maadi, F., Faraji, N., Bibalan, M.H.: A robust glaucoma screening method for fundus images using deep learning technique. In: 2020 27th National and 5th International Iranian Conference on Biomedical Engineering (ICBME), pp. 289–293. IEEE, Tehran, Iran, November 2020. https://doi.org/10.1109/ICBME51989.2020.9319434, https://ieeexplore.ieee.org/document/9319434/

11. Phasuk, S., et al.: Automated glaucoma screening from retinal fundus image using deep learning. In: 2019 41st Annual International Conference of the IEEE Engineering in Medicine and Biology Society (EMBC), pp. 904–907 (2019). https:// doi.org/10.1109/EMBC.2019.8857136

12. Ronneberger, O., Fischer, P., Brox, T.: U-net: convolutional networks for biomedical image segmentation (2015). https://doi.org/10.48550/ARXIV.1505.04597, https://arxiv.org/abs/1505.04597

13. Selvaraju, R.R., Das, A., Vedantam, R., Cogswell, M., Parikh, D., Batra, D.: Gradcam: why did you say that? visual explanations from deep networks via gradient-based localization. CoRR abs/1610.02391 (2016). http://arxiv.org/abs/1610.02391

14. Sevastopolsky, A.: Optic disc and cup segmentation methods for glaucoma detection with modification of u-net convolutional neural network. Pattern Recogn. Image Anal. **27**(3), 618–624 (2017). https://doi.org/10.1134/s1054661817030269, https://doi.org/10.1134

15. Sivaswamy, J., Krishnadas, S.R., Datt Joshi, G., Jain, M., Syed Tabish, A.U.: Drishti-GS: retinal image dataset for optic nerve head (onh) segmentation. In: 2014 IEEE 11th International Symposium on Biomedical Imaging (ISBI), pp. 53–56 (2014). https://doi.org/10.1109/ISBI.2014.6867807

16. Sreng, S., Maneerat, N., Hamamoto, K., Win, K.Y.: Deep learning for optic disc segmentation and glaucoma diagnosis on retinal images. Appl. Sci. **10**(14), 4916 (2020). https://doi.org/10.3390/app10144916, https://www.mdpi.com/2076-3417/10/14/4916

17. Coen de Vente, Koenraad A. Verrmeer, N.J.: Airogs: artificial intelligence for robust glaucoma screening challenge. In: IEEE International Symposium on Biomedical Imaging. IEEE (2022)

Fundus Photograph Defect Repair Algorithm Based on Portable Camera Empty Shot

Jun Wu[1]([✉]), Hanwen Zhang[1], Mingxin He[1], Jianchun Zhao[2], Xiaohou Shen[2], Jiankun Liu[2], Gang Yang[3], Xirong Li[3], and Dayong Ding[2]

[1] School of Electronics and Information, Northwestern Polytechnical University, Xi'an 710072, China
`junwu@nwpu.edu.cn`, {`zhanghanwen,hemingxin`}`@mail.nwpu.edu.cn`
[2] Vistel AI Lab, Visionary Intelligence Ltd., Beijing 100080, China
{`jianchun.zhao,xiaohou.shen,jiankun.liu,dayong.ding`}`@vistel.cn`
[3] Key Lab of DEKE, Renmin University of China, Beijing 100872, China
{`yanggang,xirong`}`@ruc.edu.cn`

Abstract. Fundus photograph is an important basis for ophthalmologists to diagnose retinal diseases. Due to the limitations of the optical system design for portable fundus cameras, there still exist typical image defects leading to low quality images. There are stray light defects such as atomization area, shadow ring, bright spot, central dark hole and so on. Since the camera empty shot in a dark environment can reflect important device-specific characteristics of typical defects, we propose a novel framework to execute image defects repairing by template compensation based on camera empty shots for portable fundus cameras. First, noise reduction is employed from a camera empty shot image. Then, a defect compensation template based on empty shot is generated. For each fundus image, an adjusted ratio is optimized in different defect areas of the customized compensation template. Finally, this template is applied to compensate and repair the stray light defects in order to improve image quality for the target image captured from the same camera. Experimental results show that our proposed method is effective, and it is able to obtain fundus images in better quality.

Keywords: Camera empty shot · Image defect · Image repair · Template compensate

1 Introduction

Portable fundus cameras are more convenient in screening and clinical scenarios than desktop fundus camera. Due to the limitation of the light path and lens size in the portable fundus camera, the quality of the fundus images is prone to be affected by stray light, which is not expected but reaches the surface of photosensitive equipment (e.g. charge coupled device, CCD) after propagation.

© The Author(s), under exclusive license to Springer Nature Switzerland AG 2022
B. Antony et al. (Eds.): OMIA 2022, LNCS 13576, pp. 162–172, 2022.
https://doi.org/10.1007/978-3-031-16525-2_17

In current design of optical system in portable fundus cameras, stray light still can not be eliminated completely, but it is suppressed to be in a certain extent. The images taken by portable fundus cameras are more or less affected by stray light. Strong stray light can seriously affect ophthalmologists' diagnosis and needs to be eliminated. Deep learning, such as [31,32], is not suitable for built-in processing module due to increasing costs of camera hardware. As a result, suppressing stray light defects using traditional image processing technology is necessary and crucial.

Stray light generation is related to all the optical surface and component surface of the optical system. Light sources will be more or less affected by the scattering, transmission and absorption from these surfaces during transmission to the detector. The quantitative analysis of stray light is very difficult. With the rapid development of optical technology and a variety of photoelectric detection technologies, the sensitivity of optical system increases greatly, and the detection threshold becomes lower and lower. The influence of stray light is often amplified. At the same time, the progress and development of computing ability makes it possible to analyze, locate and eliminate stray light in software level.

To the best of our knowledge, currently there is no existing work discussing the issue of stray light elimination in fundus images taken from portable cameras. In this paper, we will propose a novel algorithm for stray light elimination in fundus images captured by portable cameras.

2   Related Work

Typical image defect repairing methods include image enhancement and image inpainting. We will discuss in details as below.

2.1   Image Enhancement

The visual characteristics of stray light in fundus images are somewhat similar to the common image atomization phenomenon, which can be used for reference to remove stray light. Common defogging algorithms can be divided into algorithm based on image enhancement and algorithm based on image restoration.

Typical image enhancement methods include: histogram equalization [1], adaptive histogram equalization [2], contrast limited adaptive histogram equalization (CLAHE), Retinex algorithm [3–5], wavelet transform, homorphic filtering, etc. Histogram equalization (HLE) [1] is mainly used to enhance the contrast of images with small dynamic range by changing the histogram of the image to change the gray level of each pixel in the image. Adaptive histogram equalization (AHE) [2] can obtain more image details by changing the local histogram. CLAHE overcomes over-amplified noise problem in AHE by using contrast limiting for each small area. The Retinex-based method [3–5] is based on the consistency of color perception, removing the influence of illumination of ambient light and enhancing the reflection information of the image. Dichromatic reflection model [27, 28] is used to remove object highlights.

Haze removal algorithm based on image restoration mainly uses atmospheric degradation model. The typical algorithms are the dark channel defogging algorithm [6] proposed by He et al. and defogging algorithm based on guided filtering [22]. Other representative algorithms include single image defogging algorithm [23,24], fast image recovery algorithm [25], and Bayesian defogging algorithm [26]. Dark channel prior theory points out that there is one color channel of each pixel always has a very low gray value in the fog-free image, so the gray value of all pixels in the whole dark channel is approximately 0. The defogging model is as follows: $I(x) = J(x)t(x) + A(1 - t(x))$, in which, $I(x)$ is the existing image (to be fogged), $J(x)$ is the original fog-free image to be restored, A is the global atmospheric optical composition, and $t(x)$ is the perspective rate.

Traditional defogging algorithm in natural environment can be used for reference, but it is under the assumption of uniformly distribution of fogs. As a result, it can not be directly applied to the elimination of stray light atomization phenomenon in non-uniformly distribution in most cases.

2.2   Image Inpainting

The existing image restoration work can be divided into two main categories. The first category includes traditional diffusion-based or patch-based approaches with low-level characteristics. The second category is based on deep learning.

Traditional diffusion or patch-based methods such as [7–10,12] usually use variational algorithms or patch similarity to propagate information from the background region to the missing region. Criminisi et al. [11] uses known regions to fill the missing regions by the priority of pixel blocks. PatchMatch [13] uses a fast nearest neighbor field algorithm.

Recently, methods based on deep learning have made great achievements in the field of image inpainting. Initial work [14,15] trains convolutional neural networks for denoising and repairing small areas. Context encoder [16] uses the full connection layer in image repair work. Demir [18] et al. introduce residual learning and PatchGAN on the basis of [17]. Yu et al. [19] propose the mechanism of contextual attention. Two networks are used to refine the repair results. Dilated convolution [17], partial convolution [20] and gate convolution [21] are used to help the network to learn better learn features.

Typical image defects in fundus images include central white spot, shadow area, atomization area, etc. The existing algorithms are not targeting stray light defects in fundus images. In general, image enhancement can be used to reduce the interference of weak or partial distortion defect, and image inpainting can be used to repair serious distortion area. Due to the limitation of built-in hardware resources in portable fundus camera, deep learning is not suitable and the traditional image processing is more friendly. In addition, typical defects such as central dark ring, central dark spot and central white spot have not been investigated, where customized defect repair algorithm need to be explored further.

3 The Proposed Method

As illustrated in Fig. 1, we propose an image defect repair algorithm based on camera empty shot images, which will provide a new solution for defect repair and optimization of fundus images. The effective image information can be separated from the aliasing image signal by using empty shot image. First, we preprocess camera empty shot image to avoid the influence of noise(especially highlight noise) on subsequent processing. Then, a compensation template is determined and the defect area is located according to camera empty shot image. Using defect area and fundus image, the compensation weight of the fundus image is further determined. Finally, the defect area of fundus image is compensated by adjusting the compensation template with appropriate weights.

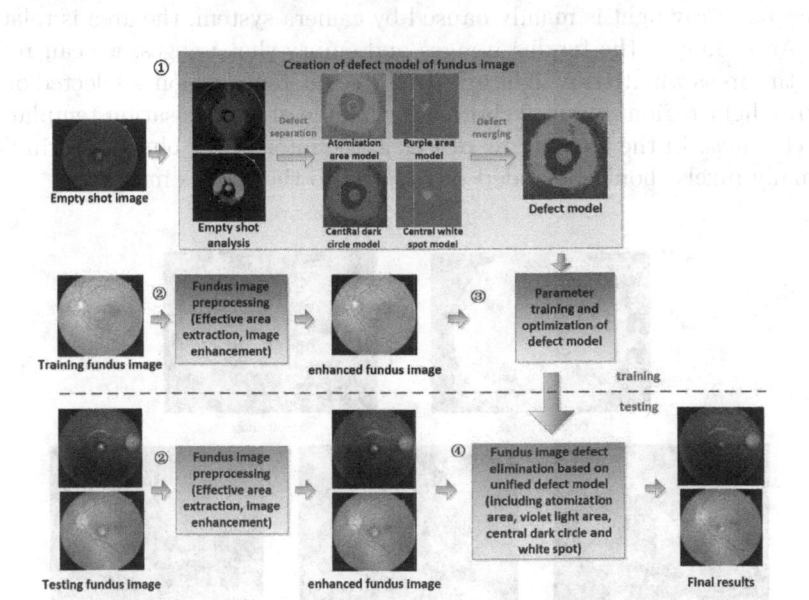

Fig. 1. The flowchart of the proposed framework.

3.1 Camera Empty Shot Image

The image taken by a fundus camera against a pure color background or even in a dark space is called a camera empty shot image. Each camera only need to capture the empty shot images once as for calibration before leaving the factory. There is no obvious illumination imbalance caused by the shooting environment and no reflection imbalance of the subject itself. It can be considered that empty shot image mainly reflects the difference of camera's imaging ability caused by hardware and the optical path design.

Ideally, the empty shot should also be a pure color image, typically in white light. The bright area in the empty shot image will appear as a bright spot in the fundus images. Dark areas in the empty shot image will appear as shadows in the fundus images. Colored backgrounds in different RGB channels presents similar pixel distribution property. As a result, we typically apply the camera empty shot captured from black background.

3.2   Compensation Template

Generating the Initial Template. Based on our observation, the distribution characteristics of stray light in the fundus image is similar and consistent to main distribution of stray light in camera empty shot image, as illustrated in Fig. 2. Inspired by this, we think the influence of stray light can be weakened with the help of camera empty shot image.

Because stray light is mainly caused by camera system, the area is relatively fixed. According to the fundus images and empty shot images, we can roughly locate the areas where stray light appears. The reference region is selected outside the stray light region. Figure 2 shows an example of compensation templates for RGB channels. In the second row of Fig. 2, the intensity of blue or red indicates how many pixels should be added or reduced to the fundus image.

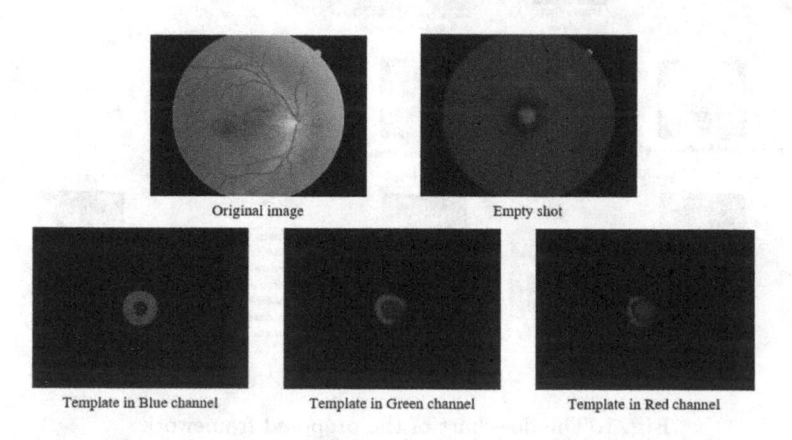

Original image   Empty shot

Template in Blue channel   Template in Green channel   Template in Red channel

Fig. 2. Comparison between fundus image and empty shot image.

The compensation method is as follows:

$$I_{result} = I - w \times I_{mask}, \tag{1}$$

where I_{result} is the optimized result of fundus image, I is the original fundus image, and I_{mask} is the template generated by the empty shot image. The parameter w is the adjustment weight of the compensation template. For the compensation template, defects that appear as bright spot correspond to a positive values in I_{mask}, and defects that appear as shadow correspond to negative values in I_{mask}. By subtraction, the bright spot in the fundus image is weakened and the shadow is enhanced to a brighter level.

Adjusting Compensation Weights. When a camera takes fundus images, the lighting conditions, the subjects' lens diopter and retinal reflection ability are all different, so stray light intensity will be different. It is difficult to find a fixed universal compensation template. Therefore, we need to adjust the compensation template according to actual situation of fundus image.

The camera imaging problem is mainly divided into the bright spot in the camera center and the shadow ring around the bright spot. Compensation template can be adjusted according to bright spot and shadow. Set different weights for bright spot and shadow, w_{bright}, w_{dark}.

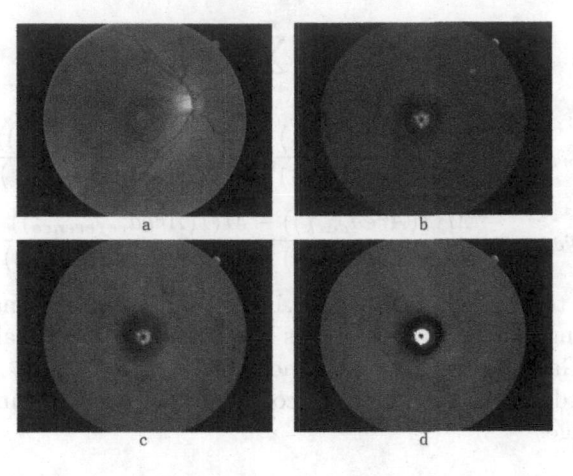

Fig. 3. Examples of camera empty shots: (a) Original fundus image (b) Empty shot image (c) Blue channel of empty shot image (d) Results locating defect area. (Color figure online)

The bright spot and shadow are mainly caused by optical path design. Although there are some differences among the devices, the distribution is roughly similar. Camera defect usually appears in the image center. As shown in Fig. 3, the bright spot defect region D_{bright} is in the green ring, and the shadow defect region D_{dark} is between the red and green ring.

$\bar{I}_{Background}$ is the reference pixel value of the empty shot image, which is the average value of $Area_{ref}$. The constant factor c is the total number of pixels in this reference area. In the defect area of the empty shot image, threshold segmentation is performed to locate the imaging bright spot $Area_{bright}$ and shadow area $Area_{dark}$ of the fundus image. The reference pixel value of empty shot image is $\bar{I}_{Background}$. (i, j) is pixel coordinate, as

$$\bar{I}_{Background} = \frac{1}{c} \sum_{i=1}^{c} I(Area_{ref}) \tag{2}$$

$$Area_{bright} = \{(i, j) | E(i, j) > \bar{I}_{Background}, (i, j) \in D_{bright}\} \tag{3}$$

$$Area_{dark} = \{(i,j)|E(i,j) < \bar{I}_{Background}, (i,j) \in D_{dark}\} \tag{4}$$

$$w = \begin{cases} w_{bright}, \text{ if } (i,j) \in D_{bright}, \\ w_{dark}, \text{ if } (i,j) \in D_{dark}, \\ 0, \text{ otherwise.} \end{cases}$$

where E is empty shot image, w_{bright} is the weight of bright spot area, w_{dark} is the weight of shadow area. According to the position of $Area_{bright}$ and $Area_{dark}$ in the image, we can get the brightness difference between defect region ($Area_{bright}$, $Area_{dark}$) and the reference region. w_{bright} and w_{dark} are adjusted based on the brightness differences of the fundus image and empty shot image:

$$M(I(Area_{ref})) = \frac{1}{m} \sum_{i=1}^{m} G(I(Area_{ref}(i))) \tag{5}$$

$$w_{bright} = \frac{M(I(Area_{bright})) - M(I(Area_{reference}))}{M(E(Area_{bright})) - M(E(Area_{reference}))} \tag{6}$$

$$w_{dark} = \frac{M(I(Area_{dark})) - M(I(Area_{reference}))}{M(E(Area_{dark})) - M(E(Area_{reference}))} \tag{7}$$

where m is the total pixels number in $Area$, I is the fundus image, $G()$ is the Gaussian filtering function, and $M()$ is to obtain the mean value in $Area$ of image I after Gaussian filtering. The adjusted weights w_{bright} and w_{dark} are calculated according to the ratio of the corresponding areas of fundus image and empty shot image.

4   Evaluations

4.1   Data Set and Experimental Setup

As a pioneer work, a private dataset is applied in this evaluation. It is collected by Beijing Hospital, captured in in 3792×2824 pixels using a portable fundus camera, HuiMouMed FC-800. It consists of 117 fundus images (20 subjects) taken by 13 different cameras with the same model. Each camera is applied to shoot its corresponding empty shot images, with a size of 3792×2824 pixels. A total 13 of camera empty shot images are collected in a dark room by photographing black color cards while the diopter of camera optical system is $0°$.

Our method is implemented in Python and C++ and it runs on the Intel Core I5 under Windows 10. Defect areas and reference areas need to be determined according to the empty shots of dataset. Based on this dataset, it is observed that the bright spot defect area is within 180 pixels from the image center, the shadow defect area is within 300 pixels from the image center, the reference area is within 700–850 pixels from the image center.

4.2   Experimental Results

We mainly use *the brightness standard deviation* (Brightness STD) and *local similarity* to measure image quality. The brightness standard deviation is calculated using defect region and mean value of reference region. The local similarity is defined as the average SSIM [30] value, which is applied to evaluate the degree of similarity between a local area and its surroundings by taking brightness, contrast and structure into consideration, as:

$$LocalSimilarity = \frac{1}{n} \sum_{i=1}^{n} SSIM(Area_{defect}, Area_i), \qquad (8)$$

where $Area_{defect}$ is the defect region, $Area_i$ is the i-th reference region near $Area_{defect}$, both in rectangle. n is the total number of reference areas (here we take $n=8$ for left, right, upper, below, upper left, upper right, lower left, lower right positions).

The greater the value is, the higher the image quality is. Since image defects are concentrated near the center of the image, the metrics are calculated with a square area with 600×600 pixels in the center of the original image.

At the same time, the existing methods such as gamma correction (GC), contrast limited adaptive histogram equalization (CLAHE) [2] and dark channel defogging [6] are used for comparison in the experiments.

Table 1. The evaluation results of our proposed method.

Methods	Original	GC [29]	CLAHE [2]	DarkChannel [6]	Ours
Brightness STD	22.99	21.71	41.31	16.11	**14.09**
Local similarity	0.659	0.472	0.362	0.653	**0.721**

As it can be seen from Table 1, compared to the original images, our proposed algorithm reduces the brightness standard deviation by 8.9, increases the local similarity by 0.062 while the overall image quality in visual representation (especially in hue) keeps unchanged. Based on our observation, other existing methods change the image hue more or less. In addition, our method weakens the bright spot area and enhances the shadow area in the fundus image. Basically, the optimized image results have higher image quality.

Figure 4 shows that the optimized image has better image quality in the central defect area, and the compensation template reduces bright spot, shadow and atomization in the original image. It proves the feasibility of the compensation template derived from camera empty shot images.

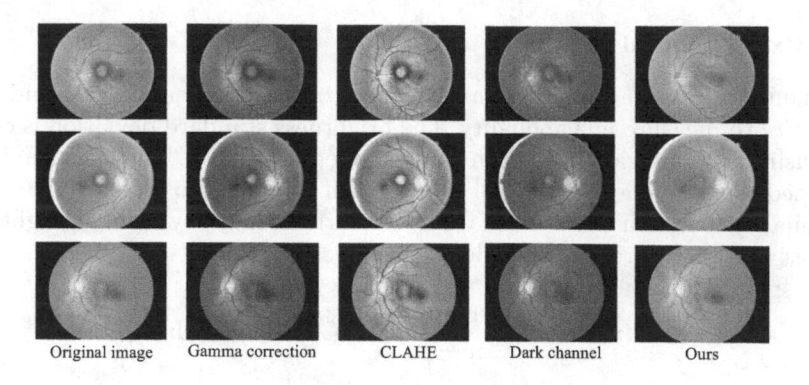

Original image   Gamma correction   CLAHE   Dark channel   Ours

Fig. 4. Comparison between different methods.

5   Conclusions

In this paper we propose an image defect repair algorithm based on camera empty shot. Camera empty shot image can reflect typical imaging defects caused by optical path and the design of optical system. Using this feature, a compensation template is generated to compensate stray light. Considering the brightness characteristics of fundus image, the compensation weight of the fundus image is adjusted and the compensation template is optimized. Finally, the template is applied to execute the final compensation step. Experimental results show that our proposed method is effective. The bright spot area is weakened, the shadow area is enhanced, and the image information entropy is improved.

Acknowledgements. This work is supported by Natural Science Basic Research Plan in Shaanxi Province of China (2020JM-129), and BJNSF (No. 4202033).

References

1. Stark, J.A.: Adaptive image contrast enhancement using generalizations of histogram equalization. IEEE Trans. Image Process. **9**(5), 889–896 (2000)
2. Kim, J.Y., Kim, L.S., Hwang, S.H.: An advanced contrast enhancement using partially overlapped sub-block histogram equalization. IEEE Trans. Circuits Syst. Video Technol. **11**(4), 475–484 (2001)
3. Land, E.H.: The retinex theory of color vision. Sci. Am. **237**(6), 108–129 (1977)
4. Jobson, D.J., Rahman, Z., Woodell, G.A.: A multiscale retinex for bridging the gap between color images and the human observation of scenes. IEEE Trans. Image Process. **6**(7), 965–976 (1997)
5. Rahman, Z., Jobson, D.J., Woodell, G.A.: Retinex processing for automatic image enhancement. J. Electron. Imaging **13**(1), 100–110 (2004)
6. He, K., Sun, J., Tang, X.: Single image haze removal using dark channel prior. IEEE Trans. Pattern Anal. Mach. Intell. **33**(12), 2341–2353 (2010)
7. Ballester, C., Bertalmio, M., Caselles, V., et al.: Filling-in by joint interpolation of vector fields and gray levels. IEEE Trans. Image Process. **10**(8), 1200–1211 (2001)

8. Bertalmio, M., Sapiro, G., Caselles, V., et al.: Image inpainting. In: Proceedings of the 27th Annual Conference on Computer Graphics and Interactive Techniques, pp. 417–424 (2000)

9. Efros, A.A., Freeman, W.T.: Image quilting for texture synthesis and transfer. In: Proceedings of the 28th Annual Conference on Computer Graphics and Interactive Techniques, pp. 341–346 (2001)

10. Efros, A.A., Leung, T.K.: Texture synthesis by non-parametric sampling. In: Proceedings of the Seventh IEEE International Conference on Computer Vision, vol. 2, pp. 1033–1038. IEEE (1999)

11. Criminisi, A., Pérez, P., Toyama, K.: Region filling and object removal by exemplar-based image inpainting. IEEE Trans. Image Process. **13**(9), 1200–1212 (2004)

12. Simakov, D., Caspi, Y., Shechtman, E., et al.: Summarizing visual data using bidirectional similarity. In: IEEE Conference on Computer Vision and Pattern Recognition, pp. 1–8. IEEE (2008)

13. Barnes, C., Shechtman, E., Finkelstein, A., et al.: PatchMatch: a randomized correspondence algorithm for structural image editing. ACM Trans. Graph. **28**(3), 24 (2009)

14. Köhler, R., Schuler, C., Schölkopf, B., Harmeling, S.: Mask-specific inpainting with deep neural networks. In: Jiang, X., Hornegger, J., Koch, R. (eds.) GCPR 2014. LNCS, vol. 8753, pp. 523–534. Springer, Cham (2014). https://doi.org/10.1007/978-3-319-11752-2_43

15. Xu, L., Ren, J.S., Liu, C., et al.: Deep convolutional neural network for image deconvolution. Adv. Neural. Inf. Process. Syst. **27**, 1790–1798 (2014)

16. Pathak, D., Krahenbuhl, P., Donahue, J., et al.: Context encoders: feature learning by inpainting. In: Proceedings of the IEEE Conference on Computer Vision and Pattern Recognition, pp. 2536–2544 (2016)

17. Iizuka, S., Simo-Serra, E., Ishikawa, H.: Globally and locally consistent image completion. ACM Trans. Graph. (ToG) **36**(4), 1–14 (2017)

18. Demir, U., Unal, G.: Patch-based image inpainting with generative adversarial networks. arXiv preprint arXiv:1803.07422 (2018)

19. Yu, J., Lin, Z., Yang, J., et al.: Generative image inpainting with contextual attention. In: Proceedings of the IEEE Conference on Computer Vision and Pattern Recognition, pp. 5505–5514 (2018)

20. Liu, G., Reda, F.A., Shih, K.J., Wang, T.-C., Tao, A., Catanzaro, B.: Image inpainting for irregular holes using partial convolutions. In: Ferrari, V., Hebert, M., Sminchisescu, C., Weiss, Y. (eds.) ECCV 2018. LNCS, vol. 11215, pp. 89–105. Springer, Cham (2018). https://doi.org/10.1007/978-3-030-01252-6_6

21. Yu, J., Lin, Z., Yang, J., et al.: Free-form image inpainting with gated convolution. In: Proceedings of the IEEE/CVF International Conference on Computer Vision, pp. 4471–4480 (2019)

22. He, K., Sun, J., Tang, X.: Guided image filtering. IEEE Trans. Pattern Anal. Mach. Intell. **35**(6), 1397–1409 (2012)

23. Fattal, R.: Single image dehazing. ACM Trans. Graph. **27**(3), 1–9 (2008)

24. Tan, R.: Visibility in bad weather from a single image. In: IEEE Conference on Computer Vision and Pattern Recognition (CVPR), pp. 1–8 (2008)

25. Tarel, J.P., Nicolas, H.: Fast visibility restoration from a single color or gray level image. In: IEEE 12th International Conference on Computer Vision (ICCV), pp. 2201–2208 (2009)

26. Wang, Y., Fan, C.: Single image defogging by multiscale depth fusion. IEEE Trans. Image Process. **23**(11), 4826–4837 (2014)

27. Xia, W., Chen, E.C.S., Pautler, S.E., et al.: A global optimization method for specular highlight removal from a single image. IEEE Access **7**, 125976–125990 (2019)

28. Guo, J., Zhou, Z., Wang, L.: Single image highlight removal with a sparse and low-rank reflection model. In: Ferrari, V., Hebert, M., Sminchisescu, C., Weiss, Y. (eds.) ECCV 2018. LNCS, vol. 11208, pp. 282–298. Springer, Cham (2018). https://doi.org/10.1007/978-3-030-01225-0_17

29. Huang, S.C., Cheng, F.C., Chiu, Y.S.: Efficient contrast enhancement using adaptive gamma correction with weighting distribution. IEEE Trans. Image Process. **22**(3), 1032–1041 (2012)

30. Wang, Z., Bovik, A.C., Sheikh, H.R., et al.: Image quality assessment: from error visibility to structural similarity. IEEE Trans. Image Process. **13**(4), 600–612 (2004)

31. Huang, X., Liu, M.-Y., Belongie, S., Kautz, J.: Multimodal unsupervised image-to-image translation. In: Ferrari, V., Hebert, M., Sminchisescu, C., Weiss, Y. (eds.) ECCV 2018. LNCS, vol. 11207, pp. 179–196. Springer, Cham (2018). https://doi.org/10.1007/978-3-030-01219-9_11

32. Zhang, T., et al.: Noise adaptation generative adversarial network for medical image analysis. IEEE Trans. Med. Imaging **39**(4), 1149–1159 (2019)

Template Mask Based Image Fusion Built-in Algorithm for Wide Field Fundus Cameras

Jun Wu[1]([⊠]), Mingxin He[1], Yang Liu[1], Hanwen Zhang[1], Jianchun Zhao[2], Xiaohou Shen[2], Jiankun Liu[2], Gang Yang[3], Xirong Li[3], and Dayong Ding[2]

[1] School of Electronics and Information, Northwestern Polytechnical University, Xi'an 710072, China
junwu@nwpu.edu.cn, {hemingxin,2021202082, zhanghanwen}@mail.nwpu.edu.cn
[2] Vistel AI Lab, Visionary Intelligence Ltd., Beijing 100080, China
{jianchun.zhao,xiaohou.shen,jiankun.liu,dayong.ding}@vistel.cn
[3] Key Lab of DEKE, Renmin University of China, Beijing 100872, China
{yanggang,xirong}@ruc.edu.cn

Abstract. When a typical wide field fundus camera takes two fundus images as a pair, two patterns of illumination beams (the top and bottom, left and right) are turned on respectively. Due to the influence of the illumination beams, the reflected and scattered light haze are observed in neighboring regions, which results in partial or even complete occlusion of retinal structures. In this paper, we propose a novel template mask based image fusion algorithm for wide field fundus cameras, which splices available higher-quality regions from these two images in one pair, and fuses them into a single high-quality image, which tries to keep complete retinal structure. First, the region of interest (ROI) are obtained based on the Hough circle transform, and these two images are adjusted by color and brightness normalization based on Poisson fusion. Then, a customized template mask is designed to fuse the higher-quality regions from this image pair. Finally, image enhancement in brightness is carried out to further improve final image quality. Experimental results on a variety of wide field fundus image pairs demonstrate that the proposed method is effective, our method increases information entropy by 0.051, standard deviation by 1.726, average gradient by 0.148 and spatial frequency by 0.233.

Keywords: Wide field fundus camera · Image processing · Image fusion

1 Introduction

In typical wide field fundus cameras, there will be a strong stray light effect (fog-like phenomenon) close to the built-in light sources, resulting in occlusion and irreversible interference to retinal structures or lesions, so that the wide field fundus camera cannot shoot only once to achieve high-quality imaging. A typical solution is to divide the

© The Author(s), under exclusive license to Springer Nature Switzerland AG 2022
B. Antony et al. (Eds.): OMIA 2022, LNCS 13576, pp. 173–182, 2022.
https://doi.org/10.1007/978-3-031-16525-2_18

four illumination beams around the observation axis into two lighting patterns (top and bottom, left and right), and turn them on alternately to capture two wide field fundus images as a capturing pair, as shown in Fig. 1. Therefore, it is necessary to develop an image fusion algorithm for wide field fundus cameras to obtain a high-quality fundus image with relatively complete retinal structures.

In traditional image fusion problems, the corresponding pixel pairs of two input images are generally aligned (after image registration) and complementary. However, wide field fundus camera images belong to a different case. High-quality central areas of the image pair can be both retained and complementary. However, low-quality areas close to light sources are almost unusable, only the relatively high-quality area in the other image can be reserved. From this viewpoint, they are choose-one-from-two as the same image area is in different light states in two patterns. In addition, the global and local brightness of two input images are significantly different due to two different lighting patterns. As a result, the boundary effects between reserved and discarded regions are prone to produce obvious visual differences, resulting in unsatisfactory overall image fusion results.

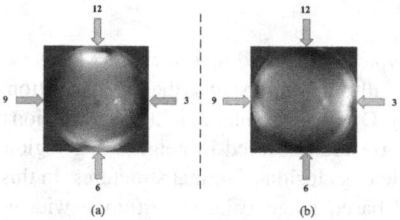

Fig. 1. A pair of wide field fundus images. (a) The first image (top and bottom light sources at 6 and 12 o'clock). (b) The second image (left and right light sources at 3 and 9 o'clock)

In this paper, we propose a template mask based image fusion algorithm for wide field fundus cameras to obtain high-quality wide field fundus images. It was observed that two wide field fundus images in the same pair are spatially complementary. That is to say, there is a low-quality region near the light source in one image, a corresponding better-quality region occurs in the other image at the same position. To take full advantage of this property, an image fusion algorithm based on template mask is proposed, which splices the available parts of two wide field fundus images and fuses them into a relatively complete and high-quality fundus image.

2   Related Work

To preserve original accurate information as much as possible, pixel-wise image fusion algorithms can be applied [1, 2], which can be divided into two categories: image fusion based on spatial domain and image fusion based on transform domain.

Image fusion based on spatial domain is generally performed directly on the gray space of image pixels. A most straightforward method is to use the maximum method or the weighted average method [4] to select the pixel from two input images, which operates directly on the target pixel without considering the correlation between neighboring pixels. When there is large information complementarity between images to be fused, a region-based image fusion method can be applied, the fusion coefficients of different to-be-used images can be determined according to the feature relations between the pixels in a rectangular window at a certain position. Zhang [5] obtained the Laplacian energy of the input image to measure the focusing degree, and realized the image fusion by a sliding window. However, the computational complexity of this algorithm is high. Principal component analysis is also a typical spatial domain method, Zhu [6] searched for principal components of images by dimension reduction, and determined the weight of each fusion image according to the energy of principal components. Chen [3] proposed an image fusion algorithm based on edge detection. The improved ROEWA (Ratio of Exponentially Weighted Averages) operator is used to detect image edge. Different image fusion rules are set according to the high-frequency region and low-frequency region. In addition, image fusion methods based on spatial domain also include false color image fusion [7], image fusion based on modulation [8], image fusion based on statistics [9], and so on.

Common fundus image fusion methods based on transform domain mainly include fusion based on pyramid transform [10–13, 24] and wavelet transform [14–18, 21, 23]. The image fusion based on pyramid transform extracts the image detail information on different decomposition scales and has a good fusion effect. However, after pyramid decomposition, the data between decomposition layers is redundant, and the high-frequency information might be seriously lost. The image fusion based on wavelet transform can not only extract low-frequency information, but also obtain high-frequency detailed information. However, because the wavelet transform uses row and column down sampling, the image is not translation invariant, which easily leads to the distortion of the fused image.

Different from traditional image fusion, image fusion for wide field fundus images should not only consider correlation between pixels, but also abandon low-quality regions where retinal structures near light source is covered. Paul et al. [22] proposed an image fusion algorithm, where a mask generated by spectral analysis is used to score the visibility of each pixel from source image, and each pixel in output image takes the corresponding source pixel with the highest score. Its mask derived bigger transmission region, unfriendly to strong fog-effect images. In this paper, based on the complementarity between two images from the same pair, an image fusion algorithm based on well-defined template mask is proposed.

3   The Proposed Method

The proposed image fusion algorithm for wide field fundus cameras is shown in Fig. 2. The algorithm consists of four parts: wide field fundus image pre-processing, color and brightness normalization, image fusion based on template mask, and adaptive brightness adjustment. For the input wide field fundus image pair, pre-processing is applied first to improve image quality. Then, the color and brightness of the two pre-processed images are normalized by Poisson fusion to reduce color and brightness differences. Next, the high-quality regions of the two images are selected for fusion based on a template mask.

Finally, the fusion image with low brightness is enhanced to further improve the overall image quality.

3.1 Wide Field Fundus Image Pre-processing

Image Defogging and Registration. Due to the imaging characteristics of wide field fundus cameras, the reflected and scattered light haze are observed in images, and there is a difference of capturing times between the two wide field fundus images, leading to possible offsets. Therefore, the image should be defogged and registered first. In this paper, dark channel prior-based defogging algorithm [19] is used to obtain a wide field fundus image with better quality to see clearer retinal structures. An image registration algorithm based on SIFT feature points is used. Firstly, the brightness and contrast of the image are improved to highlight the retinal detail. The SIFT feature points are detected, which are filtered by RANSAC, and then the input images are registered. Through registration, the center consistency of the two images can be guaranteed, the pixel error at the joint after image fusion can be effectively reduced, and the stitching accuracy can be improved.

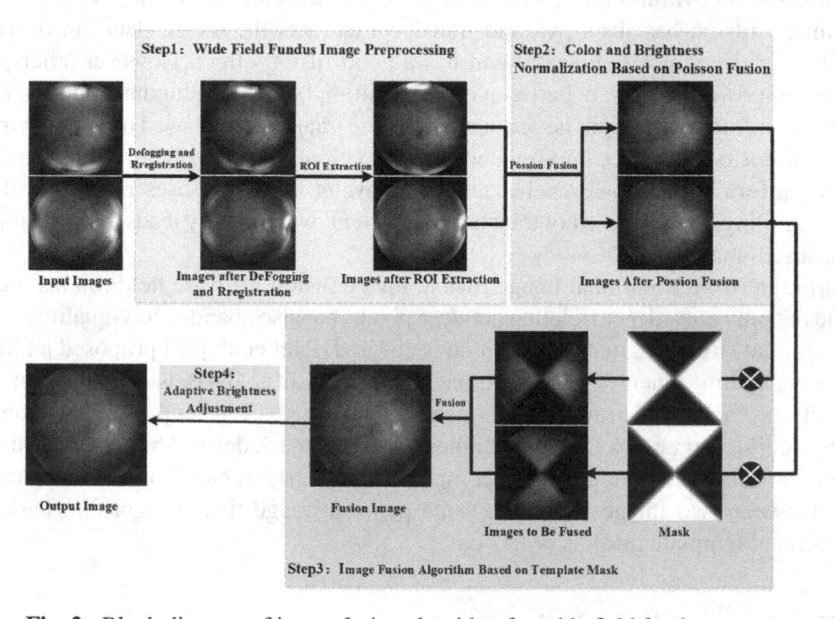

Fig. 2. Block diagram of image fusion algorithm for wide field fundus cameras.

Region of Interest (ROI) Extraction. The effective retinal area of wide field fundus image is approximately circular. In order to avoid the interference of useless areas outside the retina, the circular retinal field of view (FOV) is extracted through Hough circle detection. To ensure that the two images remain registered, they must use the same circle to extract the FOV, so the average of the detected center and the average ROI size of the two images is taken as the final result, and ROI of the two images is extracted with this result. As shown in Fig. 3, the retinal structures of the fundus become visible and they are of better quality after pre-processing.

3.2 Color and Brightness Normalization Based on Poisson Fusion

Different light sources are used in the shooting of two wide field fundus images in the same pair, which easily results in differences in brightness and color between these two images, and obvious boundary is traced in the fusion result. In order to reduce the influence of color and brightness differences on the fusion result, it is necessary to normalize the color brightness of these two images.

During the Poisson fusion process, these two images are considered as foreground and background respectively. It adjusts the color of the foreground image to that of the background image, effectively reducing the brightness and color difference between two images, weakening the image splicing boundary effect, and ensuring the overall color balance of the fusion result.

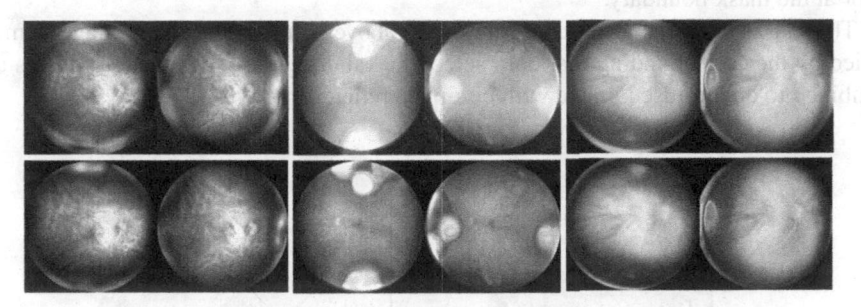

Fig. 3. Results before (the first row) and after (the second row) pre-processing.

3.3 Image Fusion Based on Template Mask

Two fundus images of the same subject have spatial complementarity. In the low-quality regions that must be discarded close to the light source, the image quality is relatively better at the corresponding position of the other image. The images are divided using a temple mask according to the distribution characteristics of stray light. An image fusion algorithm based on a diagonal mask is proposed. The high-quality regions of the original image are selected for fusion based on this template mask.

As shown in Fig. 4, according to the presence of stray light, the wide field fundus images along the diagonal are divided into four parts. The top and bottom regions of Image A (A_1, A_2) and the left and right areas of Image B (B_3, B_4) are the area without stray light, which can be retained. Other areas are abandoned due to strong stray light.

Figure 4 (c) shows the corresponding relationship between the fusion result and the two input images in each region. If the mask is directly generated according to the above method for fusion, there will be obvious boundaries on the diagonal of the fused image.

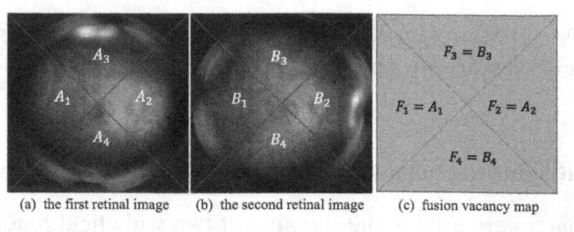

(a) the first retinal image   (b) the second retinal image   (c) fusion vacancy map

Fig. 4. Region division method of wide field fundus image and fusion image

To further improve image quality, the width w is expanded outward along the direction perpendicular to the boundary line of the image to be fused, so as to ensure that there are overlapping regions between two images to be fused. The weighted average method is applied to adjust the weight of pixel to eliminate the boundary effect. As shown in Fig. 5, for the diagonal overlapping region S_1, reduce the weight of Image A and increase the weight of Image B along the arrow direction to make the boundary transition be smooth. Similarly, for S_2, S_3 and S_4, the same method is employed realize smooth transition of color at the mask boundary.

The masks are generated according to the above method, and input image is multiplied by the corresponding masks to select the valid region. Finally, these images are combined to obtain fused image with complete retinal structures.

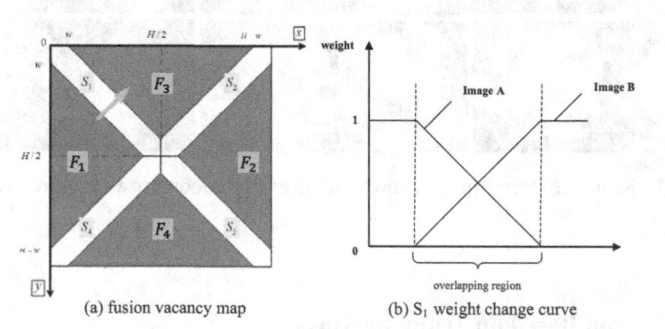

(a) fusion vacancy map   (b) S_1 weight change curve

Fig. 5. Set the overlapping regions. (a) fusion vacancy map; (b) the weight change curve of the overlapping region S_1. Along the arrow direction, the weight of Image A in the fusion image decreases from 1 to 0, and that of Image B in the fusion image increases from 0 to 1;

3.4   Adaptive Brightness Adjustment

Generally, the brightness of wide field fundus images is relatively low, which requires a suitable image enhancement step. To avoid the influence of low-quality area, the average pixel value in center region of Y channel in YUV color space is defined as the brightness. The average brightness of the fused image from the training set data is taken as the threshold. First, the gray values of all pixels in the 1% and 99% quartile are used as the pixel minimum P_{min} and maximum P_{max} respectively. Then, the pixel values greater than P_{max} and less than P_{min} are truncated as P_{max} or P_{min}. Finally, the image is stretched to 0–255 to obtain the final image enhancement result.

4 Evaluations

4.1 Data Set and Experimental Setup

The dataset used in our evaluation is a private dataset captured using Retivue with Olympus Air A01, a Portable Wide Field Fundus Camera. It consists of 56 pairs of image in 1920 × 1920 pixels, and each pair contains two wide field fundus images of the same subject, the shooting time interval between the two images is about 100 ms. The dataset is divided into two subsets: 26 image pairs as a training set (to determine the threshold in module 4) and 30 image pairs as a test set.

It is conducted in Intel Core I5 under Win10 based on Python 3.7 and Opencv3.4.2. The image fusion algorithm based on template mask has an adjustable parameter: overlapping area width w. If w is too small, there will still has boundary effect in the fusion result. If w is too large, the stray light region in the original images that should have been abandoned will still exist in the fusion result. Based on our experimental verification, $w = 100$ is the most appropriate value for the target data set.

4.2 Results and Analysis

The proposed image fusion algorithm for wide field fundus cameras includes four modules: module 1 - wide field fundus image pre-processing, module 2 - image color and brightness normalization based on Poisson fusion, module 3 - image fusion based on template mask, and module 4 - adaptive brightness adjustment.

Validation of Each Module. First, the effectiveness of the image fusion algorithm based on template mask (module 1 + module 3) is verified. Then, taking this as the baseline, the effectiveness of module 2 and module 4 are verified.

Table 1. Results of this algorithm and traditional image fusion algorithm.

Fusion Algorithm	Information Entropy	Standard Deviation	Average Gradient	Spatial Frequency
Image Fusion Algorithm Based on Pixel Definition [21]	6.017	38.050	0.523	1.429
Image Fusion Algorithm Based on Diagonal Mask Pairs(**baseline**)	**6.068**	**39.776**	**0.671**	**1.662**

According to Table 1, compared to the image fusion algorithm based on Pixel Definition [21], our proposed method is more effective, which increases information entropy by 0.051, standard deviation by 1.726, average gradient by 0.148 and spatial frequency by 0.233. Further, the module 2 and module 4 are successively added to the baseline. Results are shown in Table 2. All evaluation indexes increase, indicating that the image color and brightness normalization and adaptive brightness adjustment based on Poisson fusion can effectively improve the quality of fusion results.

Table 2. Results of each experiment scheme.

Experiment Scheme	Brightness	Information Entropy	Standard Deviation	Average Gradient	Spatial Frequency
module 1 + module 3	-	6.068	39.776	0.671	1.662
module 1 + module 2 + module 3	101	6.214	40.459	0.684	1.671
module 1 + module 2 + module 3 + module 4	110	6.328	43.773	0.747	1.832

Validation of the Overall Algorithm. In order to verify the effectiveness of the algorithm, three domain experts scores the fusion results from three aspects of image authenticity, image clarity and overall quality. The image authenticity is based on whether there is obvious noise or color distortion in images. Image clarity is according to whether images are clearly visible, and whether the details are legible, blurred, or even lost. Overall quality is combined with general features (such as brightness and contrast) and structural features (such as vascular clarity, vascular density, and macular area contrast) to comprehensively evaluate images. Since our method is aiming at a specific wide-field fundus camera and there is no common overlap area in images, it is difficult to directly compare with existing image fusion methods, so we mainly compare to a realted work [22] in a similar strategy.

We compare them with Paul et al. [22] to evaluate the effectiveness of the algorithm. According to Table 3, The proposed method is slightly lower than that in Paul et al. [22] in terms of image authenticity, because there are still obvious traces in the diagonal transition area of some images. But the image clarity and overall image quality are both higher than those in Paul et al. [22]. It can be seen that our proposed method is better and more effective. Some visual examples are provided in Fig. 6.

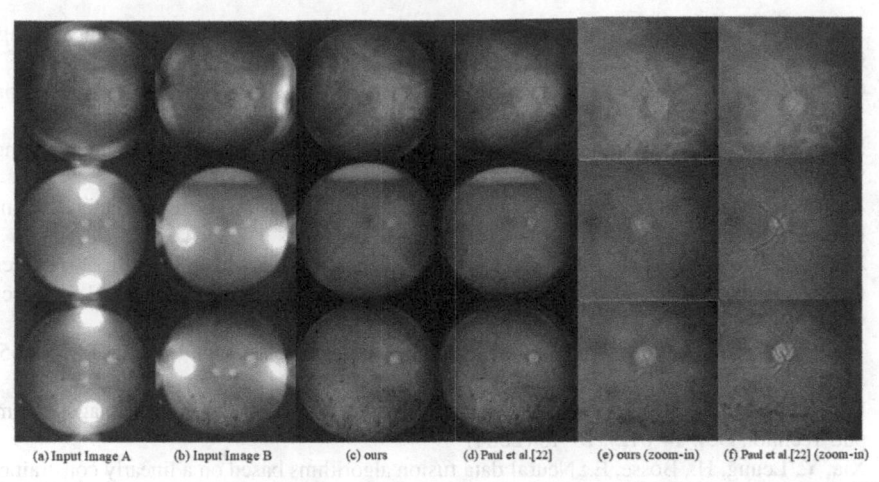

(a) Input Image A   (b) Input Image B   (c) ours   (d) Paul et al.[22]   (e) ours (zoom-in)   (f) Paul et al.[22] (zoom-in)

Fig. 6. Examples of original images and the comparison between our method and Paul's [22].

Table 3. Expert evaluation results (average of 30 pairs of data).

	Image clarity (0–10)	Image authenticity (0–10)	Overall quality (0–10)	Total (0–30)
Paul et al. [22]	7.944	**7.756**	7.676	23.356
Ours	**8.144**	7.589	**7.711**	**23.444**

5   Conclusions

In this paper, an image fusion algorithm for wide field fundus cameras is proposed. Image pre-processing is first conducted to eliminate the interference of invalid areas. An image fusion algorithm based on template mask is applied, which selects high-quality regions of wide field fundus images, and reduces the boundary effect of image fusion by weighted average method. Aiming at low brightness of wide field fundus images, a brightness adaptive image enhancement step is used to improve the information entropy of fused images and finally output a clear and high-quality wide field fundus image. Experimental results show that the proposed algorithm for wide field fundus cameras is effective and it has a better fusion results.

Acknowledgements. This work is supported by Natural Science Basic Research Plan in Shaanxi Province of China (2020JM-129), and BJNSF (No. 4202033).

References

1. Yang, B., Jing, Z.L., Zhao, H.T.: Review of pixel-level image fusion. J. Shanghai Jiaotong Univ. (Sci.) **15**(1), 6–12 (2010). https://doi.org/10.1007/s12204-010-7186-y

2. Singh, S., Anand, R.S.: Ripplet domain fusion approach for CT and MR medical image information. Biomed. Signal Process. Control **46**, 281–292 (2018)
3. Chen, J., Chen, L., Shabaz, M.: Image fusion algorithm at pixel level based on edge detection. J. Healthc. Eng. **7**, 1–10 (2021)
4. Min, X.: Application of improved weighted fusion in eliminating image stitching ghosting. Softw. Eng. **20**(5), 27–29 (2007)
5. Zhan, K., Teng, J., Li, Q., et al.: A novel explicit multi-focus image fusion method. J. Inf. Hiding Multimedia Signal Process. **6**(3), 600–612 (2015)
6. Zhu, Y. L, Liu, R. L., et al.: Research on medical image fusion based on PCA. In: 2018 International Conference on Computational, Modeling, Simulation and Mathematical Statistics, vol. 4 (2018)
7. Toet, A., Walraven, J.: New false color mapping for image fusion. Opt. Eng. **35**(3), 650–658 (1996)
8. Lv, X., Zhang, W.: Contrast modulation fusion method applied to medical images. Comput. Technol. Dev. **14**(012), 16–15 (2004)
9. Xia, Y., Leung, H., Bosse, E.: Neural data fusion algorithms based on a linearly constrained least square method. IEEE Trans. Neural Netw. **13**(2), 320–329 (2002)
10. Burt, P.J., Adelson, E.H.: The laplacian pyramid as a compact image Code. IEEE Trans. Commun. **31**(4), 532–540 (1983)
11. Toet, A., Ruyven, J.J.V., Valeton, J.M.: Merging thermal and visual images by a contrast pyramid Opt. Eng. **28**(7), 789–792 (1989)
12. Toet, A.: A morphological pyramidal image decomposition Pattern Recogn. Lett. **9**(4), 255–261 (1989)
13. Burt, P.J.: A gradient pyramid basis for pattern-selective image fusion. In: Proceedings of the Society for Information Display Conference. SID Press, San Jose, USA, pp. 467–470 (1992)
14. Li, H., Manjunath, B.S., Mitra, S.K.: Multi-sensor image fusion using the wavelet transform. Graph. Models Image Process. **57**(3), 235–245 (1995)
15. Chipman, L.J., Orr, T.M., Graham, L.N.: Wavelets and image fusion. In: Proceedings International Conference on Image Processing, pp. 248–251(1995)
16. Guixi, L., Wanhai, Y.: Image fusion method and performance evaluation based on wavelet decomposition. Acta Automatica Sin. **28**(6), 927–934 (2002)
17. Wang, H.H.: A new multiwavelet-based approach to image fusion. J. Math. Imaging Vis. **21**(2), 177–192 (2004). https://doi.org/10.1023/B:JMIV.0000035181.00093.e3
18. Liu, D., Yang, F., Wei, H., et al.: Remote sensing image fusion method based on discrete wavelet and multiscale morphological transform in the IHS color space. J. Appl. Remote Sens. **14**(1), 016518 (2020)
19. He, K.M., Sun, J., Tang, X.O.: Single image haze removal using dark channel prior. IEEE Trans. Pattern Anal. Mach. Intell. **33**(12), 2341–2353 (2011)
20. Pérez, P., Gangnet, M., Blake, A.: Poisson image editing. Acm Trans. Graph. **22**(3), 313–318 (2003)
21. Jing, Z., Xiao, G., Li, Z.: Image Fusion: Theory and Application. Higher Education Press, Beijing (2007)
22. Yates, P.A., Lai, M., Yi, T.W., Martinez, A.: Wide Field Fundus Camera with Auto-montage at a Single Alignment. US Patent: US2019/0159673 A1, PCT/US2017/038560. 30 May 2019
23. Talbar, S.N., Chavan, S.S., Pawar, A.: Non-subsampled complex wavelet transform based medical image fusion. In: Arai, K., Bhatia, R., Kapoor, S. (eds.) Advances in Intelligent Systems and Computing, vol. 880, pp. 548–556. Springer, Cham (2019). https://doi.org/10.1007/978-3-030-02686-8_41
24. Fu, J., Li, W., Du, J., et al.: A multiscale residual pyramid attention network for medical image fusion. Biomed. Signal Process. Control **66**(9) (2021)

Investigating the Vulnerability of Federated Learning-Based Diabetic Retinopathy Grade Classification to Gradient Inversion Attacks

Christopher Nielsen[1,2]($\boxtimes$), Anup Tuladhar[1,3], and Nils D. Forkert[1,3,4]

[1] Department of Radiology, University of Calgary, Calgary, AB, Canada
csnielse@ucalgary.ca
[2] Biomedical Engineering Program, University of Calgary, Calgary, AB, Canada
[3] Hotchkiss Brain Institute, University of Calgary, Calgary, AB, Canada
[4] Alberta Children's Hospital Research Institute, University of Calgary, Calgary, AB, Canada

Abstract. Diabetic retinopathy (DR) is a serious vision-threatening condition associated with diabetes and is the leading cause of visual impairment for working-age adults worldwide. Smartphone-based fundus imaging (SBFI) has the potential to be combined with machine learning-based DR screening procedures to simultaneously improve global health equity and the prognosis of DR by increasing patient accessibility to low-cost DR screening services. Federated learning is a promising method to train machine learning models for DR grade classification using large amounts of SBFI data, which can protect the privacy of sensitive patient data at the same time. However, gradient inversion attacks have been shown to be able to reconstruct private data using the model parameter gradient information transmitted during federated learning updates. The purpose of this paper is to investigate the privacy threat that gradient inversion attacks pose for reconstructing identifiable retinal fundus images during federated learning-based DR grade classification training. Specifically, a novel metric called "Segmentation Matching Score" (SMS) is proposed to quantify clinically relevant features present in fundus images reconstructed during a gradient inversion attack that could be exploited for patient identification information. Experimental results based on the FGADR dataset demonstrate that reconstructed images could be correctly matched to their corresponding source images using the SMS metric with a top-1 accuracy of 72.0%. These findings indicate that gradient inversion attacks pose a significant threat for federated learning-based DR grade classification models and warrant further investigation into viable defense strategies.

Keywords: Diabetic retinopathy · Gradient inversion attack · Federated learning

1 Introduction

Diabetic retinopathy (DR) is the leading global cause of visual impairment for working-age adults, and it is estimated that 200 million individuals will suffer from DR by 2040 [1]. The DR severity grade is typically determined by assessing the presence and magnitude of specific features clinically associated with the progression of the disease

© The Author(s), under exclusive license to Springer Nature Switzerland AG 2022
B. Antony et al. (Eds.): OMIA 2022, LNCS 13576, pp. 183–192, 2022.
https://doi.org/10.1007/978-3-031-16525-2_19

within color retinal fundus images as shown in Fig. 1 [2]. As visible features such as hard exudates, microaneurysms, and hemorrhages are used to monitor disease progression, it is critical that diabetic patients perform regular DR screening procedures to maximize potential treatment options for vision loss prevention.

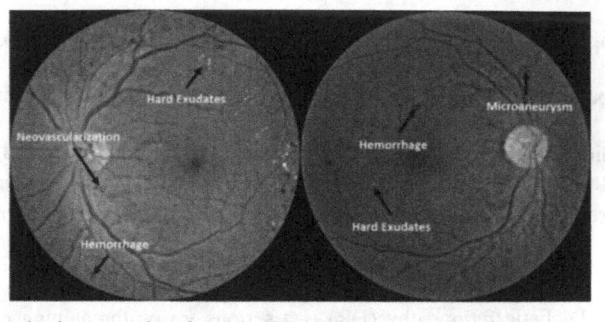

Fig. 1. Retinal fundus images taken from the FGADR dataset with associated annotations showing examples of clinical features used for quantifying the DR severity grade.

Recently, there has been tremendous progress in applying machine learning models for the task of DR grade classification [3–5]. The success of machine learning-based systems for DR screening procedures opens a wide range of possibilities for patient-centric precision medicine. The benefits of using precision medicine to improve the standard of care have been demonstrated in several medical disciplines [6]. Unfortunately, the cost of DR screening may be prohibitive for some socioeconomic regions, contributing to global health inequity [7]. However, advances in mobile technology have made it possible to capture detailed retinal fundus images using smartphone-based fundus imaging (SBFI) [8–11]. The combination of SBFI and autonomous DR screening procedures could dramatically improve the prognosis of DR globally by increasing patient accessibility to low-cost DR screening services.

Although machine learning models have displayed exceptional capability on specific benchmark datasets, several challenges have to be overcome to successfully deploy and integrate these models within the context of a SBFI patient-centric precision medicine system for autonomous DR screening. Of particular importance is ensuring rigorous patient privacy protection given the large volume of patient data that is required for machine learning models to achieve robust and generalizable performance [12]. Retinal fundus image data is especially sensitive to privacy violations as retinal recognition is a reliable form of biometric identification and is used within many security systems for identity verification [13, 14]. To help protect the privacy of patient data, federated learning paradigms have been proposed, which mitigate privacy risks by ensuring that during model training, the patient data never leaves the location where it is stored [15–17]. Instead, the parameters of the machine learning model are sent to the location of the data where training is performed on the local patient data and the updated parameters of the machine learning model are sent back to the server. In the context of training a model for DR grade classification using SBFI data stored locally on a patient's smartphone, each patient can be considered to represent their own federated learning institution. During training, the model parameters are sent to the patient's smartphone and updated on that device using the patient's SBFI data. Zerka et al. demonstrated how 1-patient-per-institution federated learning could be achieved in the extreme case where federated institutions have only a single patient sample [18]. Such a training paradigm would enable the inclusion of SBFI data from individual patients during model training without requiring the potentially privacy compromising transport of their sensitive data to a central location.

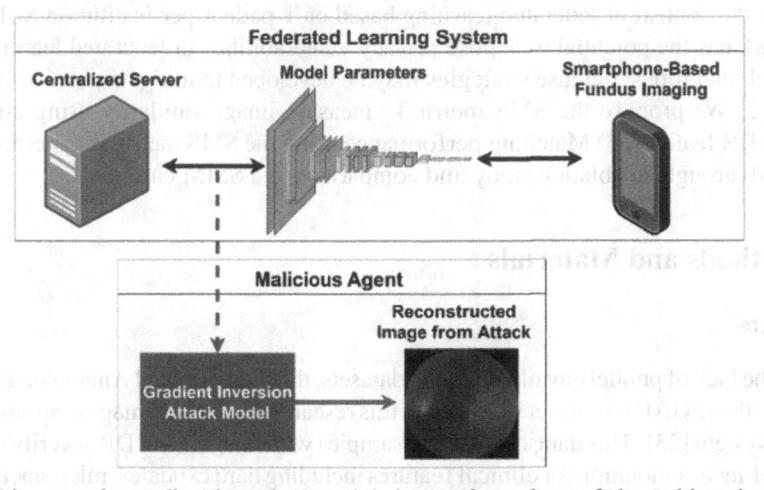

Fig. 2. Diagram of a gradient inversion attack being performed on a federated learning system using parameter gradient updates intercepted by a malicious agent.

Despite the success of federated learning, it has been shown that sensitive patient data used to train a federated model may be reconstructed from the underlying model parameter gradient updates as shown in Fig. 2. This reconstruction process is known as a gradient inversion attack [19, 20]. Of particular concern, in the context of training a federated learning system using personal SBFI data, is that the 1-patient-per-institution case has been shown to be especially vulnerable to gradient inversion attacks [21, 22]. Should a gradient inversion attack be successful, it may be possible for a malicious agent to exploit sensitive patient information. Privacy breaches of this magnitude could lead to a decreased willingness by patients to share their data, inevitably impeding the development and deployment of potentially lifesaving medical machine learning models. Therefore, it is imperative that such vulnerabilities are thoroughly understood so that robust defense strategies may be used to mitigate potential privacy threats.

The purpose of this work is to investigate the privacy threat posed by gradient inversion attacks when training a 1-patient-per-institution federated learning model for DR severity grade classification. Specifically, we are interested in measuring the amount of information present in reconstructed images that can be exploited for patient identification. Most image similarity metrics such as the structural similarity index (SSIM) do not explicitly incorporate clinically relevant features into their computation. However, prior research has shown the benefit of using clinical features such as the topology of retinal vessel structures for identity verification, and it is foreseeable that clinical features pertinent to DR grade classification, such as hard exudates, microaneurysms, and hemorrhages may also be valuable for patient identification [13]. Therefore, to quantify the threat posed by gradient inversion attacks, we propose a novel metric called "Segmentation Matching Score" (SMS), which assesses the capacity to correctly match the patient identity of reconstructed images using the topology of several clinical features relevant for DR grade classification extracted from these images. The main contributions of this work can be summarized as follows: 1) To the best of our knowledge, this is the first attempt to analyze the quality of images reconstructed using a gradient inversion attack in the context of federated learning based on 1-patient-per-institution SBFI data. This work has the potential to expose privacy vulnerabilities in federated learning systems such that robust defense strategies may be developed to mitigate potential privacy threats. 2) We propose the SMS metric to measure image similarity using clinically relevant DR features. 3) Matching performance using the SMS metric is experimentally validated through an ablation study and comparison to a SSIM baseline.

2 Methods and Materials

2.1 Data

Due to the lack of publicly available SBRI datasets, the Fine-Grained Annotated Diabetic Retinopathy (FGADR) dataset was used in this research to emulate images captured from a SBRI system [23]. This dataset has 1842 samples with image-level DR severity grading and pixel-level annotation for clinical features including hard exudates, microaneurysms, and hemorrhages. The image-level DR grade and pixel-level segmentation labels were manually provided by a panel of ophthalmologists. Each image in the dataset has three color channels and a spatial resolution of 1280×1280 pixels. Similar to the gradient inversion attack framework proposed by Qu et al., all images were resized to a spatial resolution of 224×224 pixels for experimental efficiency [24]. Data was partitioned into training/testing sets using an 80/20 split respectively (1473 training images and 369 testing images). As 83.5% of the images within the test set had more-than-mild DR (mtmDR), many of these images contained significant lesion features. Forty-six unique source images were randomly selected to serve as candidates for reconstruction.

2.2 Federated Learning and Gradient Inversion Attack Framework

The specific network architecture chosen for the DR severity grade classification was VGG16 [25], as this architecture has been heavily researched for deployment on smartphone computing hardware [26]. Weights pretrained on ImageNet were used to initialize the network. Before the federated learning updates were employed for the gradient inversion attack process, model fine-tuning was performed for 100 epochs using the Adam optimizer with a learning rate of 10^{-5}. The purpose of this fine-tuning was to establish model weights that could represent the likely training state of a DR grade classification model during a gradient inversion attack. The federated learning updates were computed using federated stochastic gradient descent (SGD) where each institution performed a single step of SGD before returning the parameter gradient updates to the server. The gradient inversion attack optimization was performed using the state-of-the-art inverting gradients framework proposed in [27]. This framework optimizes the pixel parameter values of each reconstructed image to maximize the cosine similarity between the model parameter gradient updates sent over the federated learning communication channel and the gradient updates computed from each reconstructed image directly. Given the clinical 1-patient-per-institution context, each gradient inversion attack was performed using a batch size of 1, where each batch contained one of the source images randomly selected from the test set to serve as a reconstruction candidate. The hyperparameters used for the inversion attack were set as the defaults recommended by Geiping et al. [27]. Specifically, the attack optimization was performed with total variation regularization for 24000 iterations. The output of this process was a set of reconstructed images, each corresponding to a specific source image sampled from the test set as described in Sect. 2.1. All model architectures were implemented using PyTorch and trained on an NVIDIA RTX 3090 GPU.

2.3   Segmentation Matching Score

The goal of the SMS metric is to quantify the amount of clinically relevant information present in the reconstructed images that is informative for patient identification. Therefore, using the training data split described in Sect. 2.1, three segmentation models employing feature pyramid network (FPN) architectures with Resnet34 encoders were trained to segment the spatial location of hard exudates, hemorrhages, and microaneurysms [28]. The segmentation models were trained for 100 epochs to minimize the Dice loss. Optimization was performed using the Adam optimizer with a learning rate of 10^{-4}. For each of the three segmentation models, Dice scores were computed as a measure of similarity between the extracted segmentation masks for each reconstructed image and all images in the test set. A k-NN proximity search was used to find the top-k most similar images in the test set for each reconstructed image using these Dice scores. A reconstruction was considered to be successfully matched if the corresponding source image used to generate the reconstruction was within the top-k most similar results. An overview of the processing to compute this metric is shown in Fig. 3, where clinical features are first extracted from reconstructed and test set images, and then used to match the top-k most similar images.

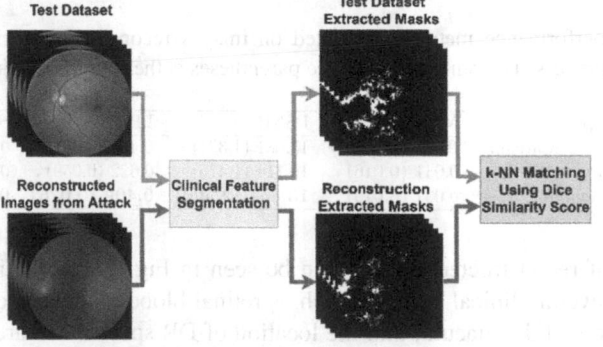

Fig. 3. Overview of the process to match images reconstructed from the gradient inversion attack with their corresponding source images using the SMS metric.

2.4 Evaluation

Several image-based metrics were used to measure the quality of the images reconstructed during the gradient inversion attack process, including the mean squared error (MSE), peak signal-to-noise ratio (PSNR), learned perceptual image patch similarity (LPIPS), and the structural similarity index measure (SSIM) [29, 30]. To evaluate the performance of the segmentation models trained to compute the SMS metric, the similarity between the corresponding computed segmentation masks from the source and reconstructed images was calculated using the Dice and intersection over union (IoU) score metrics. Furthermore, SSIM was chosen as the baseline for image matching performance due to its widespread use throughout the research community as an established image similarity metric [31], and image-based biometric comparison metric [32].

3 Results

3.1 Gradient Inversion Attack Performance

The average image-based similarity metrics computed to assess the quality of the reconstructed images are shown in Table 1. The first row shows the average metrics computed between each reconstructed image and the corresponding source image from the test set. Two baselines were developed for comparison by calculating the evaluation metrics between each reconstructed image and all test set images (row 2), and 20000 randomly selected pairs of images from the test set (row 3). These results show an increase in average image similarity as measured across all metrics when each reconstruction was compared against its corresponding source image versus other images from the test set. When comparing the mean performance metrics between rows 1 and 3 in Table 1, it becomes apparent that there is a significant difference in the average SSIM similarity (0.342 ± 0.032 versus 0.504 ± 0.047) while the difference in the average MSE similarity was negligible (0.029 ± 0.009 versus 0.031 ± 0.019). This discrepancy may indicate that the structural information extracted by the SSIM similarity metric is not adequately represented in the reconstructed images. As such, SSIM may not be optimal for measuring the similarity between images produced from a gradient inversion attack and their corresponding source images.

Table 1. Mean performance metrics calculated on images reconstructed during the gradient inversion attack process. The number inside the parentheses is the standard deviation.

Comparison Type	MSE	PSNR	LPIPS	SSIM
Reconstruction vs. Matching	**0.029 (0.009)**	15.581 (1.324)	0.455 (0.071)	0.342 (0.032)
Reconstruction vs. All	0.041 (0.016)	14.114 (1.478)	0.622 (0.059)	0.284 (0.031)
Random vs. Random	0.031 (0.019)	**15.854 (2.500)**	**0.409 (0.075)**	**0.504 (0.047)**

Examples of reconstructed images can be seen in Fig. 4. Qualitatively, it can be observed that several clinical features such as retinal blood vessel structures, location of the optic disc and the macula, and the location of DR specific features such as hard exudates are clearly present in the reconstructed images. Several differences between the reconstructions and their corresponding source images can also be observed. For example, as seen in Fig. 4, parts of the retina appear darker in the reconstructed images than in the source images, especially the retinal vessel structure.

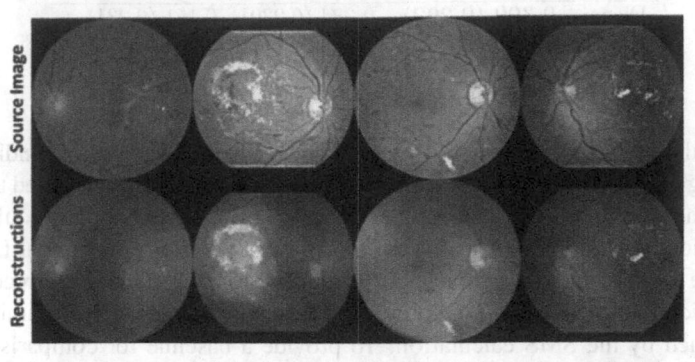

Fig. 4. Examples of reconstructed fundus images produced from the gradient inversion attack process. Each column shows an image pair where the top row shows the source image from the FGADR dataset, and the bottom row shows the gradient inversion attack reconstruction.

3.2 Extracting Identifiable Clinical Features from Reconstructed Images

The Dice scores computed for each segmentation model during evaluation on the ground truth test set were 0.371, 0.408, and 0.030 for hard exudates, hemorrhages, and microaneurysms, respectively. The poor performance of microaneurysm segmentation may likely be due to the sparsity of microaneurysms in the images compared to hard exudates and hemorrhages. The segmentation model performance comparing the extracted masks from the reconstructed fundus images and corresponding source images were computed as shown in Table 2. Microaneurysm segmentation performed worst, with average Dice and IoU scores of 0.151 and 0.103, respectively. An example of a hard exudate segmentation is shown in Fig. 5. The average Dice and IoU scores for hard exudate segmentation were 0.390 and 0.283, respectively. These results demonstrate how a significant number of clinical features captured in the source image segmentation masks are also represented in the segmentation masks extracted from the reconstructed images.

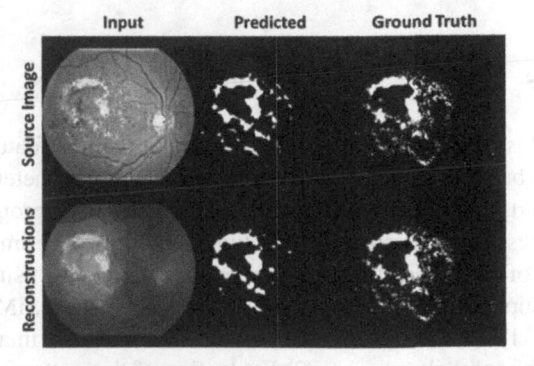

Fig. 5. Segmentation predictions for hard exudate features. The top row shows the segmentation results for a source image sampled from the test set. The bottom row shows the segmentation results for the corresponding image reconstructed from the gradient inversion attack.

Table 2. Mean IoU and Dice scores comparing the extracted segmentation masks from reconstructed images and source images. The standard deviation is shown within the parenthesis.

Metric	HardExudate	Hemorrhage	Microaneurysm
Dice	**0.390 (0.292)**	0.334 (0.239)	0.151 (0.231)
IoU	**0.283 (0.233)**	0.225 (0.177)	0.103 (0.173)

The ability to correctly match a reconstructed image to its corresponding source image using clinical features extracted by the segmentation models was used to measure how well the extracted clinical features from the reconstructed images could be used for patient identification. Specifically, the matching performance was quantified by calculating the top-k matching accuracy, corresponding to the percentage of reconstructed images which had their matching source image within the top-k most similar results as determined by the SMS calculation. To provide a baseline for comparison, image matching was also computed using the SSIM measure as the similarity matching metric. Additionally, an ablation study was performed to compute the matching performance using hard exudate, hemorrhage, and microaneurysm features independently. The matching performance results are shown in Table 3. The SMS metric performs best overall with a top-1 matching accuracy of 72.0% while, the matching performance using the SSIM measure performed worst overall with a top-1 matching accuracy of 10.0%. These results indicate that the clinical features embedded within the reconstructed images can provide pertinent information for patient identification.

Table 3. Matching accuracy describing the percentage of reconstructed images that can be successfully matched with their corresponding source image using clinically relevant features.

Metric	SSIM	SMS Ensemble	Hard Exudate	Hemorrhage	Microaneurysm
Top-1 Accuracy	10.0%	**72.0%**	67.5%	69.2%	24.3%
Top-3 Accuracy	15.0%	**76.1%**	72.5%	74.5%	29.7%
Top-5 Accuracy	17.5%	**78.2%**	75.0%	77.0%	32.4%

4   Conclusions

The results from this work demonstrate that important clinical features within retinal fundus images can be reconstructed from federated model parameter gradient updates using state-of-the-art gradient inversion attack approaches. The proposed SMS metric was shown to successfully match reconstructions to their source images with a top-1 matching accuracy of 72.0%. Furthermore, the matching accuracy using the SMS metric was shown to be superior to the matching accuracy using the SSIM measure. Future work will include: 1) Qualitative analysis of the reconstructed images using quality ratings from clinical ophthalmologists. 2) Evaluation of the performance of DR grade classification using reconstructed images. 3) Identification matching will be extended using non-lesion-based features such as the segmentation of retinal vessels, the optic cup, and the optic disc. 4) The relationship between the choice of gradient inversion attack loss function and the resulting SSIM similarity between the reconstructed images and the corresponding source images will be investigated.

References

1. Dai, L., et al.: A deep learning system for detecting diabetic retinopathy across the disease spectrum. Nat. Commun. **12**, 3242 (2021)
2. Staurenghi, G., et al.: Impact of baseline diabetic retinopathy severity scale scores on visual outcomes in the VIVID-DME and VISTA-DME studies. Br. J. Ophthalmol. **102**, 954–958 (2018)
3. Gulshan, V., et al.: Development and validation of a deep learning algorithm for detection of diabetic retinopathy in retinal fundus photographs. JAMA **316**, 2402 (2016)
4. Ruamviboonsuk, P., et al.: Deep learning versus human graders for classifying diabetic retinopathy severity in a nationwide screening program. npj Digit. Med. **2**, 1–9 (2019)
5. Abràmoff, M.D., Lavin, P.T., Birch, M., Shah, N., Folk, J.C.: Pivotal trial of an autonomous AI-based diagnostic system for detection of diabetic retinopathy in primary care offices. npj Digit. Med. **1**, 1–8 (2018)
6. MacEachern, S.J., Forkert, N.D.: Machine learning for precision medicine. Genome **64**, 416–425 (2021)
7. Byrne, M.M., et al.: Cost of a community-based diabetic retinopathy screening program. Diabetes Care **37**, e236–e237 (2014)
8. Iqbal, U.: Smartphone fundus photography: a narrative review. Int. J. Retina Vitreous **7**, 44 (2021)
9. Nazari Khanamiri, H., Nakatsuka, A., El-Annan, J.: Smartphone fundus photography. J. Vis. Exp., 55958 (2017). https://doi.org/10.3791/55958
10. Wintergerst, M.W.M., Jansen, L.G., Holz, F.G., Finger, R.P.: Smartphone-based fundus imaging-where are we now? Asia Pac. J. Ophthalmol. **9**, 308–314 (2020)
11. Parasuraman, S., Sam, A.T., Yee, S.W.K., Chuon, B.L.C., Ren, L.Y.: Smartphone usage and increased risk of mobile phone addiction: a concurrent study. Int. J. Pharm. Investig. **7**, 125–131 (2017)
12. Willemink, M.J., et al.: Preparing medical imaging data for machine learning. Radiology **295**, 4–15 (2020)
13. Farzin, H., Abrishami-Moghaddam, H., Moin, M.-S.: A novel retinal identification system. EURASIP J. Adv. Sig. Process. **2008**(1), 1 (2008). https://doi.org/10.1155/2008/280635
14. Akram, M.U., Abdul Salam, A., Khawaja, S.G., Naqvi, S.G.H., Khan, S.A.: RIDB: a dataset of fundus images for retina based person identification. Data Brief **33**, 106433 (2020)
15. Tuladhar, A., Gill, S., Ismail, Z., Forkert, N.D.: Building machine learning models without sharing patient data: a simulation-based analysis of distributed learning by ensembling. J. Biomed. Inform. **106**, 103424 (2020)
16. Konečný, J., McMahan, H.B., Ramage, D., Richtárik, P.: Federated optimization: distributed machine learning for on-device intelligence (2016). https://doi.org/10.48550/arXiv.1610.02527
17. McMahan, B., Moore, E., Ramage, D., Hampson, S., Arcas, B.A.Y.: Communication-efficient learning of deep networks from decentralized data. In: Proceedings of the 20th International Conference on Artificial Intelligence and Statistics, pp. 1273–1282. PMLR (2017)
18. Zerka, F., et al.: Privacy preserving distributed learning classifiers – sequential learning with small sets of data. Comput. Biol. Med. **136**, 104716 (2021)

19. Yin, H., et al.: See through Gradients: image batch recovery via GradInversion. In: 2021 IEEE/CVF Conference on Computer Vision and Pattern Recognition (CVPR), pp. 16332–16341. IEEE (2021). https://doi.org/10.1109/CVPR46437.2021.01607

20. Zhu, L., Liu, Z., Han, S.: Deep leakage from gradients. In: Advances in Neural Information Processing Systems, vol. 32, Curran Associates, Inc. (2019)

21. Huang, Y., Gupta, S., Song, Z., Li, K., Arora, S.: Evaluating gradient inversion attacks and defenses in federated learning. In: Advances in Neural Information Processing Systems, vol. 34, pp. 7232–7241. Curran Associates, Inc. (2021)

22. Subbanna, N., Wilms, M., Tuladhar, A., Forkert, N.D.: An analysis of the vulnerability of two common deep learning-based medical image segmentation techniques to model inversion attacks. Sensors **21**, 3874 (2021)

23. Zhou, Y., Wang, B., Huang, L., Cui, S., Shao, L.: A benchmark for studying diabetic retinopathy: segmentation, grading, and transferability. IEEE Trans. Med. Imaging **40**, 818–828 (2021)

24. Qu, L., Balachandar, N., Zhang, M., Rubin, D.: Handling data heterogeneity with generative replay in collaborative learning for medical imaging. Med. Image Anal. **78**, 102424 (2022)

25. Simonyan, K., Zisserman, A.: Very deep convolutional networks for large-scale image recognition (2015). https://doi.org/10.48550/arXiv.1409.1556

26. Wang, P., Hu, Q., Fang, Z., Zhao, C., Cheng, J.: DeepSearch: a fast image search framework for mobile devices. ACM Trans. Multimedia Comput. Commun. Appl. **14**, 1–22 (2018)

27. Geiping, J., Bauermeister, H., Dröge, H., Moeller, M.: Inverting gradients - how easy is it to break privacy in federated learning? In: Advances in Neural Information Processing Systems, vol. 33, pp. 16937–16947. Curran Associates, Inc. (2020)

28. Lin, T.-Y., et al.: Feature pyramid networks for object detection. In: 2017 IEEE Conference on Computer Vision and Pattern Recognition (CVPR), pp. 936–944. IEEE (2017). https://doi.org/10.1109/CVPR.2017.106

29. Wang, Z., Bovik, A.C., Sheikh, H.R., Simoncelli, E.P.: Image quality assessment: from error visibility to structural similarity. IEEE Trans. Image Process. **13**, 600–612 (2004)

30. Zhang, R., Isola, P., Efros, A.A., Shechtman, E., Wang, O.: The unreasonable effectiveness of deep features as a perceptual metric. In: 2018 IEEE/CVF Conference on Computer Vision and Pattern Recognition, pp. 586–595. IEEE (2018). https://doi.org/10.1109/CVPR.2018.00068

31. Nilsson, J., Akenine-Möller, T.: Understanding SSIM. arXiv preprint arXiv:2006.13846 (2020)

32. Hofbauer, H., Rathgeb, C., Uhl, A., Wild, P.: Image metric-based biometric comparators: a supplement to feature vector-based Hamming distance? In: 2012 BIOSIG - Proceedings of the International Conference of Biometrics Special Interest Group (BIOSIG), pp. 1–5 (2012)

Extraction of Eye Redness for Standardized Ocular Surface Photography

Philipp Ostheimer[1]([✉]), Arno Lins[2], Benjamin Massow[3], Bernhard Steger[4,5], Daniel Baumgarten[1], and Marco Augustin[5]

[1] Institute of Electrical and Biomedical Engineering,
UMIT TIROL - Private University for Health Sciences,
Medical Informatics and Technology, Hall in Tirol, Austria
`philipp.ostheimer@umit-tirol.at`
[2] Department of Medical and Health Technologies,
MCI - The Entrepreneurial School, Innsbruck, Austria
[3] Department of Mechatronics, MCI - The Entrepreneurial School,
Innsbruck, Austria
[4] Department of Ophthalmology and Optometry, Medical University of Innsbruck,
Innsbruck, Austria
[5] Occyo GmbH, Innsbruck, Austria

Abstract. Color photography is the basis to evaluate ocular surface imaging biomarkers such as eye redness. Different grading scales are hereby used clinically to examine the severity of eye redness ranging from a white to a red eye. Currently used imaging and grading is time consuming and subjective. In this work we propose a baseline pipeline to assess the ocular redness based on standardized images of the ocular surface. Images were acquired using a novel ocular surface photography system, specifically tailored for standardized imaging in terms of lighting, focus and position. The pipeline comprises three major steps in extracting the eye redness: (i) defining a region-of-interest in the image of the ocular surface, (ii) detection of scleral tissue by tiling the high-resolution images and subsequent classification of the tiles and (iii) quantification of ocular redness based on image features. The pipeline was evaluated on a data set containing external eye images of healthy subjects and showed promising results on the detection of scleral tiles, which can subsequently be used for eye redness extraction. The performance and the simplicity of the approach makes the baseline pipeline a suitable candidate for further development and translating the concept to clinical patient data.

Keywords: Ophthalmic photography · Ocular surface · Sclera · Classification · Feature extraction · Machine learning · External eye

1 Introduction

Bulbar redness becomes visible due to the enlargement of conjunctival and episcleral blood vessels. The redness can occur either by inflammation and irritation

B. Antony et al. (Eds.): OMIA 2022, LNCS 13576, pp. 193–202, 2022.
https://doi.org/10.1007/978-3-031-16525-2_20

of the bulbar conjunctiva or sclera, or by systemic disease [8]. Reference-image-based grading scales were introduced to clinical practice since the 1980 s s in order to ease the comparison during follow-up visits. Grading the redness allows to track changes and consequently enables to confirm or alter treatment plans [11]. Reference-image-based grading scales usually contain a range of images of the ocular surface. Each grading is showing a different severity from a white to a red eye. The reference images of a visual grading scale are either drawings (e.g., Efron [3]) or photographs (e.g., DBR [6]). The scales also differ from each other by the number of divisions in severity, e.g., Efron offers five grades, whereas IER only has four and the MC-D scale has even six grades [11]. Furthermore, Efron et al. [3] recorded significant discrepancy between observers and challenging interchangeability between his investigated scales. Hence, one can conclude that comparability of judging ocular redness is challenging when these subjective grading of ocular redness is used. Hence a different approach to grade bulbar redness is to use digital images in combination with algorithms to extract different redness features. Currently the Oculus Keratograph 5M (Oculus Optikgeraete GmbH, Wetzlar, Germany) is the only commercially available imaging device offering a standardized way of imaging the ocular surface, which is the key requirement for objective grading based on digital images [9]. Other approaches include detailed description on how to image and grade bulbar redness with slit lamps equipped with a camera sensor [7,13]. Objective quantification based on digital images here is mainly based on the red color intensity extraction and/or vessel edge detection [11]. Furthermore, the approaches differ in the region-of-interest (ROI) to be evaluated, e.g., consider all visible sclera [2,12] or predefined regions such as rectangles, which are placed manually [1,10,13].

In this work we propose a pipeline to assess the ocular redness based on high-resolution images acquired with a novel ocular surface photography system. The clinical prototype used to gather the image data is specifically designed to acquire photographs of the ocular surface in a standardized fashion in terms of location, focus, illumination and operator-independence. The baseline pipeline contains a fixed definition of the ROI placed nasally and temporally of the pupil center, tiling the ROIs in multiple non-overlapping patches, which are consequently classified as sclera and non-sclera. Eventually, an intensity based redness feature is determined for all sclera tiles.

2   Methods

An automated baseline pipeline for the extraction of eye redness is proposed and was verified on a data set containing ocular surface images from healthy volunteers. The major components of the pipeline are depicted in Fig. 1 and described in detail in the following.

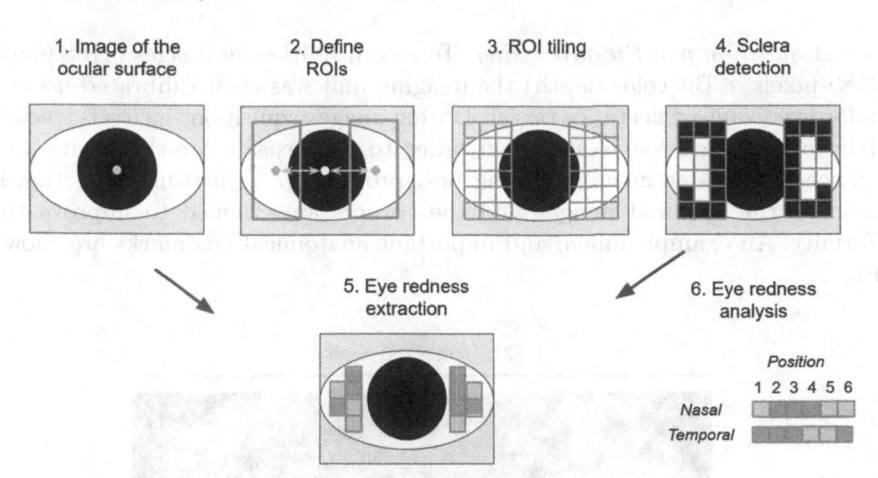

Fig. 1. Sketch of the proposed baseline pipeline for the automated determination of the eye redness based on ocular surface photography. Standardized, high-resolution ocular surface images (1) are hereby split into temporal and nasal ROIs (2). The ROIs are further split in smaller tiles (3), which are automatically classified as sclera or non-sclera (4). Eventually, the eye redness is determined for the sclera patches (5) before the results are forwarded for further interpretation and analysis (6).

2.1 High-Resolution, Standardized Ocular Surface Photography System

A clinical prototype of an ophthalmic imaging system enabling standardized ocular surface photography was utilized in this work. Based on a novel lens design the prototype enables high-resolution imaging of the ocular surface for a field-of-view of 21.3 mm × 16.0 mm with a lateral resolution of approx. 15 μm. The system includes a fixation target, an integrated eye tracker and a single acquisition mode illumination unit. The device aims to provide reproducible and centered photographs of the ocular surface, which are independent of environmental conditions such as room lighting and also operator-independent. Hence, standardized imaging regarding focus, position and lighting is ensured, which paves the way for automated analysis of ocular surface imaging biomarkers such as ocular redness.

2.2 Image Data Set

Both eyes of healthy volunteers were imaged for the verification of the proposed pipeline. The research project was approved by the Research Committee for Scientific Ethical Questions from the UMIT TIROL (RCSEQ, 3012/22). Informed consent was obtained from all volunteers prior to inclusion into this study. The image data set comprised 17 volunteers of different sex (12 males/5 females), iris color (11 brown, 2 blue, 4 green), age (26 to 46 years) and skin color.

Image Acquisition and Pre-processing. To record RGB color images (4768 pixels × 3580 pixels; 8 Bit color depth) the imaging unit was color calibrated using a standardized white reflectance target. During image acquisition the iris is tracked and its central position is stored in order to compensate for the positioning tolerance allowed for imaging during post-processing. Vignetting correction is applied to the acquired images and the corners are cropped to improve the uniformity. An example image and important anatomical landmarks are shown in Fig. 2.

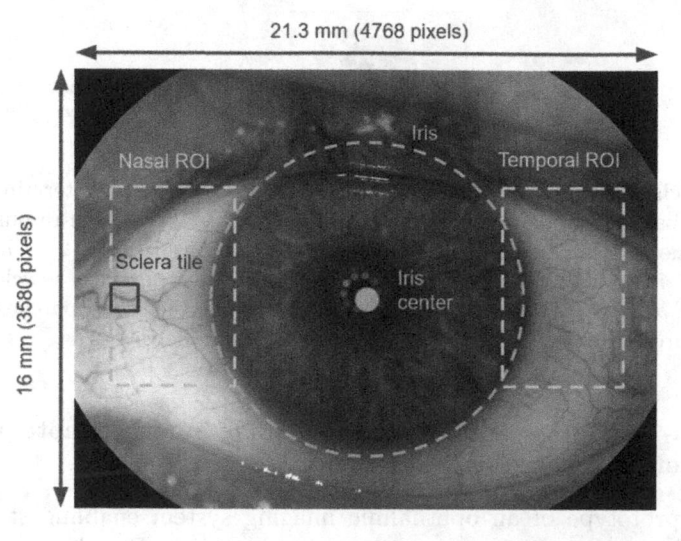

Fig. 2. Ocular surface image of a healthy left eye and anatomical regions as defined and used for the automated extraction of the eye redness.

2.3   Automated Sclera Detection

ROI Determination and Image Tiling. A temporal and nasal ROI with a size of 1600 pixels × 1000 pixels is defined in a horizontal distance of 1600 pixels from the center of the iris to the center of the ROI. Each ROI is consequently subdivided into 8 × 5 tiles with a tile size of 200 pixels × 200 pixels. The tiles are smoothed with a Gaussian filter (7×7; $\sigma = 1$) to reduce noise.

Image Tile Annotation and Classification. In a next step the tiles are classified as sclera or non-sclera as anatomical differences, e.g., iris size or different abilities of the subjects to open their eyes can affect the areas, which can be used to determine the eye redness eventually. As a baseline model a random forest based on first order intensity features and texture based features (Haralick) was trained after manually annotating all tiles by two observers. A split of 76.5% and 23.5% for the training and test data set was defined. This split was chosen to investigate the tile correlation and randomly apply training in leave-entire-subjects-out manner (13 training subjects to 4 test subjects).

2.4 Eye Redness Extraction

The eye redness is determined for each sclera image tile. For the verification of the proposed approach the eye redness is determined as defined by Fieguth et al. [4] based on the color intensity level

$$f_r(S) = \frac{1}{|S|} \sum_{i \in S} \frac{2(S_R)_i - (S_G)_i - (S_B)_i}{2[(S_R)_i + (S_G)_i + (S_B)_i]} , \qquad (1)$$

where S is the sub-image to input with composite components (S_R, S_G and S_B for each color channel) and without black pixels. The redness is normalized by the denominator in a range of $-0.5 < f_r < 1$, where a completely red image equals a value of 1.

2.5 Ocular Surface Tile Annotation

To label the image tiles a custom-made tool was developed for rapid and reliable annotation. The annotation tool is showing the whole image as well as the tile to be annotated side-by-side enabling a quick annotation for the majority of the tiles. Image tiles were annotated as sclera if only the sclera was visible and as non-sclera if no sclera, e.g., skin (including eyelashes), iris or a mix of them was visible. A screenshot of the annotation tool is shown in Fig. 3 next to some exemplary tiles of each class.

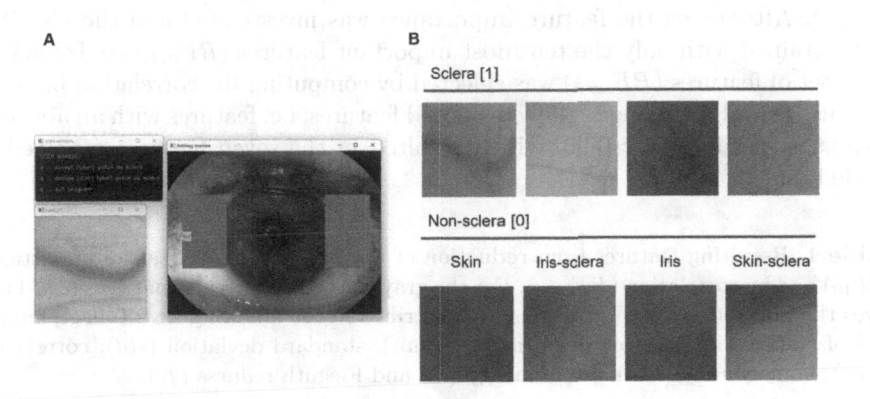

Fig. 3. (A) A custom-made annotation tool was used to label the image tiles. The whole image as well as a zoom-in of the current patch to be labeled is shown. Using the keyboard the tiles can be efficiently labeled. (B) Exemplary image tiles and their annotation (1: sclera; 0: non-sclera). A mix of structures, e.g., sclera and skin was labeled as non-sclera.

3   Experiments and Results

3.1   Ocular Surface Tile Annotation

Tiling the 34 images resulted in 2720 non-overlapping image patches. Each tile was manually annotated by two observers and classified as either sclera or non-sclera. The annotation process took less then one hour for the two observers and showed an agreement of 96.99%. The two observers disagreed on 82 tiles which were consequently removed from the data set for the subsequent steps, resulting in 2638 tiles for further analysis. The chosen ROIs and the used definition resulted in 47.57% sclera and 52.43% non-sclera tiles.

3.2   Automated Tile Classification

For the classification of the tiles a random forest was trained on intensity- and texture- based features. These features include six gray level co-occurrence matrices features (contrast, correlation, dissimilarity, homogeneity, angular second moment, energy) for eight different directions (every 45°) and four different pixel offsets (2, 3, 5, 7) resulting in 192 texture-based features [5]. Intensity based features comprised the mean and standard deviation for each color channel (R, G, B) as well as for the gray-scaled transformed image. Furthermore, the Fieguth redness was added resulting in a total of 201 features for each tile.

Feature Selection. The random forest was trained on the full set of features (RF_{all}). Afterwards the feature importance was investigated and the classifier was retrained with only the ten most important features (RF_{10}), see Table 1. A third set of features (RF_{corr}) was selected by computing the correlation between all features and removing highly correlated features, i.e. features with an absolute correlation coefficient >0.90, which resulted in the seven features reported in Table 1.

Table 1. Resulting features from reduction of the 201 features by feature importance (RF_{10}) and by correlation (RF_{corr}). For the gray level co-occurrence matrices based features the pixel offsets and directions are described in the following way: (offset, angle). List of features in table: channel mean (*mean*), standard deviation (*std*), correlation (*corr*), homogeneity (*homogen*), energy (E) and Fieguth redness (f_r).

Model	Features (descending order of importance for RF_{10})
RF_{10}	$mean_G$, $corr_{(7,315)}$, $corr_{(7,45)}$, $mean_R$, $corr_{(7,225)}$, std_{gray}, $mean_B$, std_G, $corr_{(5,45)}$, $corr_{(5,0)}$
RF_{corr}	$homogen_{(5,90)}$, $homogen_{(5,180)}$, $E_{(2,45)}$, $corr_{(7,90)}$, $mean_R$, std_R, f_r

Table 2. Scores of random forest classifiers with different features based on the evaluation of the test data set. Listed are the model, the number of features (n_f), the accuracy (acc), the precision $(prec)$, the recall (rec) and the F1-score $(F1)$.

Model	n_f	acc	prec	rec	F1
RF_{all}	201	0.971	**0.97**	0.97	**0.97**
RF_{10}	10	0.943	0.94	0.94	0.94
RF_{corr}	7	**0.974**	**0.97**	**0.98**	**0.97**

Training and Evaluation. A random forest was trained for each of the feature sets $(RF_{all}, RF_{10}, RF_{corr})$. The training data contained the images of both eyes from 13 subjects. The performance of the classifier on the test data set containing eight images of four subjects is shown in Table 2.

Classification Examples. Figure 4 shows examples of the automated classification based on the random forest model RF_{corr} in comparison to the labels by the two observers.

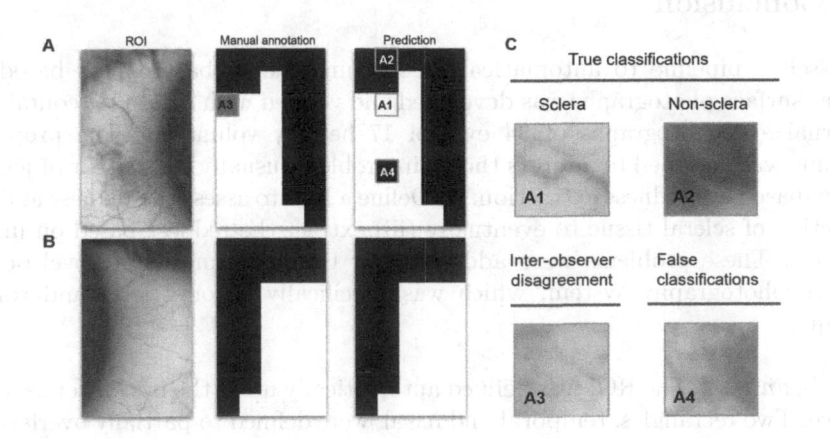

Fig. 4. (A) Shows an example of an automated tile classification with disagreements between inter-observers and false classification. (B) Shows the results of an automated tile classification with an agreement between the manual annotation and the prediction. (C) Shows an enlarged view of tile examples for true classifications, inter-observer disagreement and false classification from (A).

3.3 Redness Extraction

Based on the Fieguth redness of all tiles heatmaps were generated to investigate the results of the healthy subjects. Examples are visualized in Fig. 5(A) and (B), where in case of a birthmark the variation in determined redness is apparent. This birthmark presence is also visible as redness score outliers when the redness scores are plotted for each individual eye and also differentiated by eye color for each tile, which is shown in Fig. 5(C) and (D).

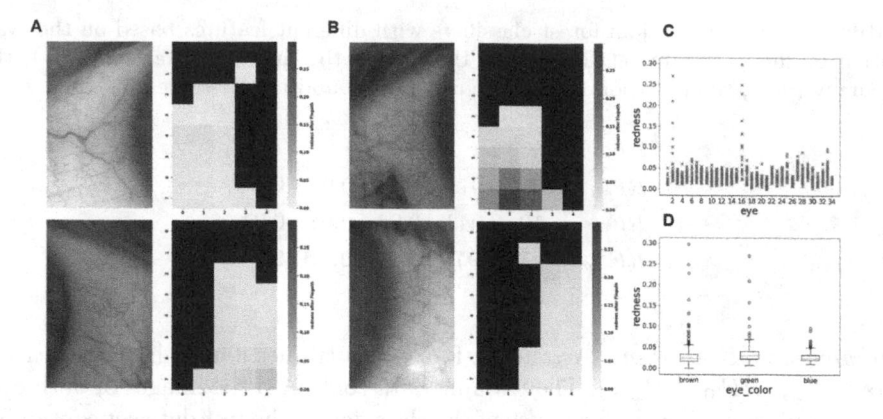

Fig. 5. (A) Shows the ROIs and the respective redness heatmaps of a subject without any ocular surface abnormality. (B) Shows the ROIs and the respective redness heatmaps of a subject with a birthmark on the ocular surface. (C) Shows Fieguth redness scores for each eye. (D) Shows the Fieguth redness scores separated by eye color.

4   Conclusion

A baseline pipeline to automatically determine the bulbar redness based on ocular surface photographs was developed and verified with a data set containing external eye photographs of 34 eyes of 17 healthy volunteers. The proposed pipeline was designed to address the main problems usually defined for objective image-based eye redness extraction: (i) Define a ROI to assess the redness and (ii) detection of scleral tissue to eventually (iii) extract the redness based on image features. These problems were addressed for the first time for a novel ocular surface photography system, which was specifically tailored for standardized imaging.

ROI Definition. The ROI was defined automatically using the iris center as a reference. Two rectangles, temporal and nasal, were defined to partially overlap the iris and cover the majority of the visible sclera. Using this definition the resulting tiles were balanced between sclera and non-sclera patches for subsequent classification. Expanding the ROI in the inferior direction as well as towards the peripheral region could be considered to expand the area for redness assessment.

Sclera Classification. External eye image tiles where classified as sclera or non-sclera using random forests. The classifiers were trained for different number of intensity and texture features after manually labeling the image tiles. The labeling process was done conservatively, i.e., tiles which did not display only sclera tissue, were labeled as non-sclera. The classifiers made wrong predictions for tiles, which showed abnormalities like birthmarks or where only small parts of non-sclera structures were present. The best performance was achieved with a model trained on three intensity- and four texture- based features (F1-score of 0.97). Adding more classes will be part of future investigation, e.g., iris, birthmarks and lesions. This would potentially improve reliability for subsequent redness interpretation. Increasing the complexity of the problem will also lead to the need to explore other models, e.g., based on deep learning.

Redness Extraction. In this work we used intensity-based redness extraction to determine the bulbar redness of tiles. The use of image tiles eases the comparison of the redness between eye images of different subjects, since the redness can be averaged based on the number of tiles labeled as sclera and their location can be compared over time. In future work this approach should be expanded to also include texture based features, e.g., based on vessel edges.

In the future, the objectively assessed redness based on the standardized photographs must be correlated to clinical reference-image-based grading of different redness for clinical evaluation. Hence, the data set must be further expanded for healthy subjects and also include patient data as the number of images currently is limited. The proposed simple baseline pipeline provided excellent results in terms of classification and feasibility for healthy subjects, which implicitly validates the standardization characteristic of the novel ocular surface photography system. Hence, standardized external eye photography can be key for reliable and high-throughput ocular surface imaging biomarker extraction.

Acknowledgements. This work was supported by the federal state of Tyrol (Austria) within the K-Regio program (project ImplEYE).

References

1. Brea, M.L.S., Barreira-Rodríguez, N., González, A.M., Evans, K., Pena-Verdeal, H.: Defining the optimal region of interest for hyperemia grading in the bulbar conjunctiva. Comput. Math. Methods Med. **2016**, 3695014:1-3695014:9 (2016). https://doi.org/10.1155/2016/3695014
2. Curti, N., et al.: A fully automated pipeline for a robust conjunctival hyperemia estimation. Appl. Sci. **11**(7), 2978 (2021). https://doi.org/10.3390/app11072978
3. Efron, N., Morgan, P.B., Katsara, S.S.: Validation of grading scales for contact lens complications. Ophthalmic Physiol. Opt. **21**(1), 17–29 (2001). https://www.ncbi.nlm.nih.gov/pubmed/11220037
4. Fieguth, P., Simpson, T.: Automated measurement of bulbar redness. Invest. Ophthalmol. Vis. Sci. **43**(2), 340–347 (2002). https://www.ncbi.nlm.nih.gov/pubmed/11818375
5. Haralick, R.M., Shanmugam, K., Dinstein, I.: Textural features for image classification. IEEE Trans. Syst. Man Cybern. **3**(6), 610–621 (1973). https://doi.org/10.1109/TSMC.1973.4309314
6. Macchi, I., et al.: A new scale for the assessment of conjunctival bulbar redness. Ocul. Surf. **16**(4), 436–440 (2018). https://doi.org/10.1016/j.jtos.2018.06.003
7. Park, I.K., Chun, Y.S., Kim, K.G., Yang, H.K., Hwang, J.M.: New clinical grading scales and objective measurement for conjunctival injection. Invest. Ophthalmol. Visual Sci. **54**(8), 5249–5257 (2013). https://doi.org/10.1167/iovs.12-10678
8. Pult, H., Murphy, P.J., Purslow, C., Nyman, J., Woods, R.L.: Limbal and bulbar hyperaemia in normal eyes. Ophthalmic Physiol. Opt. **28**(1), 13–20 (2008). https://doi.org/10.1111/j.1475-1313.2007.00534.x

9. Pérez-Bartolomé, F., Sanz-Pozo, C., Martínez-de la Casa, J.M., Arriola-Villalobos, P., Fernández-Pérez, C., García-Feijoó, J.: Assessment of ocular redness measurements obtained with keratograph 5M and correlation with subjective grading scales. Journal Francais d'Ophtalmologie **41**(9), 836–846 (2018). https://doi.org/10.1016/j.jfo.2018.03.007

10. Rodriguez, J.D., Johnston, P.R., Ousler, G.W., III., Smith, L.M., Abelson, M.B.: Automated grading system for evaluation of ocular redness associated with dry eye. Clin. Ophthalmol. (Auckland, N.Z.) **7**, 1197 (2013)

11. Singh, R.B., et al.: Ocular redness - i: etiology, pathogenesis, and assessment of conjunctival hyperemia. Ocul. Surf. **21**, 134–144 (2021). https://doi.org/10.1016/j.jtos.2021.05.003

12. Sirazitdinova, E., Gijs, M., Bertens, C.J.F., Berendschot, T.T.J.M., Nuijts, R.M.M.A., Deserno, T.M.: Validation of Computerized Quantification of Ocular Redness. Trans. Vis. Sci. Technol. **8**(6), 31 (2019). https://doi.org/10.1167/tvst.8.6.31

13. Yoneda, T., Sumi, T., Takahashi, A., Hoshikawa, Y., Kobayashi, M., Fukushima, A.: Automated hyperemia analysis software: reliability and reproducibility in healthy subjects. Jpn. J. Ophthalmol. **56**(1), 1–7 (2012). https://doi.org/10.1007/s10384-011-0107-2

Correction to: Ophthalmic Medical Image Analysis

Bhavna Antony ⓘ, Huazhu Fu ⓘ, Cecilia S. Lee ⓘ,
Tom MacGillivray ⓘ, Yanwu Xu ⓘ, and Yalin Zheng ⓘ

Correction to:
B. Antony et al. (Eds.): *Ophthalmic Medical Image Analysis*,
LNCS 13576, https://doi.org/10.1007/978-3-031-16525-2

For chapter 5
In an older version of this chapter, the title was incomplete. This has been corrected.

For chapter 8
In an older version of this chapter, there was an error on page 78. The sign "C" for Celsius was inadvertently and incorrectly added after "30°". This has been corrected. In addition, Electronic Supplementary Material (ESM) was missing. It has now been added.

The updated original version of these chapters can be found at
https://doi.org/10.1007/978-3-031-16525-2_5
https://doi.org/10.1007/978-3-031-16525-2_8

Author Index

Printed in the United States
by Baker & Taylor Publisher Services